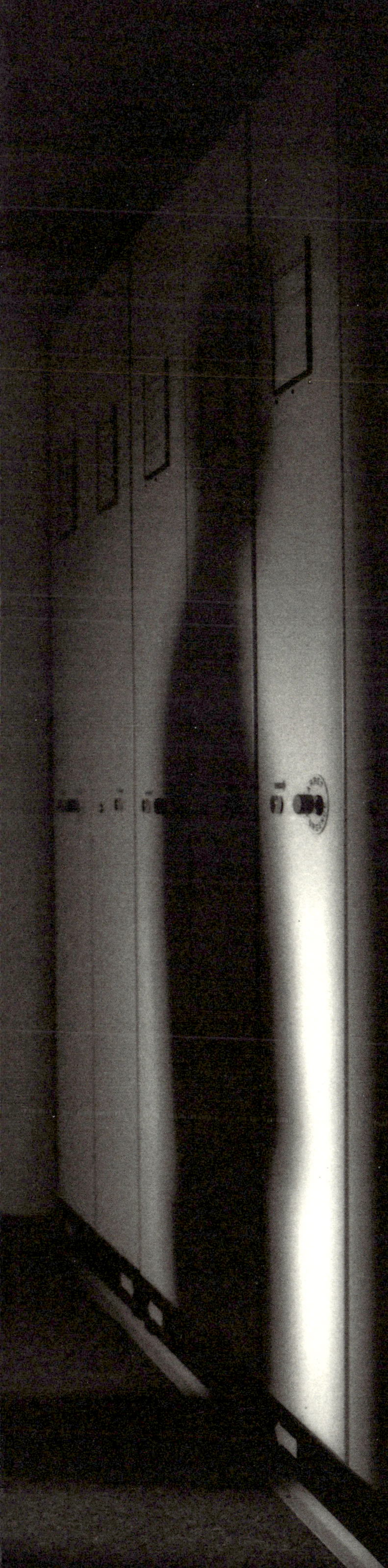

Encounters with Great Painters

Project Manager, English-language edition: Ellen Nidy
Editor, English-language edition: Julie Di Filippo
Design Coordinator, English-language edition: Tina Thompson
Jacket design, English-language edition: Michael Walsh

Library of Congress Cataloging-in-Publication Data

Encounters with great painters : the artists, Bacon...[et al.]. / photography and text by Claude Azoulay...et al.]. ; compiled by Roger Thérond.
p. cm.
Taken from the annals of Paris Match, the popular French magazine.
ISBN 0-8109-4396-4
1. Painting, European. 2. Painting, Modern—20th century—Europe.
3. Painters—Europe—Miscellanea. I. Azoulay, Claude. II. Thérond, Roger.
III. Paris-Match.

ND458 .E53 2001
759.94'09'04—dc21

00-64609

Copyright © 2000 Éditions Filipacchi—Société SONODIP—Paris-Match
English translation copyright © 2001 Harry N. Abrams, Inc.

Published in 2001 by Harry N. Abrams, Incorporated, New York
All rights reserved. No part of the contents of this book may be reproduced without the written permission of the publisher.

Printed and bound in France

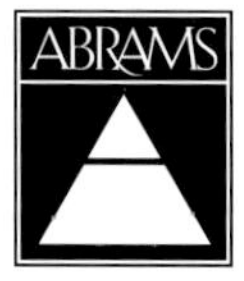

Harry N. Abrams, Inc.
100 Fifth Avenue
New York, N.Y. 10011
www.abramsbooks.com

Encounters with Great Painters

THE ARTISTS

Bacon, Balthus, Braque, Chagall, Dalí, Delvaux, Léger, Matisse, Miró, Picasso, Van Dongen

PHOTOGRAPHS AND TEXT BY

Claude Azoulay, Peter Beard, Alvaro Canovas, Walter Carone, Jean-François Chabrun, Henriette Chandet, Edmonde Charles-Roux, Jean Diwo, Robert Doisneau, David Douglas Duncan, Pépita Dupont, Christian Gibey, Julien Green, Eugène Ionesco, Izis, Pierre Joffroy, Barry Joule, Jean Leymarie, Hélène Parmelin, Maurice Rheims, Tony Saulnier, Marie-France Saurat, Hubert de Segonzac, René Vital

Translated from the French
by Molly Stevens and Anthony Roberts

Compiled from the Archives of *Paris Match* Magazine
by Roger Thérond

Harry N. Abrams, Inc., Publishers

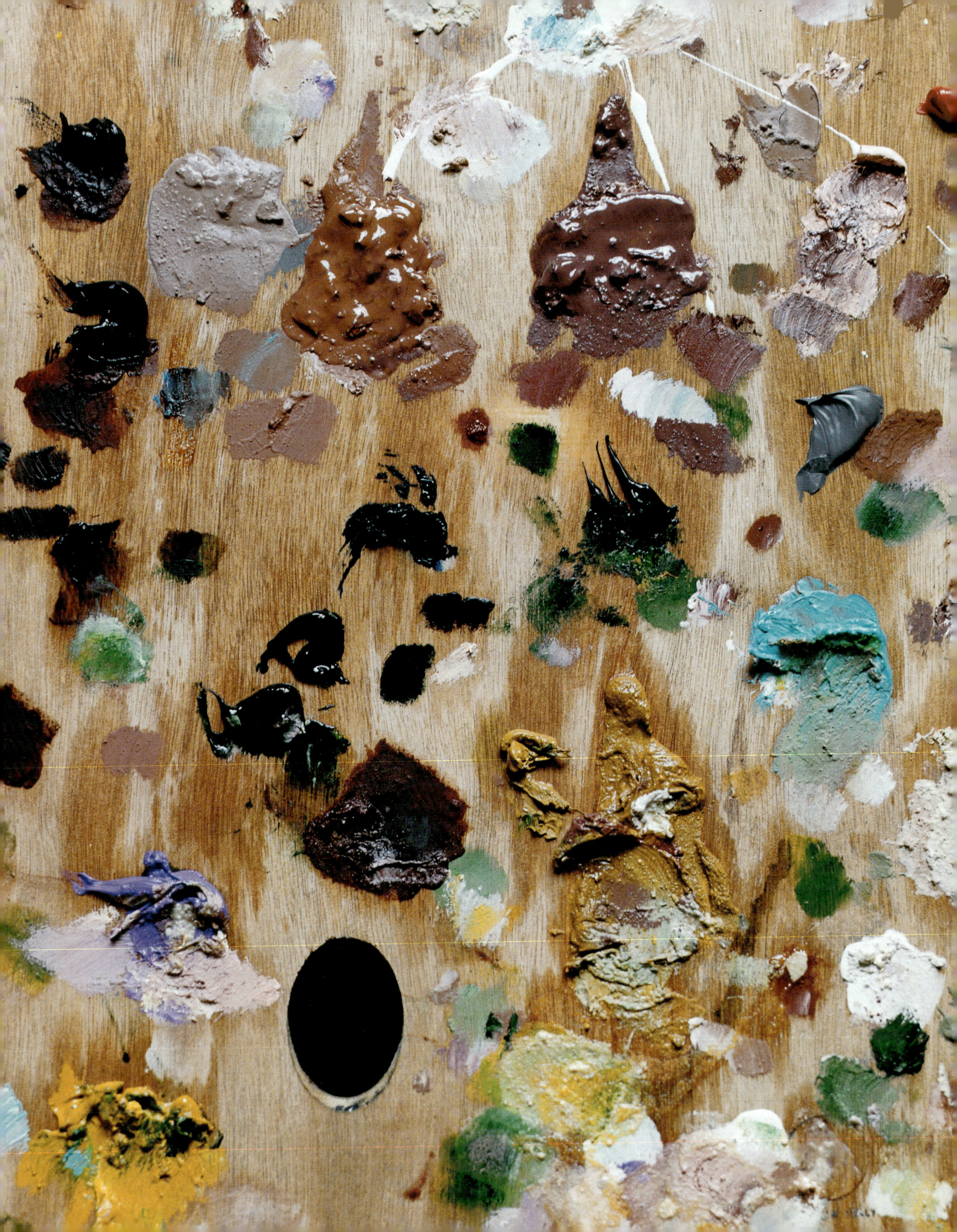

The launching of a collection is an emotional voyage. The premiere album is the first journey: Where will it take us? Our hope is that *Encounters with Great Painters* will lead the reader toward the desire to explore, toward discovery, knowledge, distraction, and pleasure. It's a grand plan, but because the *Paris Match* archives have been opened, let us slip into its vast annals. Here, millions of images reflecting decades of talent and ambition have been gathered and are to be awakened by our research. We are invited to unravel the mystery, rediscover, choose, extract, and reassemble themes recorded from the history of art.

This volume presents a three-fold segment for each of our subjects:

- a photographer
- a moment
- a painter

The moment of the encounter may be brief, last a day, stretch out over several months, or mark three key years in a painter's life.

This is an arbitrary approach, but one that is in the fine tradition of *Paris Match* magazine: to surprise, captivate, and ignite reflection through pictures. Each of the chapters in this book open with evocative captions that withhold all commentary and analysis and allow the images to speak for themselves.

I hope that you will find a few happy moments with these great, tortured, and serene artists. In these palettes, in these charcoal sticks and paintbrushes, a joy that only art can offer is harbored.

—Roger Thérond

Contents

Matisse

Walter Carone 1950

A piercing stare from underneath Henri Matisse's glasses reveals the spirit of a great professor.

"The work of a painter is different from that of a photographer; it involves expressing the feeling that the spectacle of nature provokes in him." Matisse's latest colored cut-outs convey this love for life.

Matisse, the old unrepentant Fauve, the painter of odalisques, is now concentrating on religious motifs. His mission is to decorate the Vence chapel.

Matisse is now eighty years old; moving about has become difficult. He has abandoned his huge studio and no longer leaves his bed, which stands in the middle of his room. He works at an adjustable table on wheels.

He proves to have an ardent need to create. He has found that there is only one way to conquer his immobility: a piece of charcoal attached to the end of a pole allows him to work on paper hung from the walls of his room.

Matisse traces St. Magdalen's face in one stroke.

"Now that the chapel is almost finished, I am at peace," says the artist.

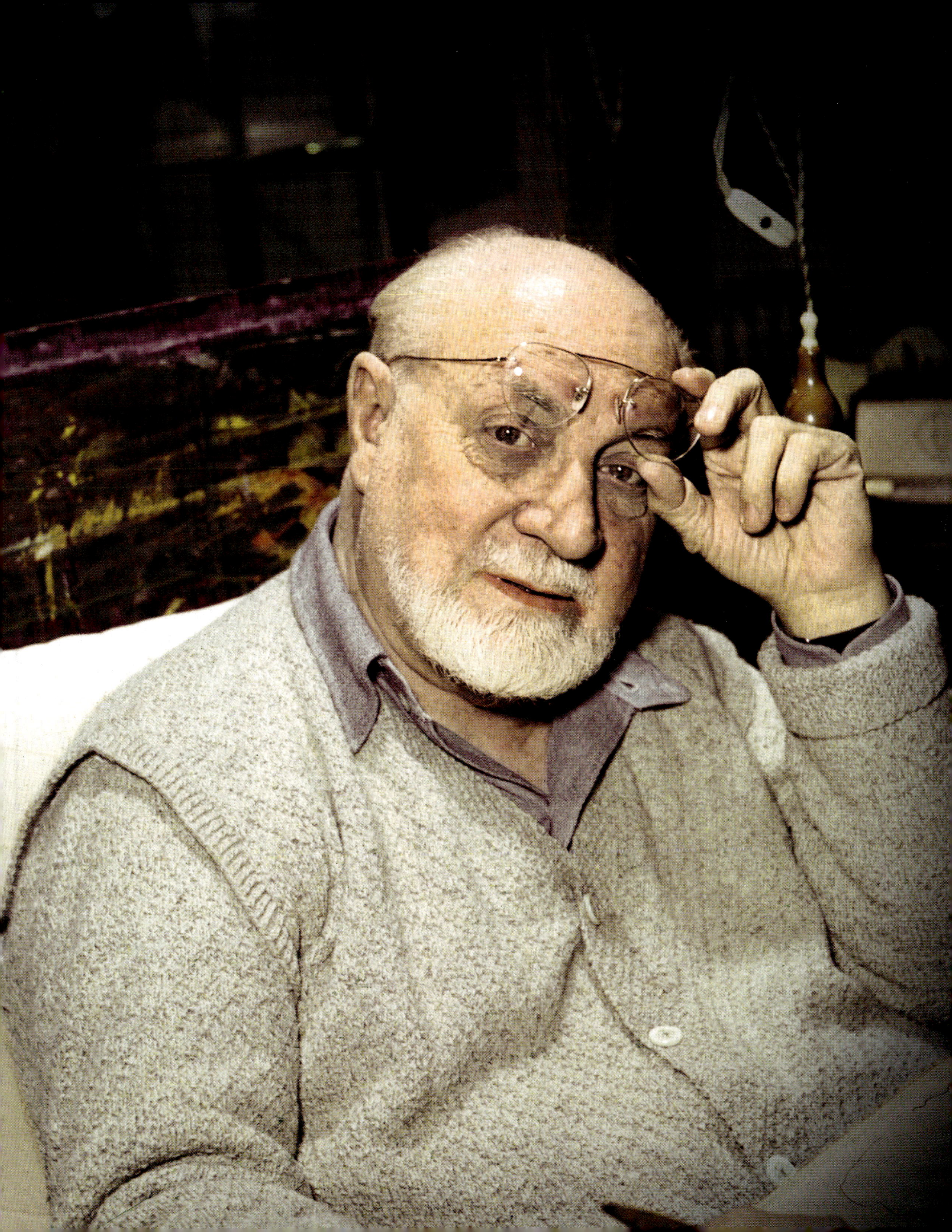

When word caught on among the initiated that Henri Matisse, the old unrepentant Fauve—and moreover a Communist sympathizer—was extending his talents to create designs for a small provincial Dominican chapel in southern France, there was an audible cry of disbelief.

To his Communist friends, united in Nice and alarmed by the news, Matisse answered: "Yes, I'm going to decorate a chapel. A chapel, a village hall, or a gathering place, what's the difference to me? I'm going to put flowers everywhere." But it did make a difference, for, during the past three years, the master painter of odalisques had only been painting saints.

Such an abrupt and complete evolution could hardly be called anything but "conversion." The French writer and active Communist Party member Louis Aragon went so far as to tell him, "When we're in power, we'll make a museum out of your chapel!" Matisse responded by securing the chapel in his will as a place strictly reserved for church services, no matter what circumstances might arise. Nevertheless Picasso, who at first turned his back on Matisse's chapel project, continued to visit the artist and criticized him less frequently. Moreover, there was a rumor going about that for some time Picasso himself had been evolving. There is a mystery about Matisse, a mystery that he himself does little to dispel. At eighty years old, he continues to cloak his feelings behind the timid shyness of an adolescent. In the Montmartre of his youth, the serious and distinguished cut of his beard lent him the nickname "the Doctor."

Today it gives him a venerable and jovial air, and his eyes sparkle with mischief upon remembering. Apparently, Matisse is the least introverted man in the world. Yet in Saint-Paul-de-Vence, where the Surrealist poet Jacques Prévert, the director Marcel Carné, and the painter Marc Chagall all live—in Saint-Paul, which has become an extension of Saint-Germain-des-Prés—Matisse sees no one.

He no longer has any theories to profess or fashion trends to spread; he has become deaf to the world's hubbub. At eighty years old, the Chapel of the Rosary of the Dominican Nuns in Vence has just revealed to him his real vocation. In truth, the seeds of this epiphany had been present for nearly a decade. In the late 1930s, Matisse was seriously affected by intestinal maladies, and when a Dr. Leriche operated, he gave the artist six months to live. A young nurse from the Vendée, filled with extraordinary devotion, came to care for the old painter. She even said that she was healing his spirit as well as his body by spreading the good Christian word. Today, for this woman who has in the meantime become Sister Jacques, the time has come to reap the benefits of her generosity.

After the Liberation many Dominican nurses, Sister Jacques included, moved to the Lacordaire residence at Vence. The old Romanesque chapel there was on the verge of crumbling. While the Sisters considered rebuilding it, they lacked sufficient funds to accomplish the task. Sister Jacques's talent for drawing had led her to begin work on a model of one of the stained-glass windows from the chapel. She wished to show her sketch to Matisse, considering it an opportunity to spark the artist's curiosity about the project.

Matisse looked at the sketch with interest, altering things here and there, and quickly volunteered to design not only the windows, but the entire chapel itself as an expression of his gratitude for the hospitality and care offered to him by Sister Jacques and the other Dominican nuns. His enthusiasm for the chapel extended to the architecture, murals, tile work, bell, altar, chandeliers, prie-dieux, vestments, and even the embroidery on the altar cloth, all expressed by designs in a fresh and joyous spirit.

A Dominican novice less than thirty years old, the Brother Rayssiguier prepared Matisse's plans for the chapel. The esteemed French architect Auguste Perret agreed to participate in the project. At first, Brother Rayssiguier showed some concern, despite his trust in Matisse's genius. The artist's last project before the chapel had been the illustration of the *Lettres portugaises*, a masterpiece from the late seventeenth century, in which the language of a very profane Passion reached new heights. Brother Rayssiguier feared that Matisse planned to work in the same spirit. "Don't worry," Matisse assured him, "whether I am depicting the Blessed Virgin or a nymph surprised by a faun in her sleep, I begin by contemplating the whole picture." Brother Rayssiguier, who was not so convinced, nevertheless gave him the benefit of the doubt. He doesn't regret doing so. Matisse was so zealous about his subject that he did fifty versions of the *Stations of the Cross*, a series of line drawings in ceramic. He works from his home in Nice while sitting in bed. With the aid of a piece of charcoal attached to the end of a pole, he draws on paper hung from the ceiling and walls. When he is displeased by his work, Lydia Delectorskaya, a young Russian woman who is both his secretary and his housekeeper, assists by erasing when necessary. Once satisfied with his mural drawings, he reproduces them with black paint on white ceramic tiles that are then re-fired and sent to the chapel. Once a month, Matisse travels to Vence by taxi to observe the chapel's progress.

Dealers estimate that a Matisse painting measuring

19½ x 23⅝" (50 x 60 cm), is worth about $283 thousand. By devoting himself exclusively to his chapel, Matisse is therefore giving up $400 to $550 thousand every year. Half of his earnings used to go to Madame Matisse, from whom he is now separated. Matisse's former wife acts as the Communist mayor in a small town located in the eastern Pyrenees mountain range. Because her husband no longer paints, the Vence chapel is costing her almost $300 thousand per year. As a Communist, it's a joke that's not funny.

This past December, the first stone was placed and blessed in a ceremony led by Monsignor Rémond, the bishop of Nice. Although he claims to be anticlerical if not anti-Catholic, Matisse was moved with pride. The chapel stands atop a hillside on the Saint-Jeannet road overlooking Vence. It is forty-five feet long, seventy-five feet high, and eighteen feet wide, with ample room for eighty prie-dieux.

Upon entering the chapel from the side door, one is led into a large rectangular room. The walls, which are as high as the choir, part slightly to form the tau cross, or St. Anthony's cross, a common ecclesiastical ornament. There is, however, one decisively modern aspect for which Matisse did not follow tradition; this was in the choir where he tilted the altar toward the congregation: "We've had enough of seeing the priest's back," he explained, smiling through his beard. Frescoes are starting to be placed on the walls. A large figure of St. Dominic stands out, a long silhouette of starkly pure line work, black on white: "At first, he resembled more of a Dominican," Matisse says bluntly. "I painted him in the grip of my Freudian complex."

What one realizes above all is that, although everything in the chapel is black on white, color flows everywhere. The ample amount of sunlight streaming through the stained-glass windows gives off the effects of a prism. Behind the altar, on the wall that faces the nave, two vivid stained-glass windows depict stylized cacti in three colors—ultramarine blue, emerald green, and lemon yellow—through which light filters dramatically. The idea of working with the sun came to Matisse while he watched light dance upon the azure-colored waters at the Blue Grotto in Capri. "Originally," he says, "stained-glass windows were simply colored light, as can be seen in the marvelous old windows at Chartres Cathedral as well as in the Orient. Artisans eventually wanted the windows to narrate the story of the saints and the history of the church. Although the ability to communicate through these works of art was reached, the beauty inherent in the light became overshadowed by the story. But a stained-glass window is in itself a luminous orchestra. There is no need for stories. As for me, I illustrate my stories in black and white on the walls. The sun coming through the windows accomplishes the rest."

Although haunted by the sea like the poet Stéphane Mallarmé, Matisse, "painter from Nice," comes from the north of France. He was born in Le Cateau-Cambrésis and worked as a lawyer's clerk in Saint-Quentin. His parents, who were grain merchants, wanted him to become a pharmacist and, to this end, they sent him to Paris. It was here that he discovered color. Art historians all agree that Fauvism was born when Matisse met André Derain, an encounter that triggered a veritable color explosion in painting in the 1900s. But Fauvism was not whole-heartedly embraced by members of the art community. A year ago, when the annual banquet of the Royal Academy let out, Sir Alfred Munnings violently attacked French painting in general and Matisse and Picasso in particular: "They are incapable of painting a tree that looks like a tree," Munnings exclaimed. Matisse then responded to an English journalist: "If one wants a tree that looks like a tree," he said, "it would be best to contact a photographer. A painter's job is something else entirely; it is to express the feeling that the spectacle of nature provokes in him. There are two kinds of painting," he continued, "There is painting that illuminates something new. At first, one doesn't find any value in it. But in time, it becomes the most prized kind. Then, there is that type of painting that one immediately accepts because, bringing nothing new, it is happy to simply flatter the taste of the public. After a few years, it is forgotten."

Matisse belongs to the first category of painters. Now that he can better understand the turning points of his evolution, he deems that there were two pivotal events in his life. One was meeting Derain and discovering the vibrant colors that took possession of his paintings. The other was the influence of the Catholic Church, which led him, as a painter, to this final subtlety: to allow color to eclipse its source, the sun, much like the artist stands in the shadow of his creation.

"Today," Matisse says, "I sense that all my work over the past sixty years has had no other profound meaning than to lead me to this chapel. Now that it is almost finished, I am at

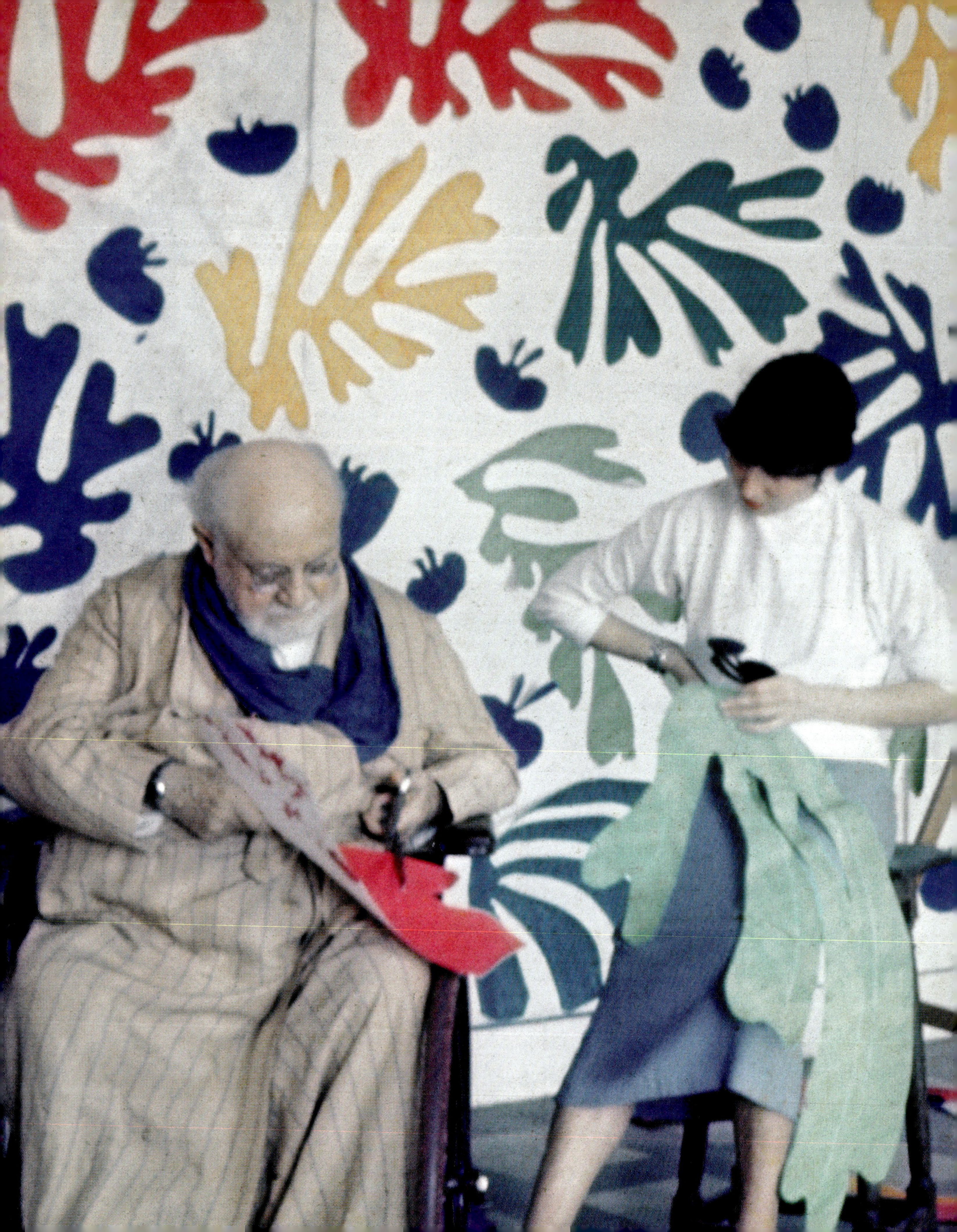

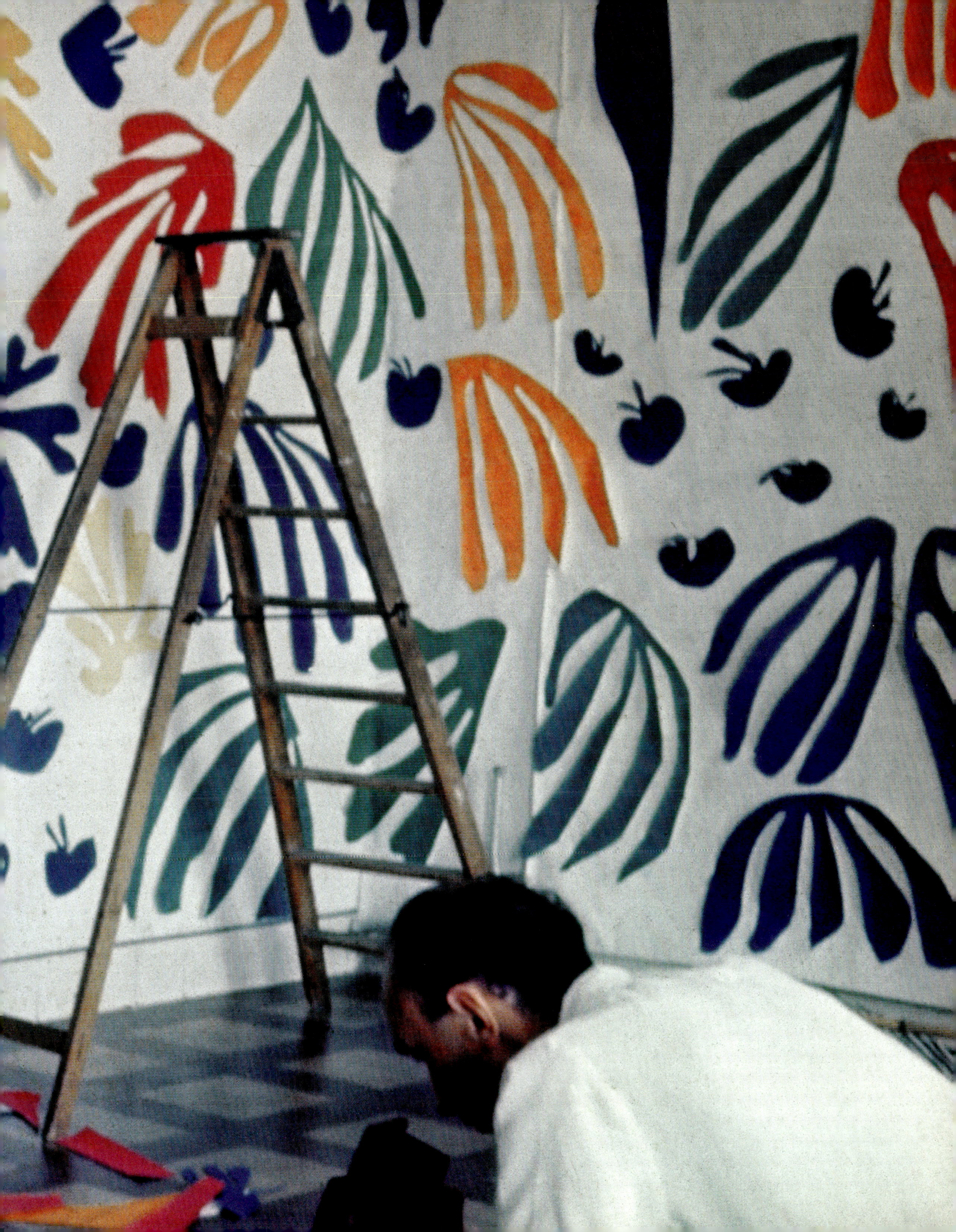

peace. My bags are packed. I have only to wait for the last train to depart."

Derain and Georges Braque fondly called Matisse "Professor." It was said in both a friendly and respectful manner, indeed with a touch of irony. It was their own way of appointing a man who, their elder by a decade, in those years represented the image of the artist they envisioned becoming. In 1946 I went to visit Matisse in Cimiez where I found him amidst his white birdcages and numerous house plants, clearly acting the part of the eponymous "Professor." But that was not all. By calling him "Professor," Derain implied that, after sharing the experience of Fauvism during that steamy summer in Collioure, Matisse continued to be "a great man" for him, even though they had pursued alternate paths. Derain admired his work and considered some of his pieces "utterly splendid." Coming from Derain, this was the highest form of praise. The title of "Professor" was a way of differentiating Matisse from his contemporaries. It perfectly suited a man with delicate spectacles, a man from the north of France with an affable smile, an educated man who, from the moment he set foot in Paris, was distinguished by his seriousness. During his years of study at the Ecole des Beaux-Arts, as with the studios he visited later on, Matisse always seemed more orderly, more reasonable than the painters of the upcoming generation. Wild times? There were hardly any for him... When he was still in training, seeking advice from the masters of the time but already married with a family, he avoided roisterers and clowns. He was already obsessed and passionate about painting; it was his greatest desire. It's impossible to imagine the "Professor" stealing a nap on the generous shoulder of the beautiful Kiki (Kees van Dongen) in Montparnasse, or on the terrace of a café as Derain often did. Could Matisse have slept so soundly, so peacefully?

When a café was about to close, Derain was sent to the coat check where he would awaken the following morning amongst the items in the lost and found. Furthermore, it would have been literally shocking to hear of Matisse perched on top of a table at the café Dôme, with a paper napkin for a peplum—as his contemporary Max Jacob would do—showing friends how Isadora Duncan danced. For a while, Matisse was an eager student, always attentive to the advice of his instructors and shamelessly acknowledging that he was still seeking his truth. His profound, irrepressible originality was immediately apparent in his tastes, his conception of décor, his interests in books and poetry, even his clothing—at least when I first met him, when his fame allowed him to fulfill his desire for discreet, refined luxury. He enjoyed fine hotels and expensive clothes and was sometimes reproached for this. Matisse's shirts!—he had them hand tailored at Charvet's. What can one say about the hats with rolled brims and the dressing gown he wore while painting in his studio? He was unique to the core.

Let's take a moment to consider his travels, for this sedentary soul has gone to several countries, sometimes reluctantly and only slightly impressed by what he encountered abroad. He went to Tahiti, New York, and Russia, among other locales, but was always ready to return home to his painting. He disliked when it was said that he was "away," preferring it be said that he was "on a business trip," mostly because he wished to distinguish himself from painters who went away in search of beautiful landscapes and tropical scenes that were simply ready to be transferred from sketchbook to canvas. He didn't go to Tangier because he was drawn to the exotic, but rather, "to let in the light..." In Tangiers, he collected rugs, objects, ceramics, jewelry, and enough embroidery, silks, and tapestries to satisfy his love for fabrics. He packed his bags with everything that he refused to paint while in Morocco, horrified by the uselessness of these objects and unwilling to have anything interfere with his flat surfaces of pure color. He was going to extract what was essential from his purchases later on, little by little, and for the rest of his life. In order to enhance a nude, he added the colorful burst of a Moroccan rug. Or, with another nude, as if left there on the ground by mistake, a pair of Chinese slippers...the hair of a French beauty held back by a vermilion silk twist, with tinkling pendants hanging from her ears. In other words, nothing, or almost nothing, just enough to accentuate these women in their roles as odalisques.

But let us go back to Matisse opening his window onto the landscape of Tangier. In the spirit of Fauvism, but in a new direction, Matisse triggered a style of painting that left behind any attempts previously made in this vein. He was the absolute innovator, the man who slammed the door in the face of his forefathers' orientalism. It wasn't that Alfred Dehodencq, Henri Regnault, Jean-Léon Gérôme, Fabius Brest, Georges Clairin, and Henri Laurens were admired less after Matisse, but rather that they were seen from a different perspective, and the place that they were given was no longer the same. In the serenity of Cimiez, Matisse seemed to be the master. Aragon showed great conviction in saying these things, and plenty of humor: "In the future, when one will want to situate a thought or a discovery, it won't cross one's mind to say 'It was the time of Emile Loubet or Emile Deschanel or Henri Lebrun...' one will say, 'It was the time of Henri Matisse.' "

—Edmonde Charles-Roux

Académie Goncourt

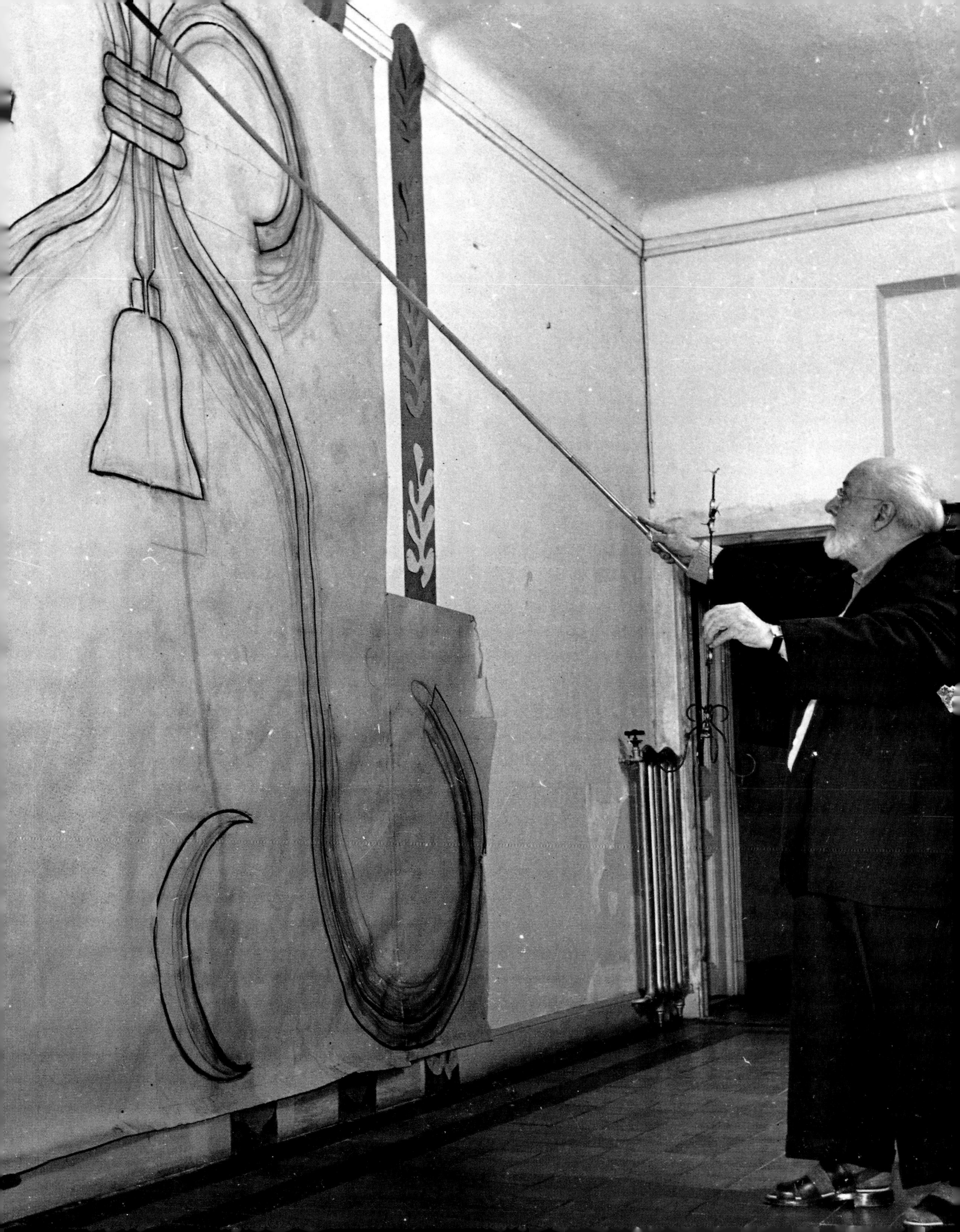

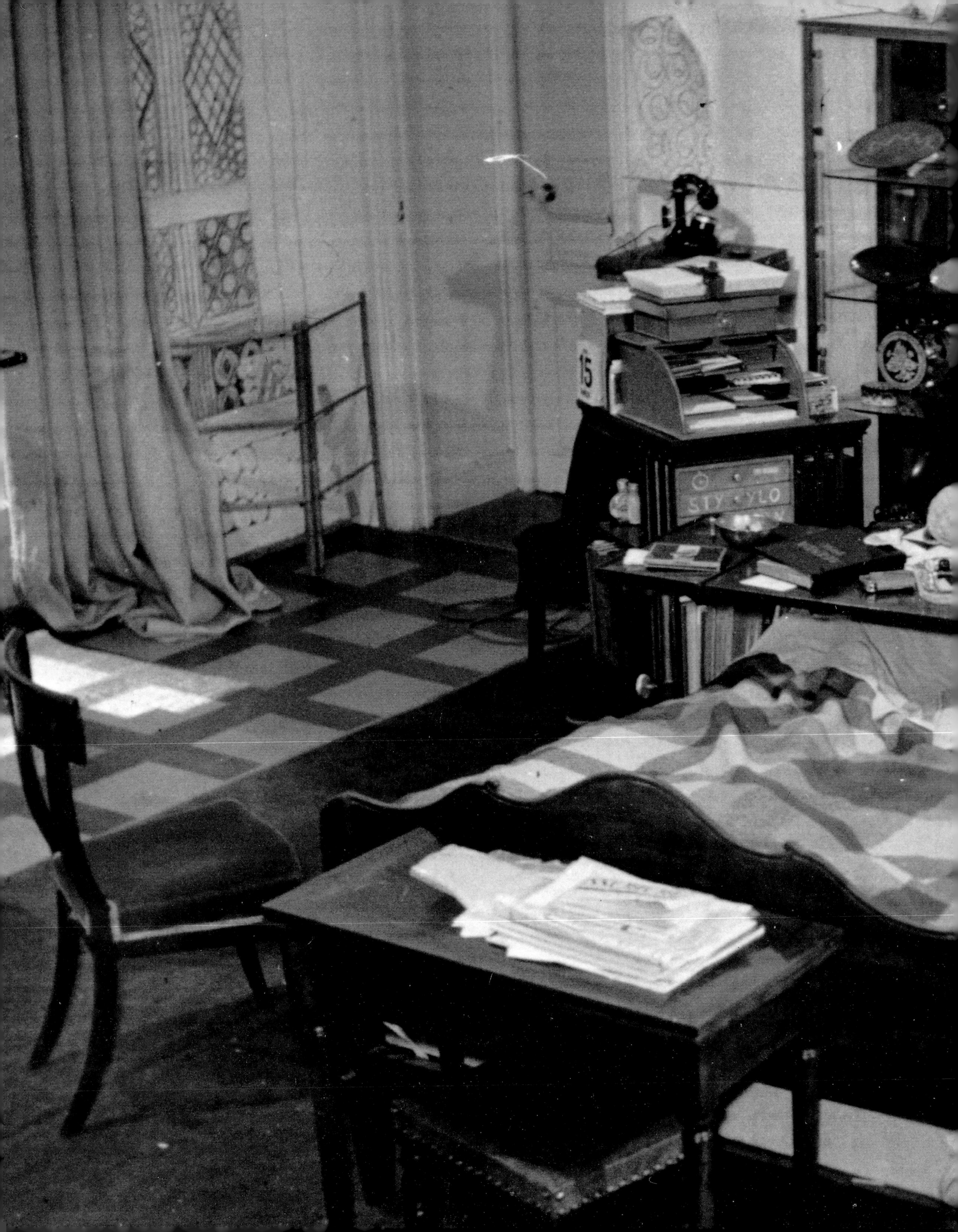
15

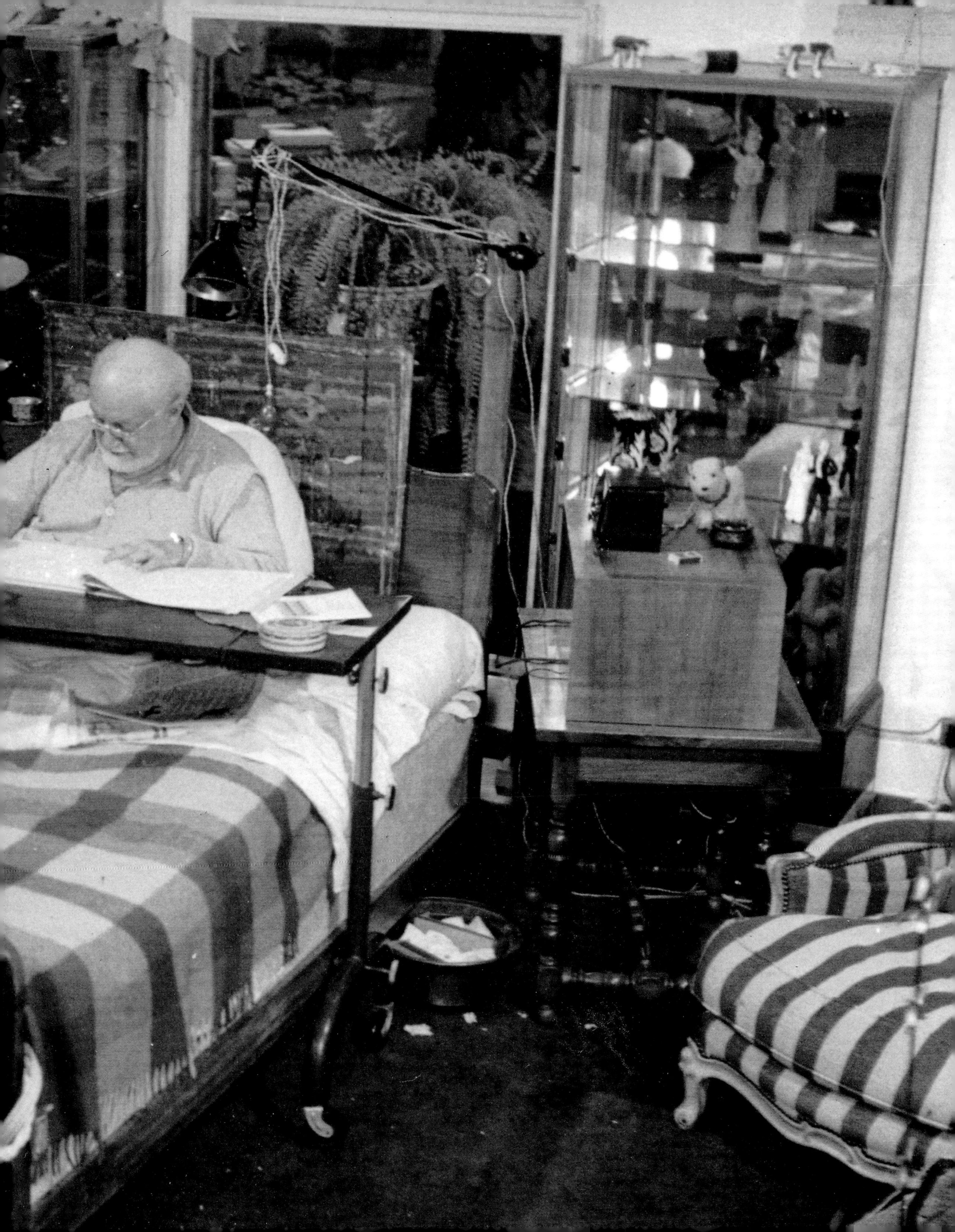

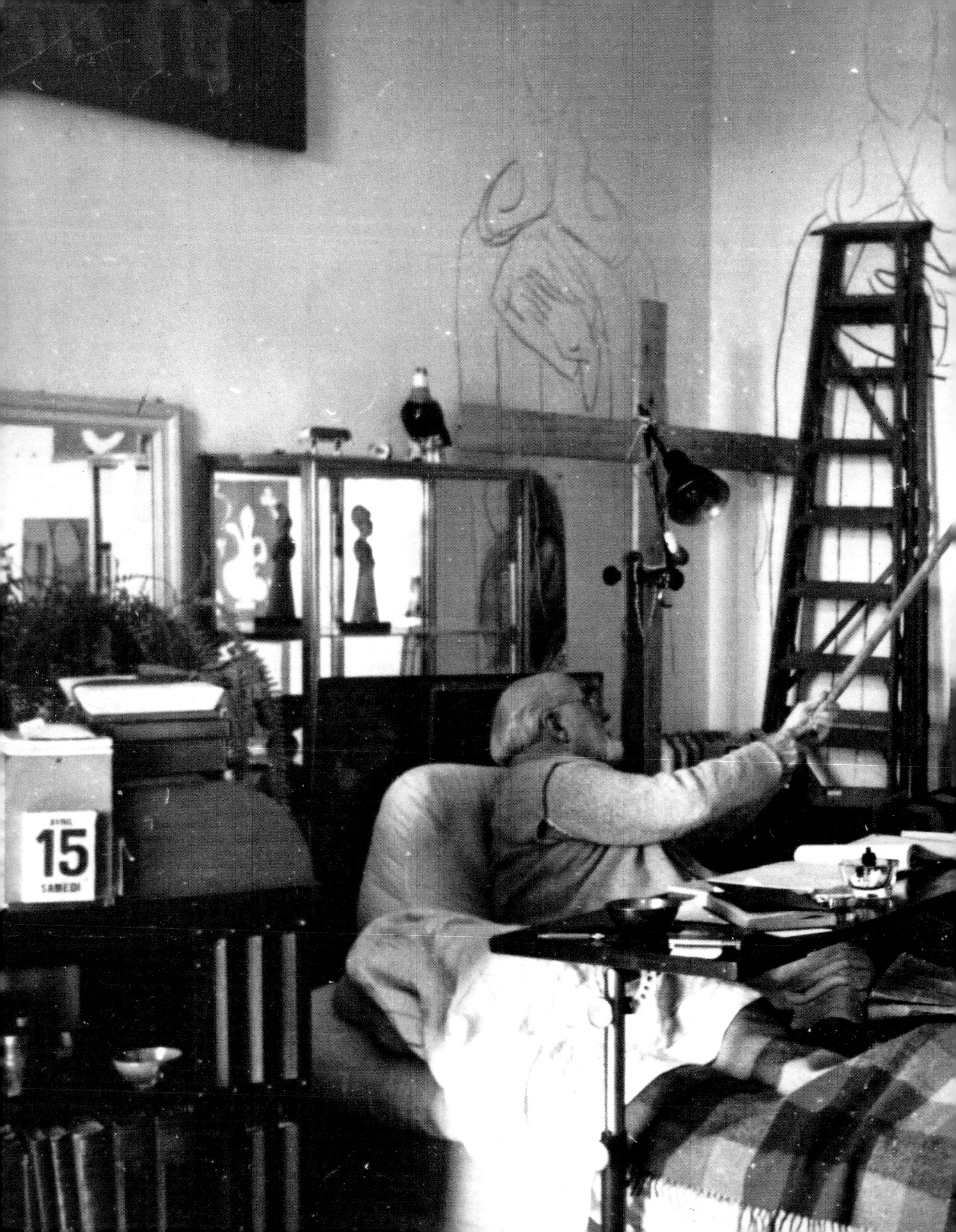
15

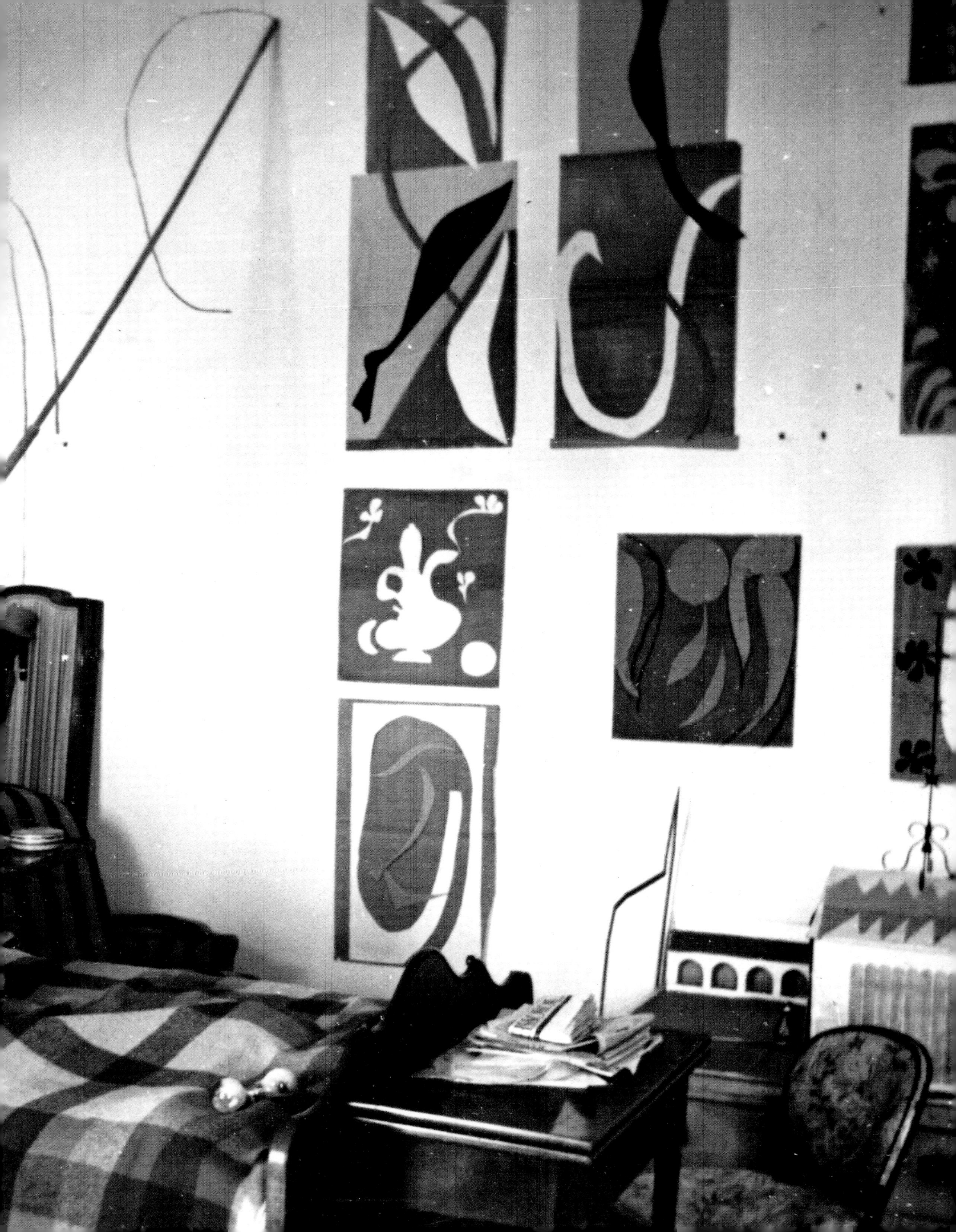

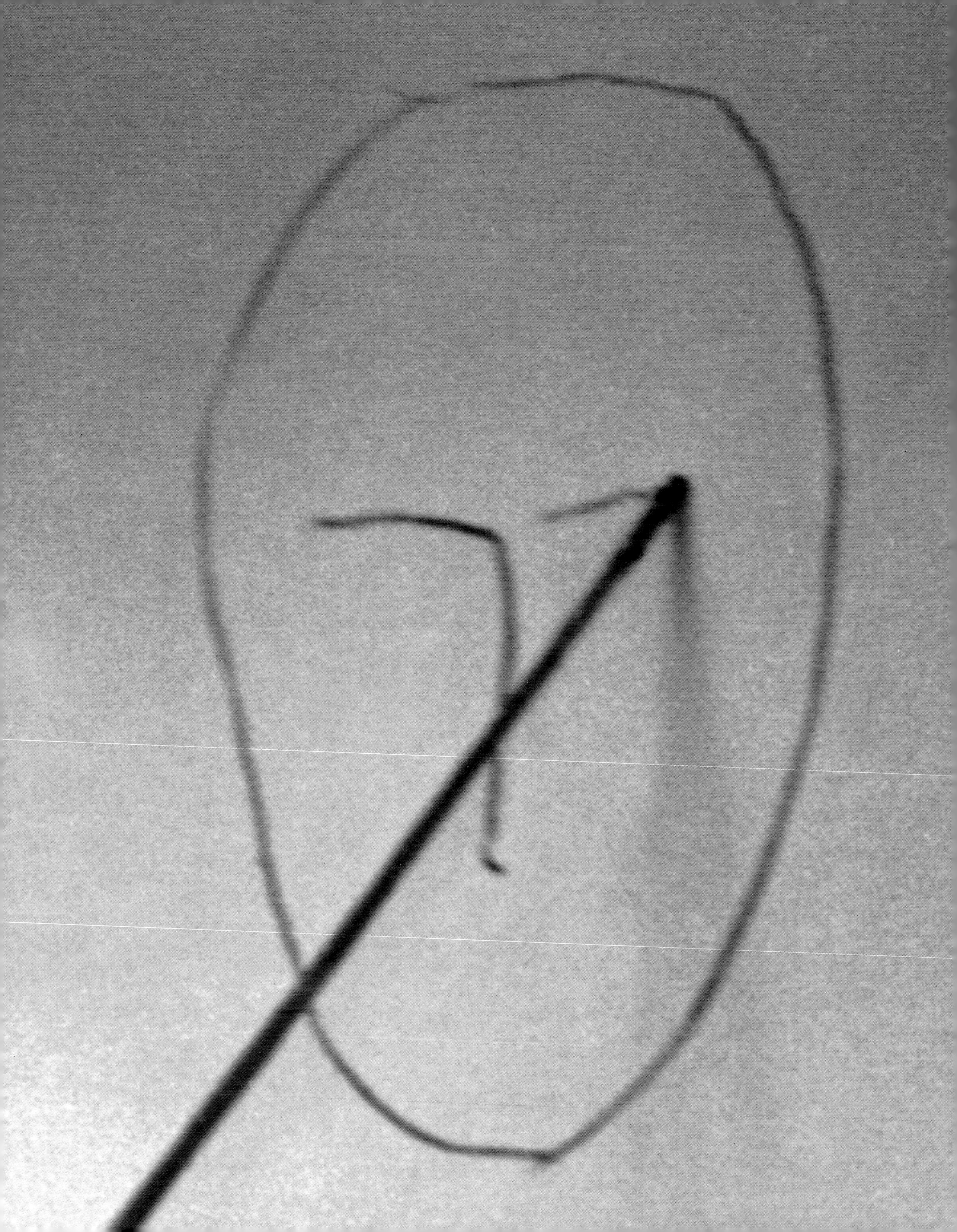

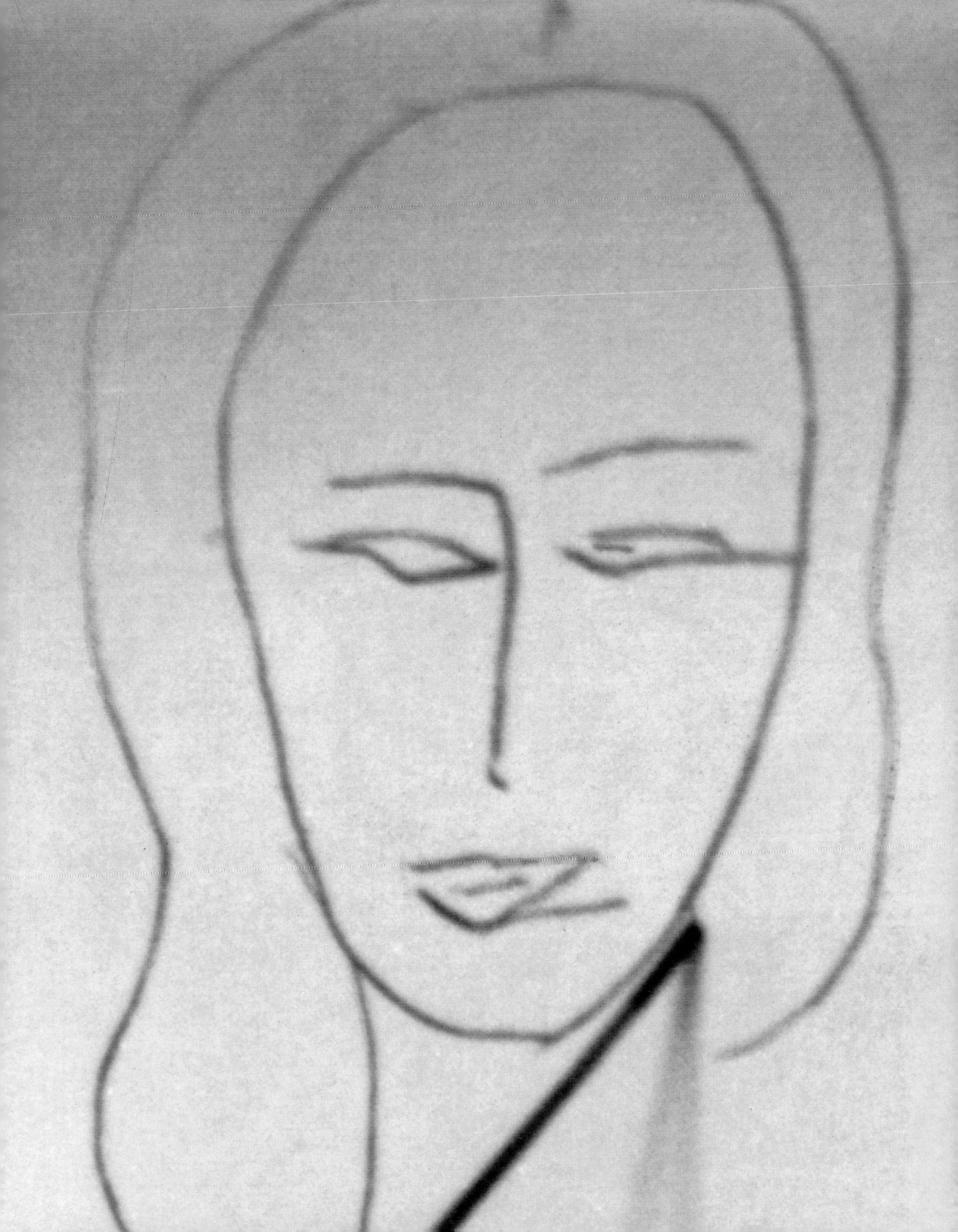

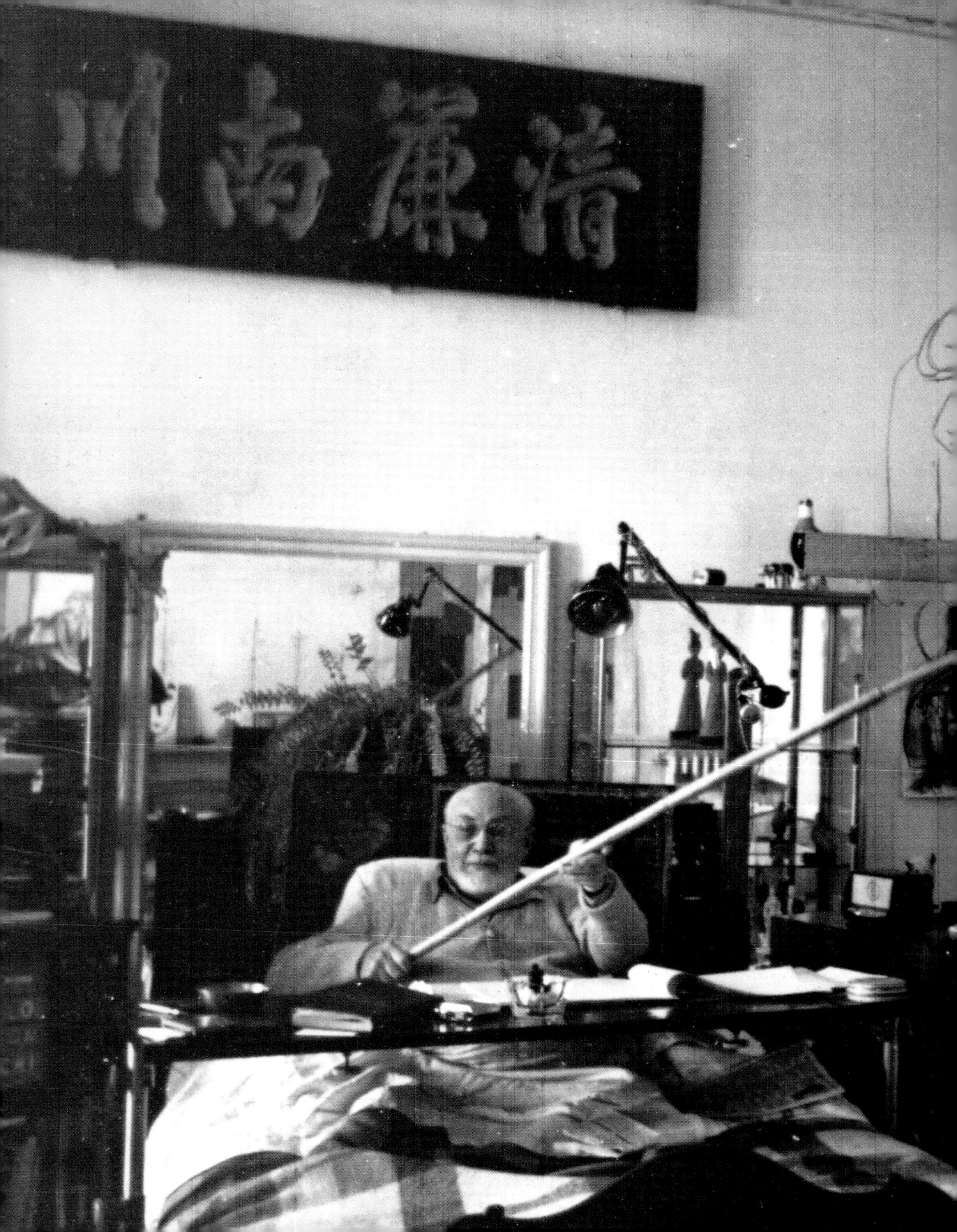

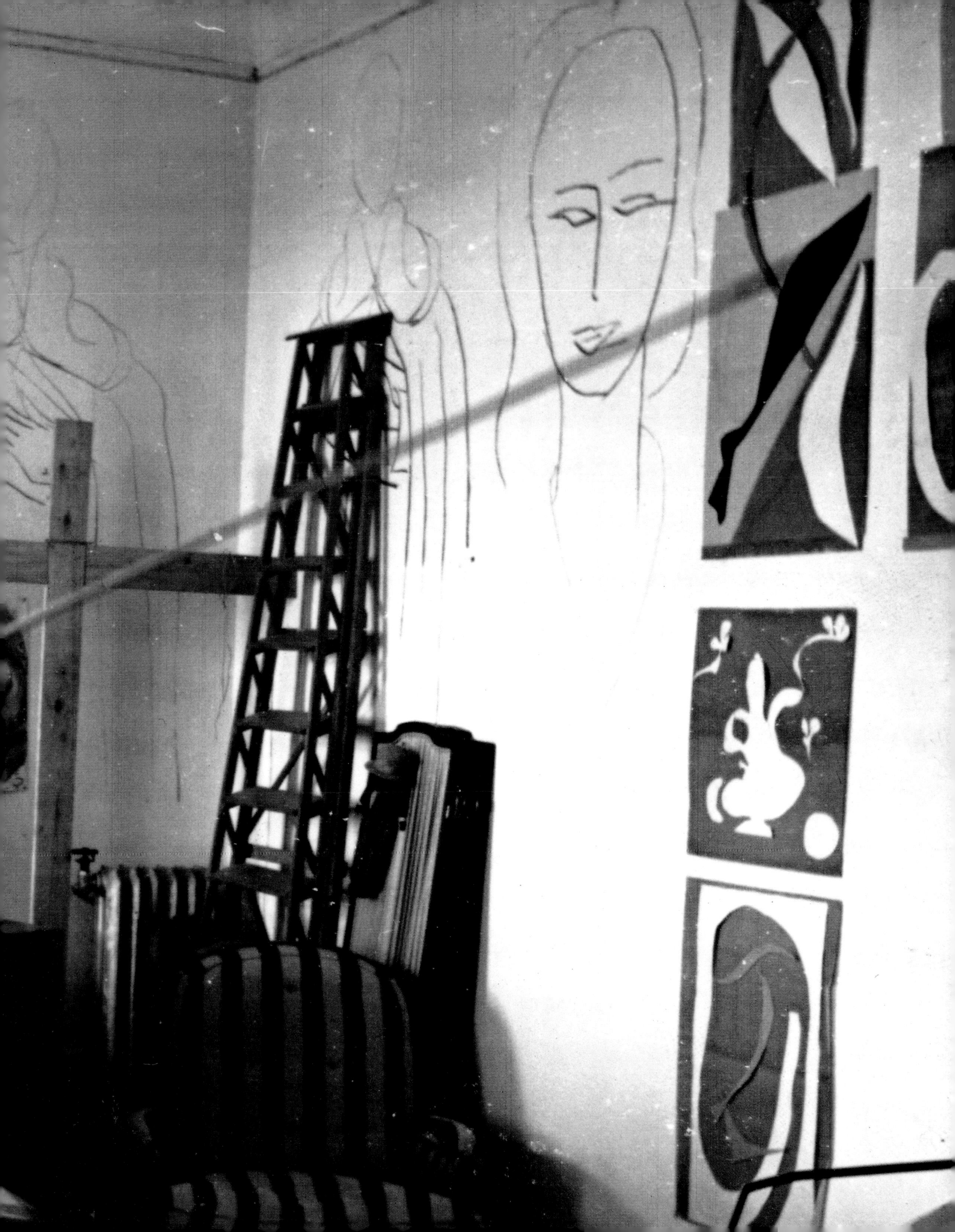

Dalí

Tony Saulnier 1965

"The Venusians have landed!" Welcome to the Dalí-fiction spectacular set in the Couliaro inlet, in Cadaqués, the very place where he shot *L'Age d'or* with the Spanish film director Luis Buñuel thirty-five years ago.

This day of creation is an ephemeral tableau observed by a photographer.

The master himself designed the spare costumes for the Venusians: plastic stretched over a wooden frame with an opening for the head, hands, and feet. "I drew inspiration from the Egyptian statues at Luxor and the Perpignan train station," says Dalí.

Dalí invites Frédérika, his invented queen of the Venusians, to dine at his table. A prisoner of her S-shaped space suit, she nevertheless remains formal throughout the course of the meal. The tablecloth is peppered with sea urchins, "the only animal," Dalí says, "capable of space travel." After their meal, the host has prepared a modest apocalypse: 132 gallons of gas poured into the sea and set on fire.

That same afternoon Dalí produces another tableau vivant: Venusians abducting Earthlings.

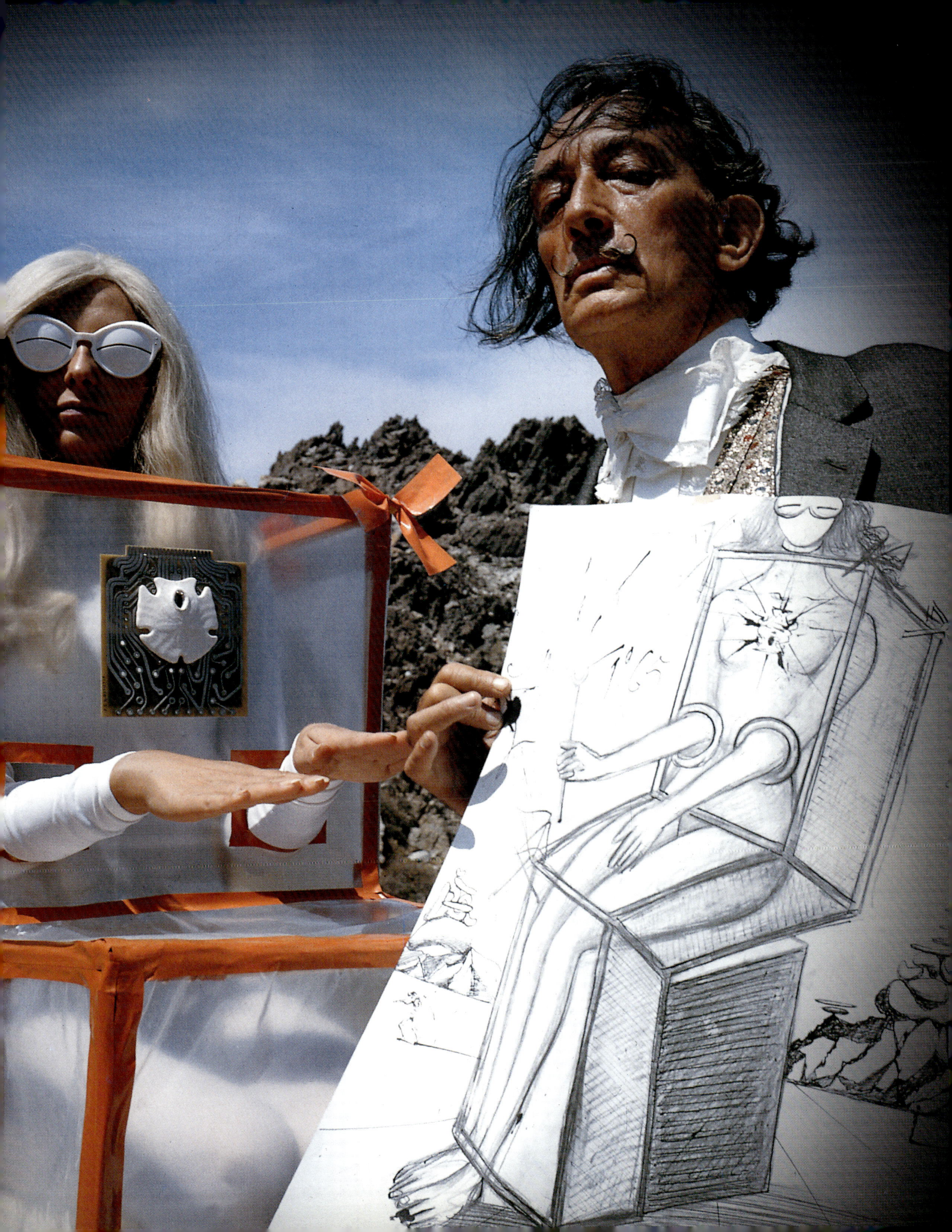

I've known Salvador Dalí since he was twenty-eight years old. Even then his appearance was striking. He was thin and had the beginnings of his signature mustache, which resembled cat whiskers at the time. His eyes were so large, they devoured his face. It's impossible for me to think of Dalí without picturing his huge, frenzied eyes staring at me. My sister, Anne Green, had already known Dalí for two years, but it was the painter Christian Bérard who brought me to see his latest painting at the Galerie Pierre Colle, in Paris, where Dalí was preparing an upcoming exhibition. Bérard introduced us and, over the last fifty-seven years, despite the time and space separating us, our friendship has remained solid. It was like love at first sight.

Four days go by. I'm in his studio and I want to have every picture I see but limit myself to one painting. I focus on a canvas that looks like a big nocturnal butterfly, blue and black against a green sky. There is a saffron-colored band at the horizon. I'm reminded of a line by Rimbaud: "Night comes, pirate black..." How does Dalí manage to convey such vast spaces that give us the impression of taking off into our dreams? The painting that enchants me has a title: *Persistence of Memory*. I take it. But I walked away with a lot more: the memory of discovering a new world and the beginning of a conversation that was like no other, one that continued in Paris and in America as if time existed less for us than it did in Dalí's canvases of color and empty space.

In 1932 Dalí was poor. What a seemingly impossible couple—Dalí and poverty! Yet they lived together despite his mad love for his wife, Gala, or perhaps because of this love—because he hadn't really grown up and did not know how to earn a living. Of course, there was the Surrealist movement, but, in those years, Paris had a population of only a hundred and, unfortunately, painting didn't provide one's daily bread. Public success was won by Bérard, but Dalí's name remained among a small circle. One day, he sent a message to my sister Anne, asking her to come see him "at once." Anne liked him and believed in his work, so she went to his modest apartment near the Parc Montsouris. To her great surprise, he took her to his bedroom and locked the door. His eyes were full of melancholy as he said, "Anne, we don't have any money." My sister came up with the Zodiac plan. Dalí's practical side emerged and the idea took shape. There were twelve of us who paid an annual allowance in exchange for a painting per month; we drew lots for our month. This afforded the artist a worry-free year and, in the meantime, twelve paintings were heading toward the most seen walls in Paris, at the Noailles', the Cuevas', the Faucigny-Lucinges', among others. In one year Dalí was famous, but he immediately understood that with genius alone one starved to death despite admiration, whereas talent was needed for a red carpet to appear under his feet. Fame depended on how much he was willing to push himself; this was the lesson he never forgot. "With talent, you can do what you want. With genius, you do what you can," André Gide said to me.

Among other gifts, Dalí received the genius of publicity. He treated it as it deserved to be treated, with eccentricity and derision. Amazed by this boldness, publicity soon fell in love with him. From that moment on, it had two idols in the world of painting: Picasso and Dalí, the macho and the androgen, both Spaniards. One painted with violence, the other with cruelty. An executioner of bodies and an executioner of minds. But because the people wanted more, Dalí gave it to them with the cold sense of a clinician, the son of Dr. Freud and the greedy and scandalous Alfred Jarry character Père Ubu. He created some of the wildest images in art history: soft watches to set time straight again, liquid desires, and female bodies resembling bedroom armoires.

There came a time when he rolled ferocious eyes, eyes of a child disguised as an ogre to scare his father. This was one of the mysteries of his life. In each one of his paintings, he explained to me that one can see "Dalí at the age of seven, holding his father's hand." Both of them tiny, heading toward the horizon. What was he searching for in his canvases? What did they mean? In his paintings the subconscious becomes tangible. Dalí transforms secret thoughts into objects so that a new world is born on top of the everyday world to the point of erasing it. Dreams enter life and reality gets the hell out through the same door. As Dalí and his father head off into the distance, childhood disappears toward the future. There, he meets up with our immortal reality.

In America, about 1942, Dalí continued to dream with his eyes wide open. He and André Breton—but separately, since they no longer spoke—were the ones I was happiest to see in New York. The Catalan painter brought Paris back to me and we took up our conversations where we had left off. He was the first to make me realize that we see things best through memory, the eye acting as a camera obscura for the mind; the mind, in the lobes of memory, freely recreating reality, "true to all of its details," Dalí said. With a slight smile he added, "A microcosmic reality." He knew how to find the irrefutable word, while all the time mocking pseudoscientific language, which he found amusing. He asked me to write a preface for his retrospective at the Museum of Modern Art in New York, but I was mobilized in the American army and therefore couldn't. Many years later, I wrote the introduction for the large retrospective at the Centre Georges Pompidou. After, I received a charming letter from Dalí exclaiming, "Finally! Time doesn't exist—you're right. And so New York is today." Enclosed was a picture of Don Quixote penetrating a windmill marked "future."

On one occasion, I found myself at one of my cousin's houses, a distant relative of George Washington. Dalí came to see me there. The man who came that day could have been a man unknown by the public; he wasn't role-playing, he was himself, the Dalí with perfect and simple manners, a gentleman. The conversation with my cousin quickly took a Dalí-esque turn, but in the most natural of ways; the world seemed to slide toward reasonable madness. We were no longer seated on winged chairs but on sheep, and the living room sofas were pregnant ewes; the pillows took on the shape of lambs. The living room transformed and the fireplace became a hillside. My cousin was fascinated by Dalí's measured voice, both soft and precise, changing everything through imagination. When he left, everything went back to normal. I was lucky enough to witness other variations of his herd, once in a library, another time in the Senate chambers at the Capitol.

That winter he designed a ballet with my sister. He wanted it to be "velocipedistic." The dancers would be cyclists on their machines. My sister asked how they would manage to dance. There was an immediate answer: the "velocipedes" would be dancers with enormous mustaches. The project was never realized, but, two years later, these cyclists appeared again, painted into the backdrop of his ballet *Colloque Sentimental,* wearing bridal veils on their heads.

Dalí was bored by Europe, as I was, and every occasion seemed right for us to get together. He traveled by car even though he despised this means of transportation. So as not to look at the road and the Coca-Cola advertisements that "riled" him, he painted his own landscapes on the windows. "There are no landscapes in America," he told me, "there are only geological accidents."

"That may be true," I answered, "but an American landscape is a Dalí painting in cosmic dimensions." He liked this interpretation very much.

It is a wonder that he was able to render immense landscapes of deserts and extensive dunes within a small format. The anxiety one senses from viewing these panels stems from beneath the lacquer of a flawless painting, as if he had imprisoned the world behind the thin veil of a dream. Who will assure us that we will be able to return from those empty beaches? In his paintings, the dog that sleeps at the bottom of the sea, the tigers that roar toward the sun—these images lure us to a world unknown and frightening. I have spoken of silent paintings, but no, they are full of ultrasounds and cries that are only perceptible to our subconscious.

There is one aspect of Dalí's work that resists all analyses, all scholarly research; an aspect that no longer has anything to do with either admiration or ambition. As spectators, we are before a man for whom the world is no longer enough, and who tries in vain to rid himself of his false identity. He makes himself up, he amuses the gallery, he accumulates provocations and honors, his cat whiskers become tiger whiskers, billions pour down upon the one who used to say, "We don't have any money." But the Catholic Spaniard is well aware that this whole circus is nothing. He was in search of Dalí, and through his dreams, he tried to discover his soul. His attempts left us fleeting and splendid visions.

—Julien Green

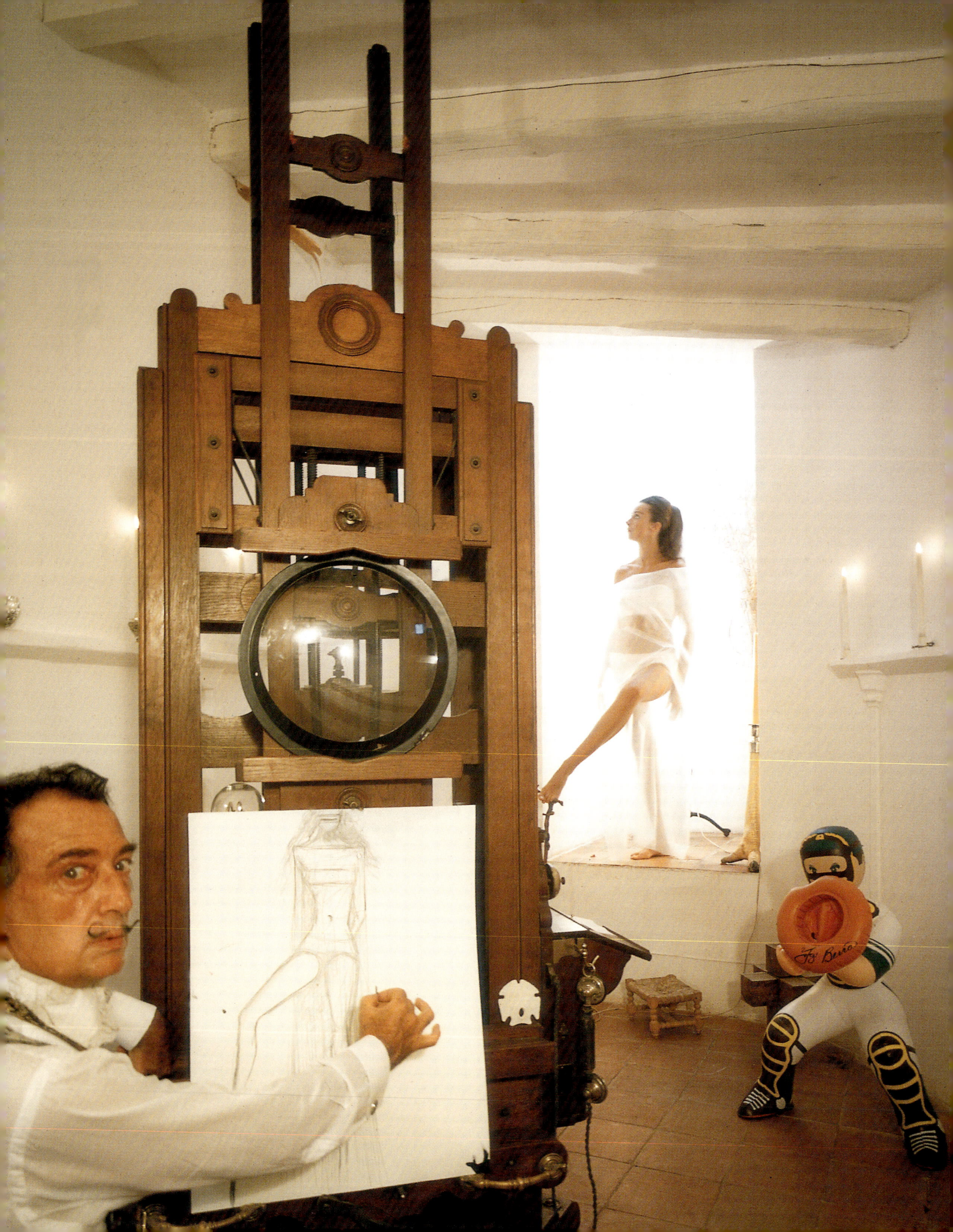

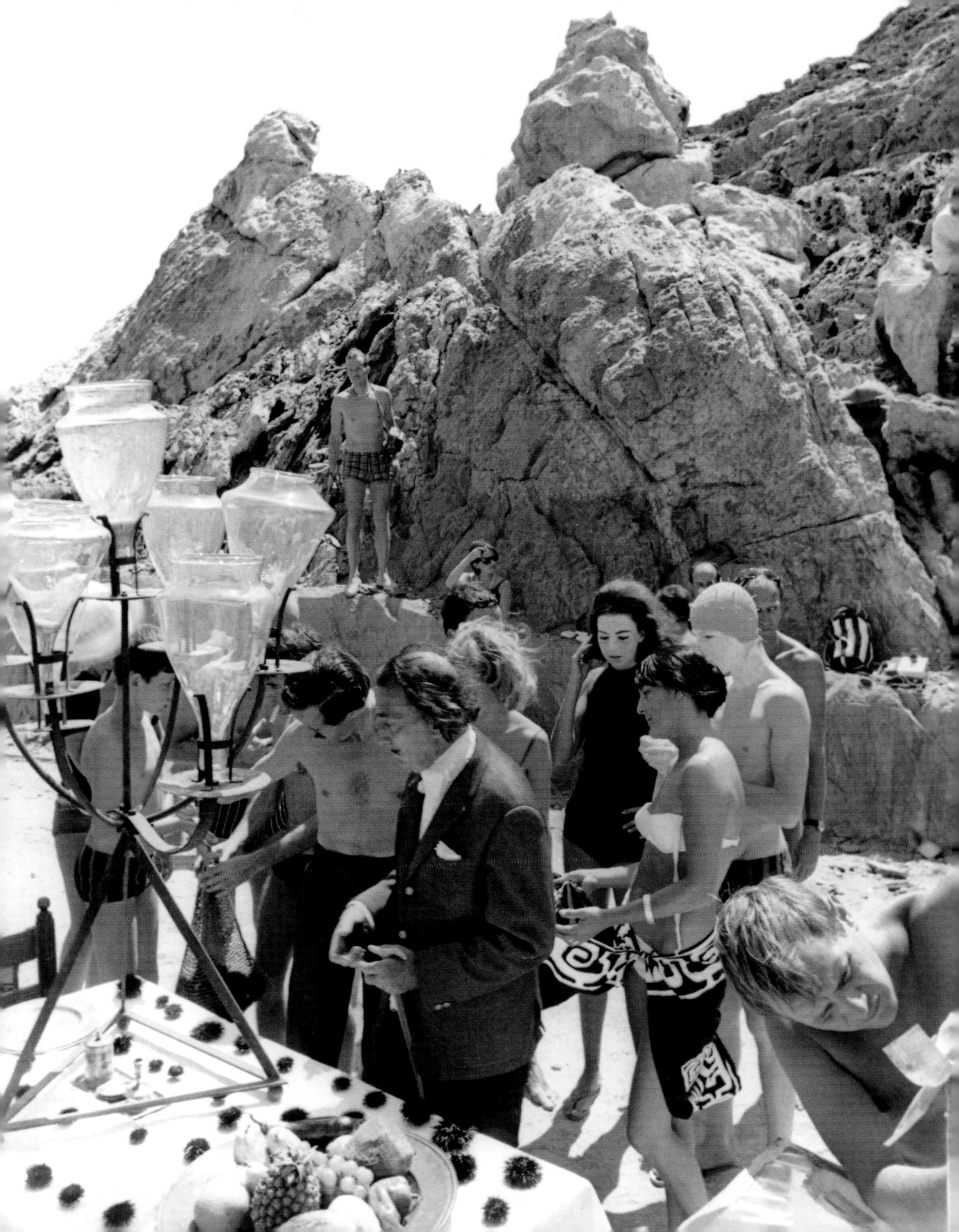

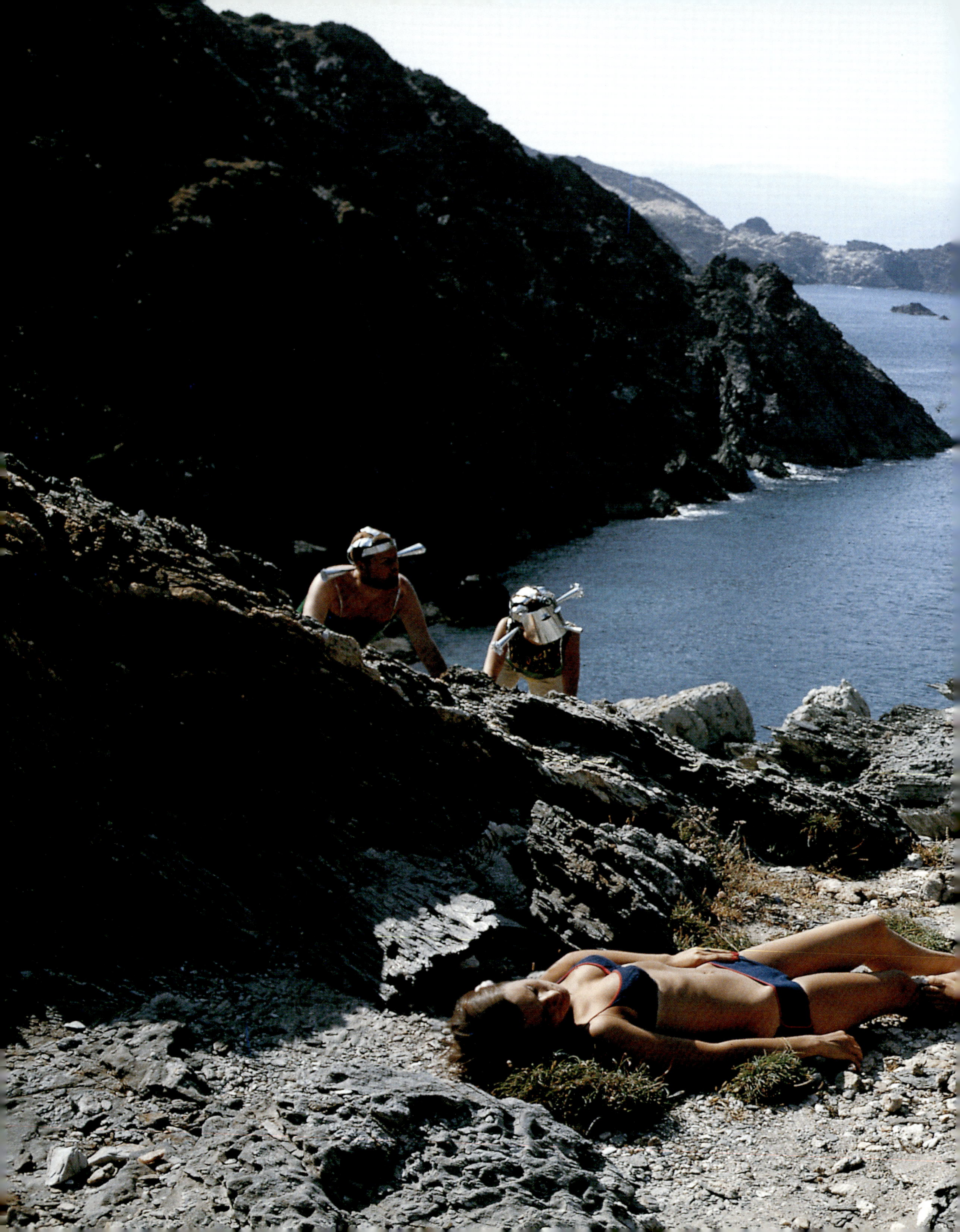

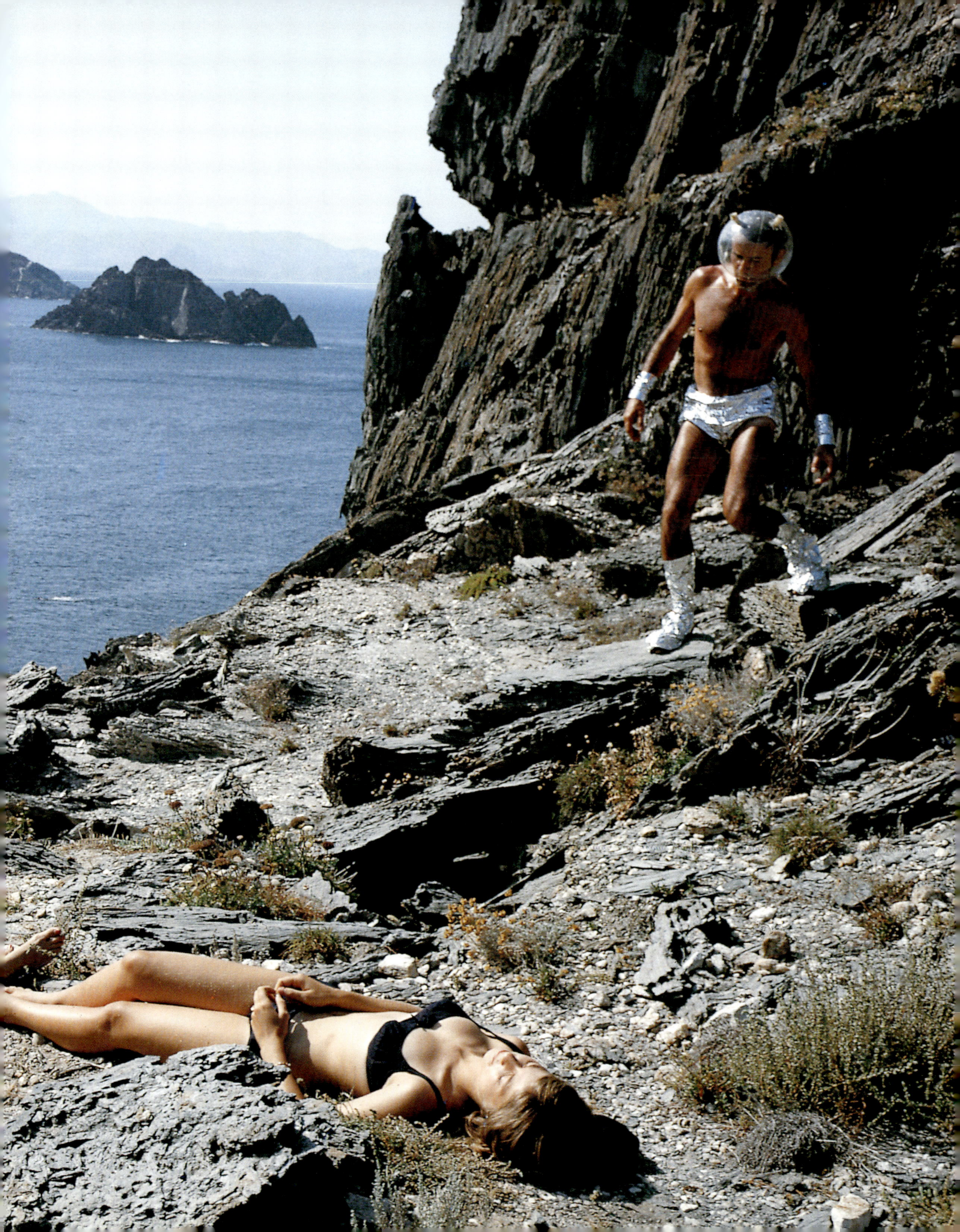

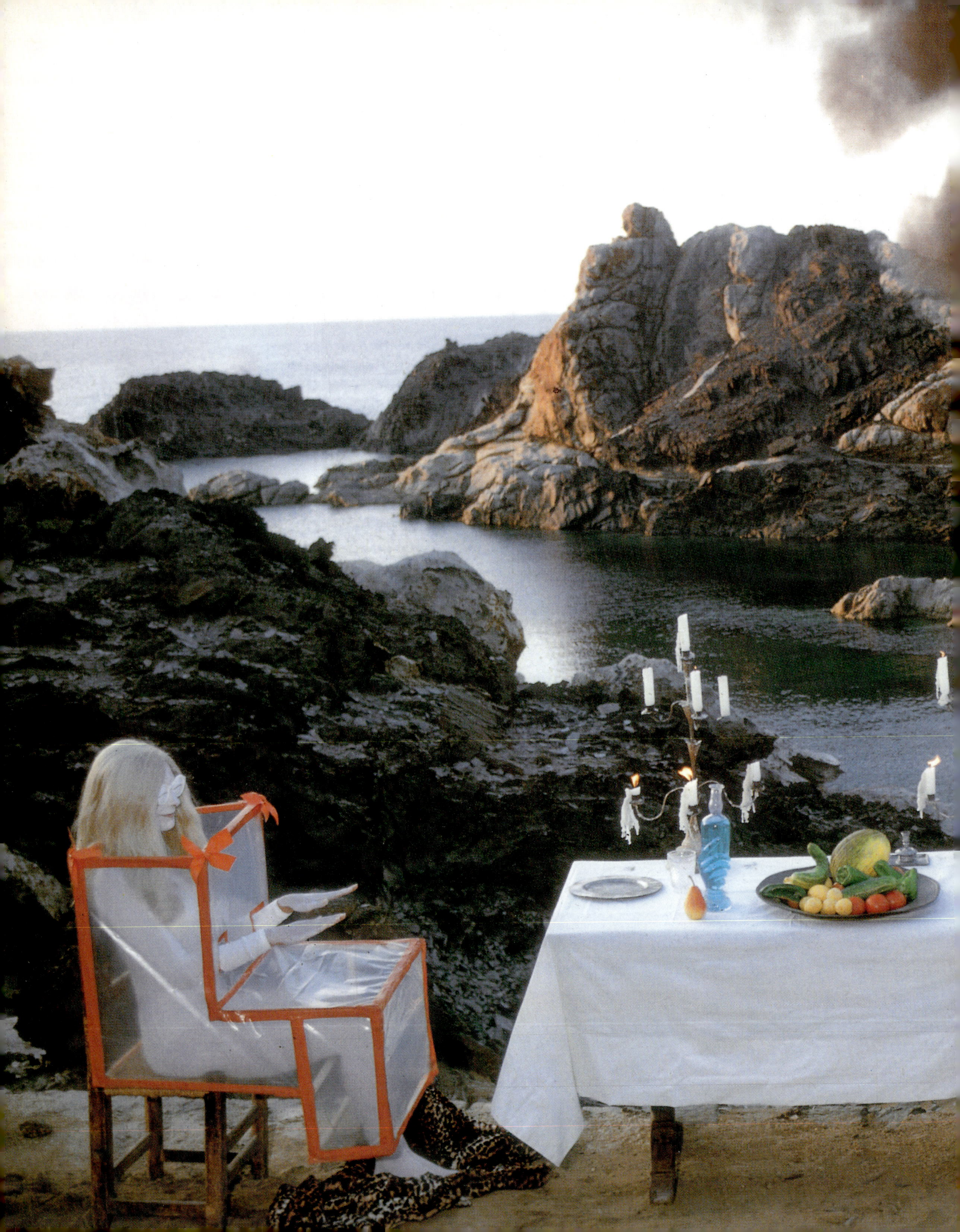

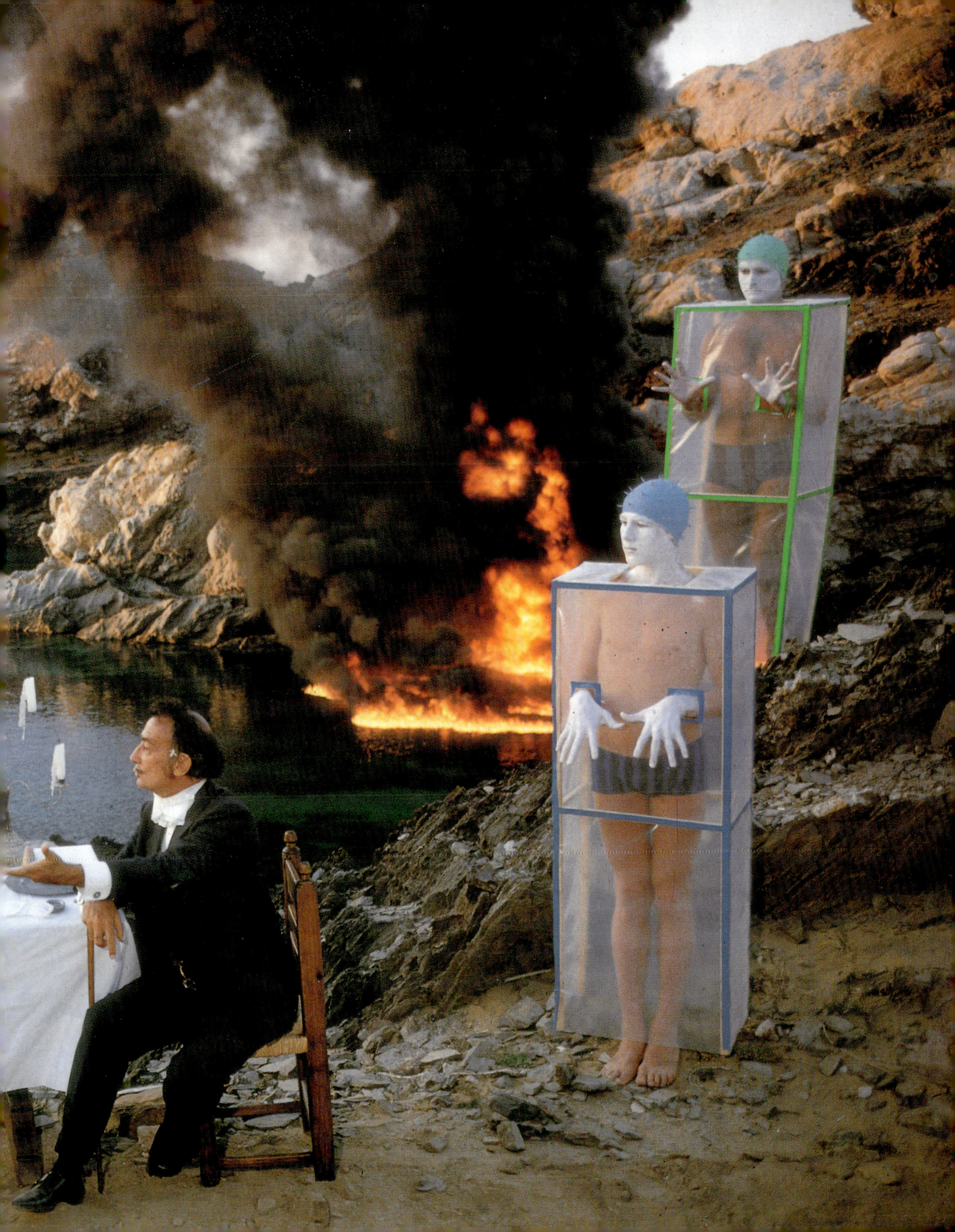

Bacon

Barry
Joule
1982

Do Francis Bacon's paintings resemble him? Or did Bacon himself end up resembling his paintings? This is the greatest mystery surrounding one of the twentieth century's most enigmatic artists.

At the door of his studio, an anguished Bacon confronts his *Human Study,* which faces him on the easel.

Bacon's flat is both his heaven and his hell. No one ever enters this space or touches anything. A sense of mingled confusion, beauty, and nightmare prevail.

He has turned one wall of the studio into a palette for mixing colors.

Alone and serene in Paris after his "onslaught of creativity," Bacon awaits the arrival of friends and lovers of his art—eight thousand of them appear at a gallery on the first day.

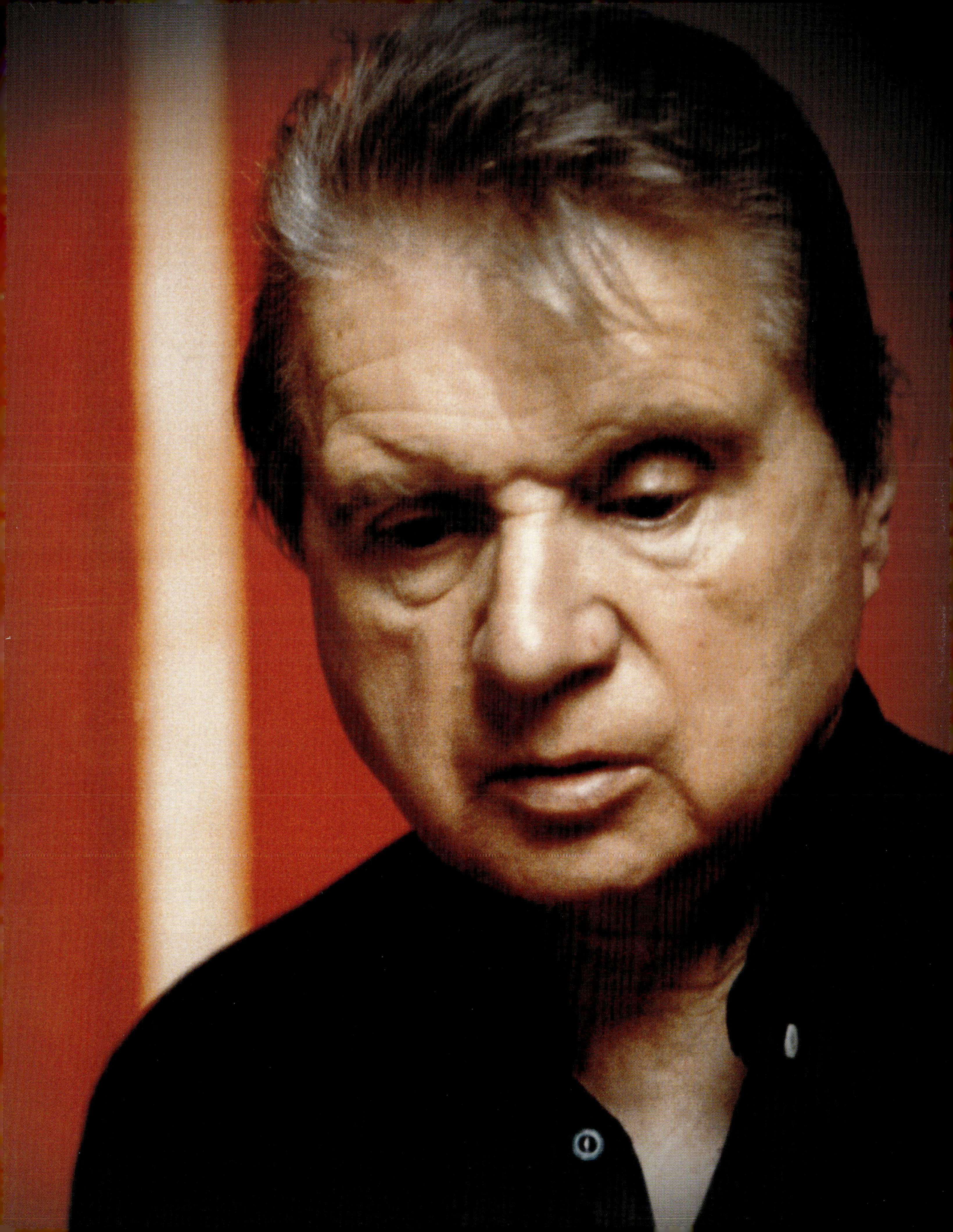

On a sweltering summer day in London 1977, I was busy washing my car in front of my Kensington house when a face appeared in the neighbor's kitchen window and called out "Hi, you!" in a refined sort of way. It was my first never-to-be forgotten glimpse of Francis Bacon. The night before he'd heard a bang on his roof and now he asked if I'd be good enough to investigate. His television aerial had keeled over. I offered to fix it, and afterward he asked me in.

The first thing I saw was a large panel representing a contorted figure with strange, piercing eyes. I was twenty-three years old and fresh from conventional Canada, which I'd left to travel the world in pursuit of life's mysteries. Now, bizarrely, I had stumbled into the Ali Baba's cave of a powerful and disturbing form of art. Still sweating from my exertions on the roof, and stupefied by the pure, prodigious energy radiating from the picture, I found myself deeply moved by it—so moved that I failed to utter a word.

Francis watched my reactions closely. Then, as if he'd read my mind, he handed me a drink and asked if there was something about the painting I didn't understand.

"Not something—everything!" I said impulsively. "What were you looking for?"

"Well, as a matter of fact, I think I found it," said Francis calmly.

I had no artistic education to speak of, and, in my present state of shock, I was hardly equipped to debate the question. Instead I stammered out something commonplace and stared uncomfortably at the book-strewn floor. Then an amazing thing happened: in the simplest, purest language imaginable, Francis began to talk about why and how he painted complex, peculiar figures like this one. He explained that with luck and by dint of manipulations and roiling brushwork, smears, deposits, and trails of paint laid on the rough side of the canvas, he'd discovered how to make new, exciting things appear.

"I'd be as boring as Canada," he said, "if I went on painting faces and bodies like painters have been doing for the last four centuries. As far as I'm concerned, there's no medium more fluid or mysterious than paint. I try to paint people and things as I feel them to be."

He quoted one of his favorite painters, van Gogh, while scribbling at the same time on a piece of paper. "My greatest desire is to learn how to change and recreate reality. I want my paintings to be *un*faithful, *ab*normal; I want them to be lies, if you like—but lies much truer than the simple truth."

He scooped up a blob of white paint with the tip of his finger and flicked it over his shoulder at the canvas, then turned to examine the result. It seemed to please him. "I gamble with life, love, and art," he said. "I think I'll just have another tiny go at this painting."

He seized a sponge soaked in purple paint and casually wiped over one half of the face. Then he stood back and tossed the sponge to the other side of the studio, where it splattered into a pile of dog-eared photographs. This explosion of creative energy took my breath away. Next he rubbed his fingers in dust, and I wondered if this too would end up on the paint surface. Not today. Francis lowered his hand and led me into the sitting room next door. It was a simple, tidy space.

"What do you do when you're unhappy with what you've done?"

"Well, if it can't be helped, I just kiss it goodbye. I destroy it and start again."

A few months later, I saw for myself exactly how ruthless Francis could be with his own work. He called me over to his house, handed me a sharp knife, and looked on while I ripped a canvas to shreds. His fame was so great at that time that he couldn't just throw his rejects away: people routinely sifted through his garbage, looking for discarded treasures. That day he gave me a book just as I was leaving. It was the first volume of his long series of interviews with David Sylvester, and for a while it was my bible.

The sale of *Human Study* was the excuse for a memorable binge of drinking and eating. By the time it was over, we were barely able to stand. At this moment Francis—drunkenly, but with great tenderness—presented me with a small self-portrait from his early years. Then he dug out an old frame and gave me that, too, but the picture was too big for the frame, and since I was roaring drunk I grabbed a saw and cut off the excess. Francis signed the frame for me, and, as I was leaving, loaded me with eight more early pieces, most of them painted on wood. Since they couldn't be torn up, he said, did I mind taking them down to the Chelsea incinerator for burning? I staggered home and shoved them under my bed.

Two days later, a chastened Francis called. Had I done as he asked? I said yes. Could he "borrow" the self-portrait he'd given me? I handed it back, without the frame, and it was swallowed forever by his studio.

Then Francis gave me three volumes of van Gogh's letters written to his brother, Theo. I reveled in this marvelous, crystal-clear correspondence. But shortly after, he commanded me to return the books, accusing me of being a "book thief." When I inquired what he'd done with the drawings that had been ripped out of them, he just said they were "raw material." He had no respect for the visual appeal of books—all he saw was the creative contribution they might make to some future work of his own.

Another time, at my house, he picked up a book of the photographer Francesco Scavullo's images of nude men, and asked if he could borrow some of them. Then to my amazement he ripped out the pages he wanted, stuffed them in his pocket and closed the book with evident satisfaction. They resurfaced years later in some boxes destined for the incinerator—torn, crumpled, and spotted with paint, victims of Francis's perpetual creative quest.

"I never know where I get my ideas," he said. "The mind is a sieve, but the brain records everything we see. I just run my memories through my nervous system, hoping an image will appear. Images can come from reading, too."

Bacon often quoted a gruesome line from the *Oresteia* by the Greek dramatist Aeschylus. "'The reek of human blood smiles out at me,' What a marvelous idea for a painting," said Francis.

Another time I watched him climb a rickety ladder to splash scarlet all over a large picture. The effect was immediate and explosive, resulting in *Blood on the Floor,* 1986, which was later shown at the Galerie Lelong in New York.

Francis was not fazed by the high prices being paid for his work. The only action that excited him was painting. He gave me one of his favorite books, an edition of T. S. Eliot's *The Waste Land* marked with Ezra Pound's original comments. The following lines from Eliot's poem provoked a visible anguish in Francis: *"...I have heard the key / Turn in the door once and turn once only..."* These lines reminded him of his close friend George Dyer, who committed suicide on the eve of the great 1971 retrospective at the Grand Palais in Paris. *Triptych—May-June 1973,* a scream of agony that memorialized Dyer's suicide, greatly shocked the art world with the violence and beauty of its grief.

"The facts leave ghosts behind them," Francis used to say. His life was strewn with such ghosts; his supreme gift was to contain them by the physical act of painting. Paris, where Dyer's tragedy took place, had been Francis's favorite city ever since 1928 when he saw a Picasso exhibition there at the Paul Rosenberg Gallery. He always acknowledged his debt to Picasso, whom he placed at the pinnacle of twentieth-century art and tried many times to paint a portrait of the Spanish master, but every attempt ended up in pieces on the studio floor. One day, when I was tape-recording him, he told me, "How awful it is, comparing oneself to Picasso!"

Although Francis had never been able to work in Paris, he always viewed the French capital city as the best place to exhibit art because the people there actually took the trouble to look. Success in Paris was for him the summit of his achievements. He dreamed of a companion who could work with him, just like Ezra Pound worked with Eliot. I secretly hoped I would be chosen, but it wasn't to be. Francis remained alone and independent to the end.

The winter of 1991–92 was a very difficult one for him. He had to grapple with the pain of a recent lost love, severe bouts of asthma, and heart problems—enough to kill even a much younger man.

At eighty-two years of age, he sensed that the end was near. "I hope I can go on painting and die at my work, as Titian and Picasso did. The most important thing is the instinct for work." But it turned out differently. He died in Madrid on April 28, 1992, still trying to recover from the loss of his love—a handsome young Spaniard I had introduced him to in 1986.

When I heard that Francis died alone in a Spanish hospital, I grieved that the last great bohemian, a man of immense spiritual generosity, had left this life in such a way. Francis went out still believing that the only thing that mattered was what one did between birth and death, the two frontiers of the Absolute. For his many friends and disciples, the vacuum left in his absence can never quite be filled by his legacy of great art. The images in his work may have encapsulated his personal sufferings and expressed a universal pain, but what about the friends he left behind? A few phrases, scribbled in French on one of the books he gave me, have partly abated my wretchedness at the loss of my great friend and mentor.

"It is easier to love a work of art sincerely than it is to love a man, for material considerations seldom penetrate a work of art. In art there is almost no risk that love will founder in sensuality."

—Barry Joule

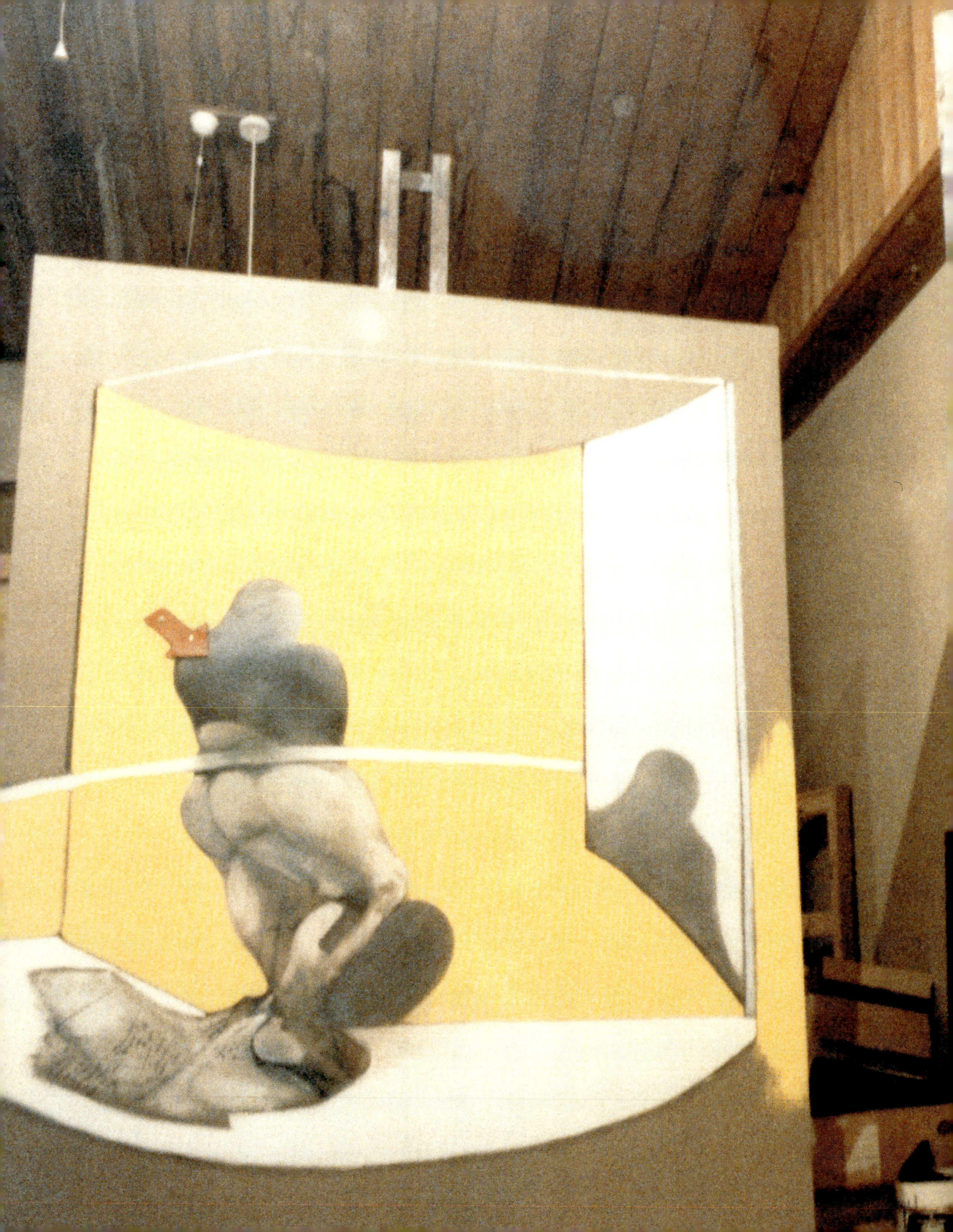

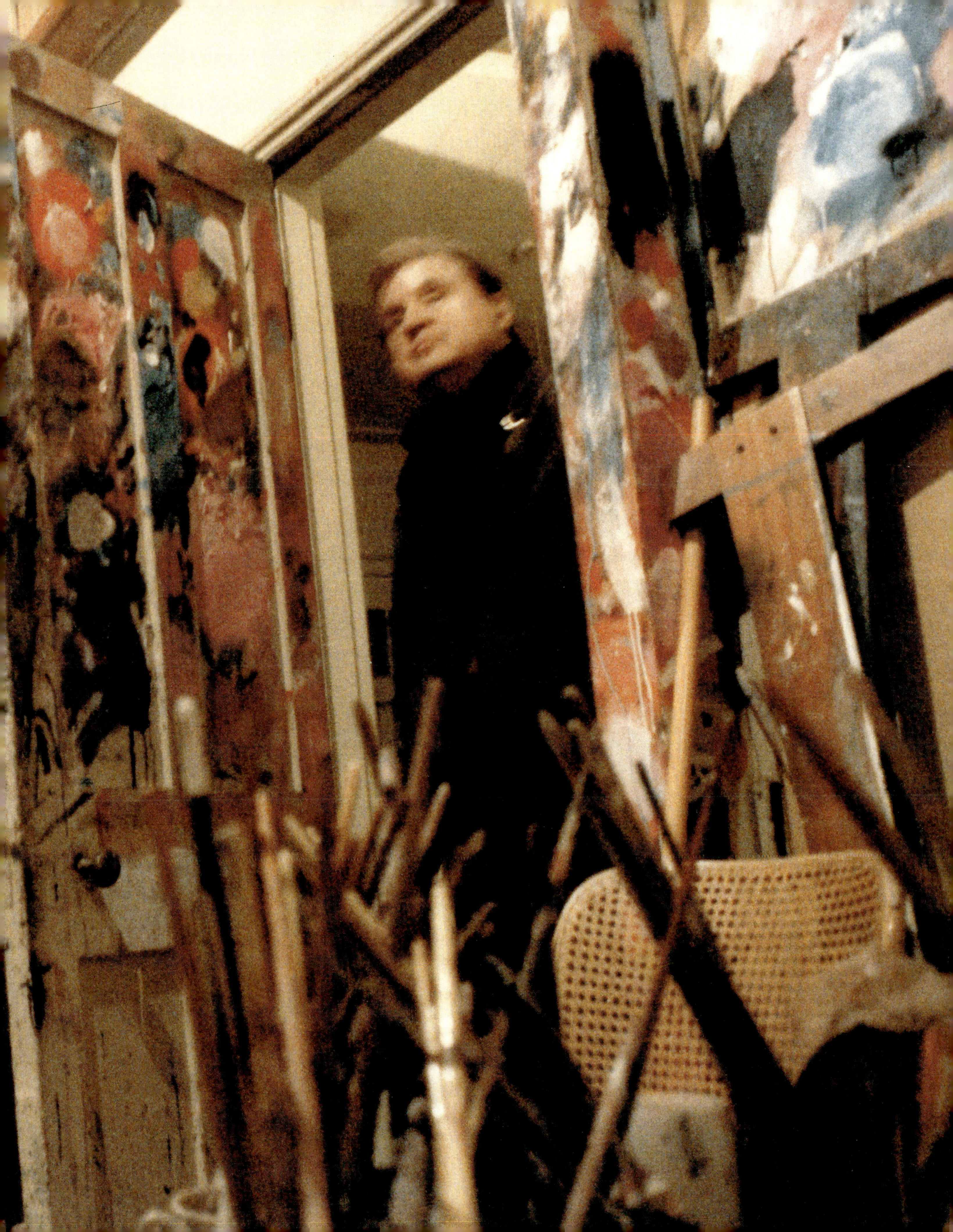

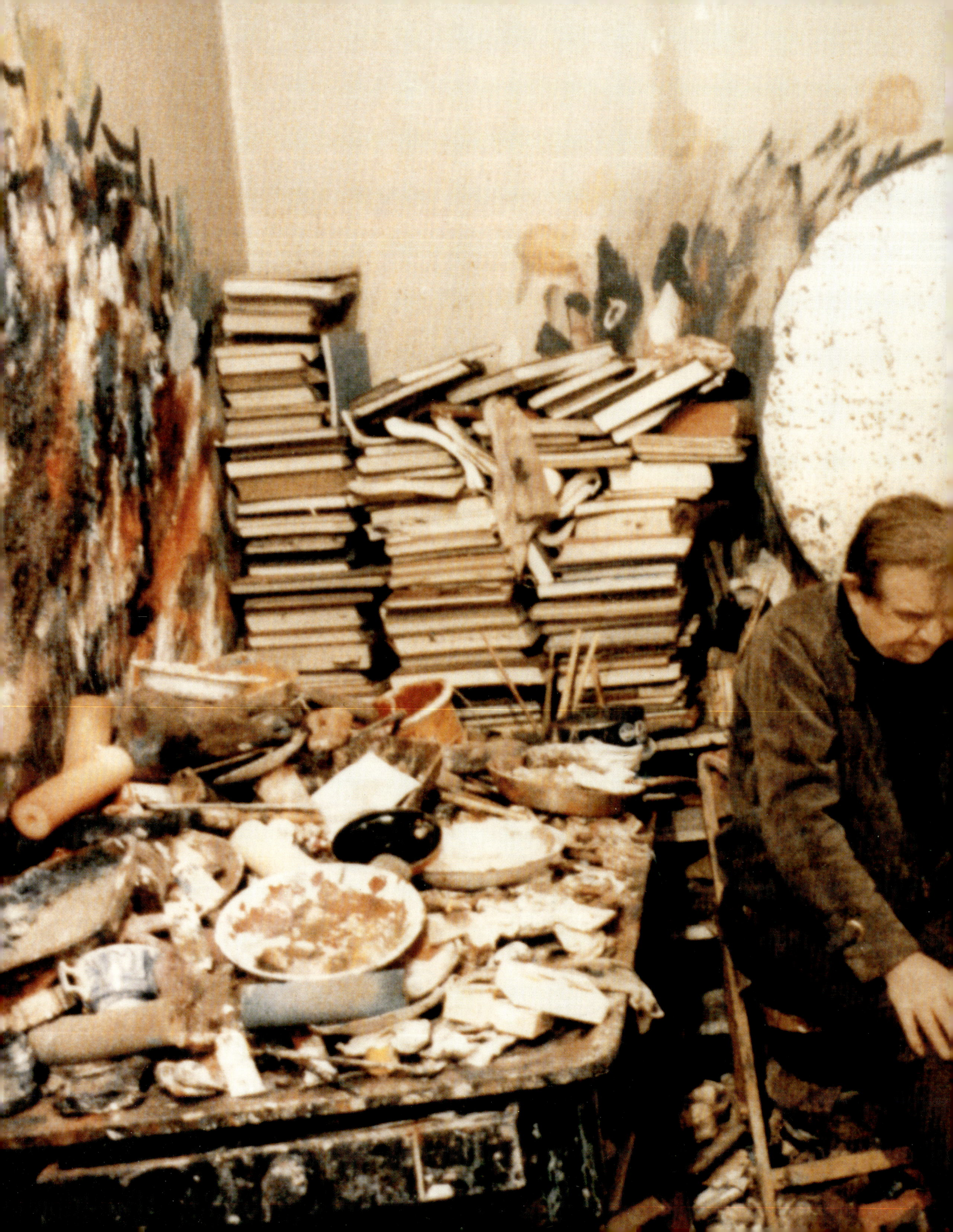

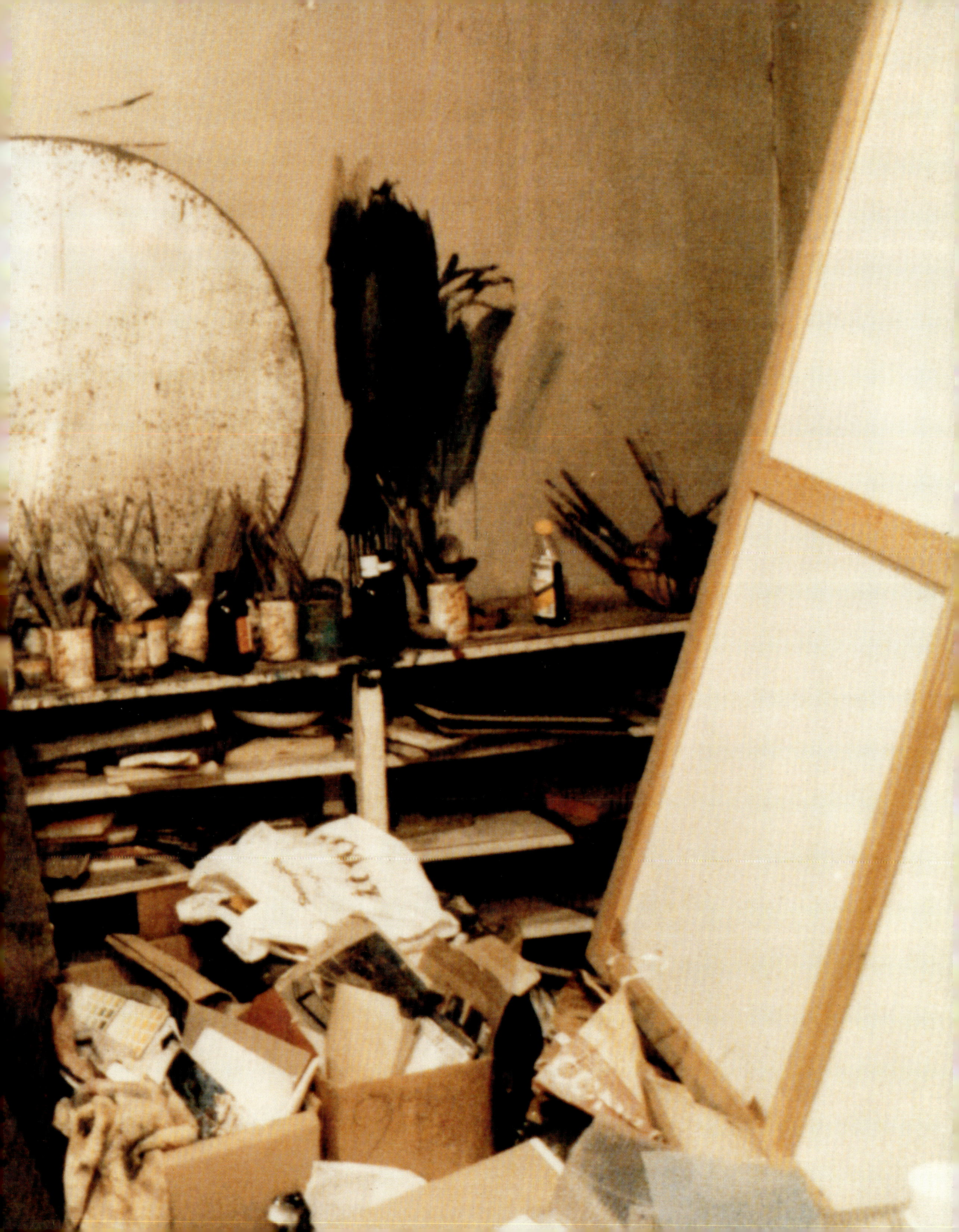

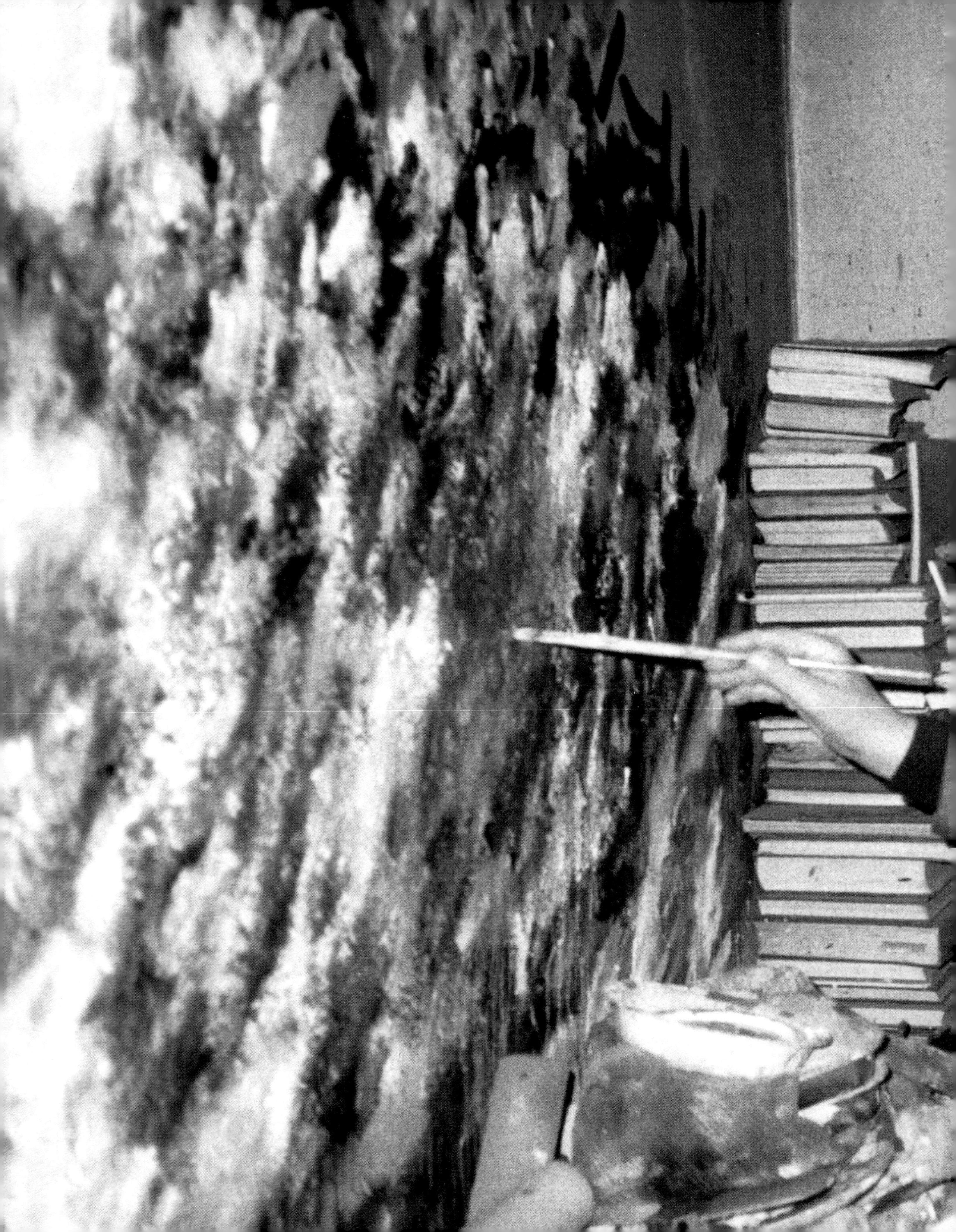

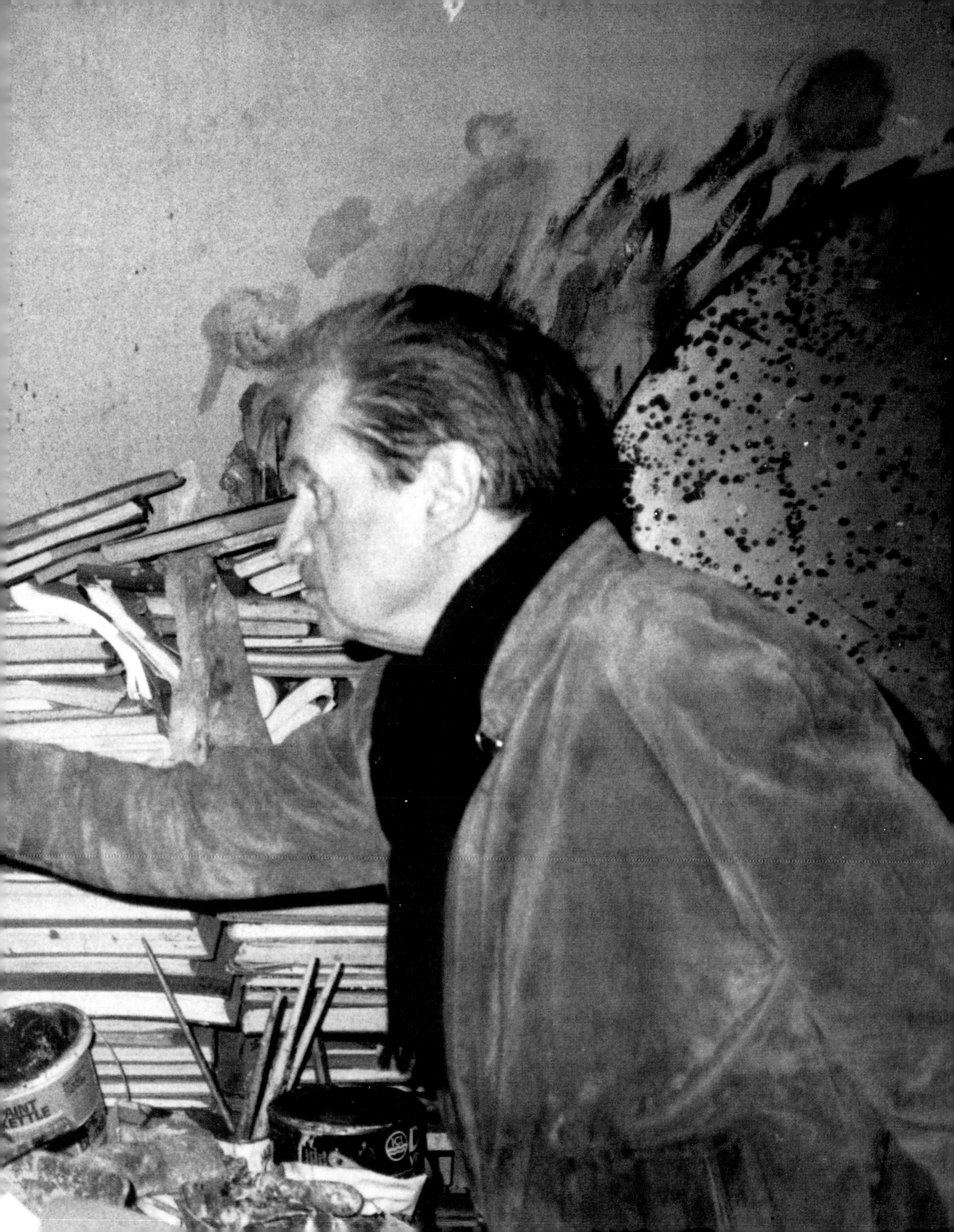
PAINT
KETTLE

During our twenty years of friendship, Francis Bacon's lucidity, absolute honesty, strong personality, and corrosive humor captivated me and helped me involve myself more closely in my own work. The only promise that great art can keep to us is that it will push us to attempt something similar.

To preserve as best I could the incalculable treasure of Francis, I began recording a disparate series of interviews—a reconstruction of the jottings in my notebooks, which had been lost in a fire—desperately, because Francis adamantly refused to waste his time repeating himself. His priorities were thought and continual work, and, as a result, he was sparing with words, preferring a very personal, intense silence. I originally wanted to write a book about Francis Bacon and his views on the evolution of our species on earth, and on the deserts we seem to leave in our wake. "Many extraordinary things have happened to me," he once said, concentrating hard and staring straight into my eyes. *"But I don't want to be extraordinary at all."*

Fortunately he agreed, as a friend, to read a series of questions I wrote, and then to meet me a little later and record his answers.

Work

"Sometimes things work, but sometimes no good comes of them at all. I see myself as a kind of cement mixer. Everything goes in, and from time to time something comes out. Sometimes the cement is quite gray. Out of every ten paintings I'm aware of, I hate nine, and that includes my own. I dislike almost everything I see. I think that if someone produces one or two exceptional pieces of work, that's already a great deal."

Portraits

"I always tried to paint portraits that went beyond the simple illustration of the person in front of me, hoping that I could render the real appearance of my subject in a non-illustrative way."

On luck

"Everything that ever worked well for me is the result of luck, of accidents with which I was able to work. I didn't start out knowing what I wanted to say here, for example" (showing a detail of a painting). "I don't think I could paint another picture if I found I knew exactly what I was doing. I simply work on, hoping luck will lend a hand. It's the same with everything I do."

Nerves

"No, I don't often think about nervous exhaustion. I can feel it inside me all the time; I think it affects me without my knowing it; but I can't say I'm consciously aware of it."

Instinct

"I'm very egotistical about my work. I freely admit that. I'm completely engrossed in my world, which perhaps reflects violent tensions, empty spaces—but none of it is conscious. We're all artificial and anguished; I just think my instincts lie in this direction. What people call 'natural' is a very relative notion, just like everything else."

Order

"My personality has several facets. For example, I like perfection. I even like perfection on a grand scale. In a sense, I'd like to live in a very grand house; but since one makes such a mess when one paints, I prefer to live in this clutter, on a pile of broken objects and memories. I think all of us have these two sides. One side craves order, the other craves chaos. We have to fight to impose order."

On luck (again)

"I'm quite sure that luck has a thousand ways of getting into people's lives. I know how it gets into mine: I'm painting a picture and suddenly I say to myself, God, that's awful, and reach without thinking for a brush or a rag, and suddenly everything tilts sideways and there's an image. From that image I can extract the thing I was instinctively after when I began. But I think all that comes from incessant work, a sort of internal programming one's quite unaware of. In a sense, one works without stopping, thinking, constantly looking at things which have nothing whatever to do with what one's trying to achieve, but which will come in useful later. One digs a great well of images inside oneself, and objects keep bubbling up to the surface. Truth comes in through the strangest doors."

Life

"I don't see painting as an equivalent of life, but oddly enough I believe the paintings I love reflect life and restore me to a more violent sense of living, like any other form of art that moves me. Most masterpieces intensify life."

Abstraction

"Almost all abstract art leaves me cold. All I see in it are shapes that are more or less beautiful. It seems to me that most abstract art is ornament, belonging to the art of decorating interiors—of making a pretty room or a beautiful hall for somebody. I know very well that most abstract painters would disagree with that, but to my mind there isn't much else in there but a kind of insipid beauty. You can't compel people to see something or ignore something in a picture. Everybody sees painting in a different way. I'll tell you how I see my own work: it lubricates the valves of sensation on several levels."

Blood

"If you see somebody lying in the sun on the pavement in a great pool of blood, the sight of it, blood on asphalt, is very invigorating and galvanizing. Whenever I've seen car accidents—all those corpses lying by the road—the first impression was one of shocking beauty, something extreme, well before it occurred to me to do something about it. That's because the sight is so exceptional. One day I saw a serious accident on a main road. Corpses were lying in a mass of broken glass, there was blood everywhere and personal things scattered all over the place and it was all tragically beautiful. I think beauty of that kind is terribly fleeting, but it was unquestionably there, in the way the bodies were distributed, in their postures, and the blood too..."

Death

"Death is the only absolute we know of in life, the only clear certainty. Artists know nothing can be done about it. They are acutely aware of their coming annihilation, and the awareness of it follows them around like a shadow. I think this is why most artists are so alert to the fragility and fatuity of life, and to the vulnerability of their lives and the lives of others."

Myself

"It's very difficult to talk about oneself and one's work, because one can't look at oneself in the objective way an outside observer can. Also it's incredibly difficult to talk about oneself, because one tends to be less hard on oneself than one is on other people.

I hate an awful lot of my paintings. I deeply dislike all those popes, for example. For me they're *aesthetic* works; I don't like their *shape*. They could have been much better. I keep on hoping something special will happen. That excites me—hope is very important to me."

Painters

"I appreciate certain paintings—even ones by artists of my own generation. I'm a great admirer of some of the work of Picasso and Duchamp, but I think that no matter who the artist is, you can only really like certain stages and certain pictures. In general, painters get better as they age. I'd like to create images that reflect a certain number of intuitions about my own species; in my own arbitrary fashion, I'd like to clear the way for an authentic approach to human beings. It's a tall order. People find my habit of deforming images, which actually gets me closer to the human being than if I were doing conventional portraits, quite disconcerting; but my approach does work—I get closer even as I distance myself."

Aesthetics

"If painting is the way it is today, it's because it's been very difficult to carry on being figurative, and because abstract art has seemed to be the logical continuation of figurative art. Nearly all abstract art resembles decoration because in abstract art the painter is left completely to his own devices and can do all kinds of pretty things. That's very difficult to carry off in figurative art, where it's virtually impossible to avoid painting the human body in the manner of an illustrator. A photographer does the job better. Describing something is an arduous task—you have to be content to speak as your own instincts dictate and not bother with the rest. The moment comes when an image seems right—right from the point of view of sensation, aesthetically right. I think it's intriguing that a man like Marcel Duchamp, who attacked everything that in his time was qualified as aesthetic, eventually became the most aesthetic artist of the twentieth century. I can only say that he must have had a profoundly aesthetic temperament, although he himself was against what was thought beautiful at the time, the contemporary aesthetic. He ended up creating a body of work that was every bit as aesthetic, perhaps even more so. Duchamp had such sensitivity that everything he did became very beautiful. He even died in an aesthetic way: first he laid down, and then he died."

Intelligence

"I've known extraordinarily intelligent people who wanted to become artists, but who never managed it. Intelligence is not the primary quality of an artist. Churchill is a case in point; although he was quite brilliant, there's no trace of his intelligence in his paintings. Nietzsche was the Cassandra of the nineteenth century who foresaw the future. He said the world was so absurd that in the coming times we would be completely free to be extraordinary."

—Peter Beard

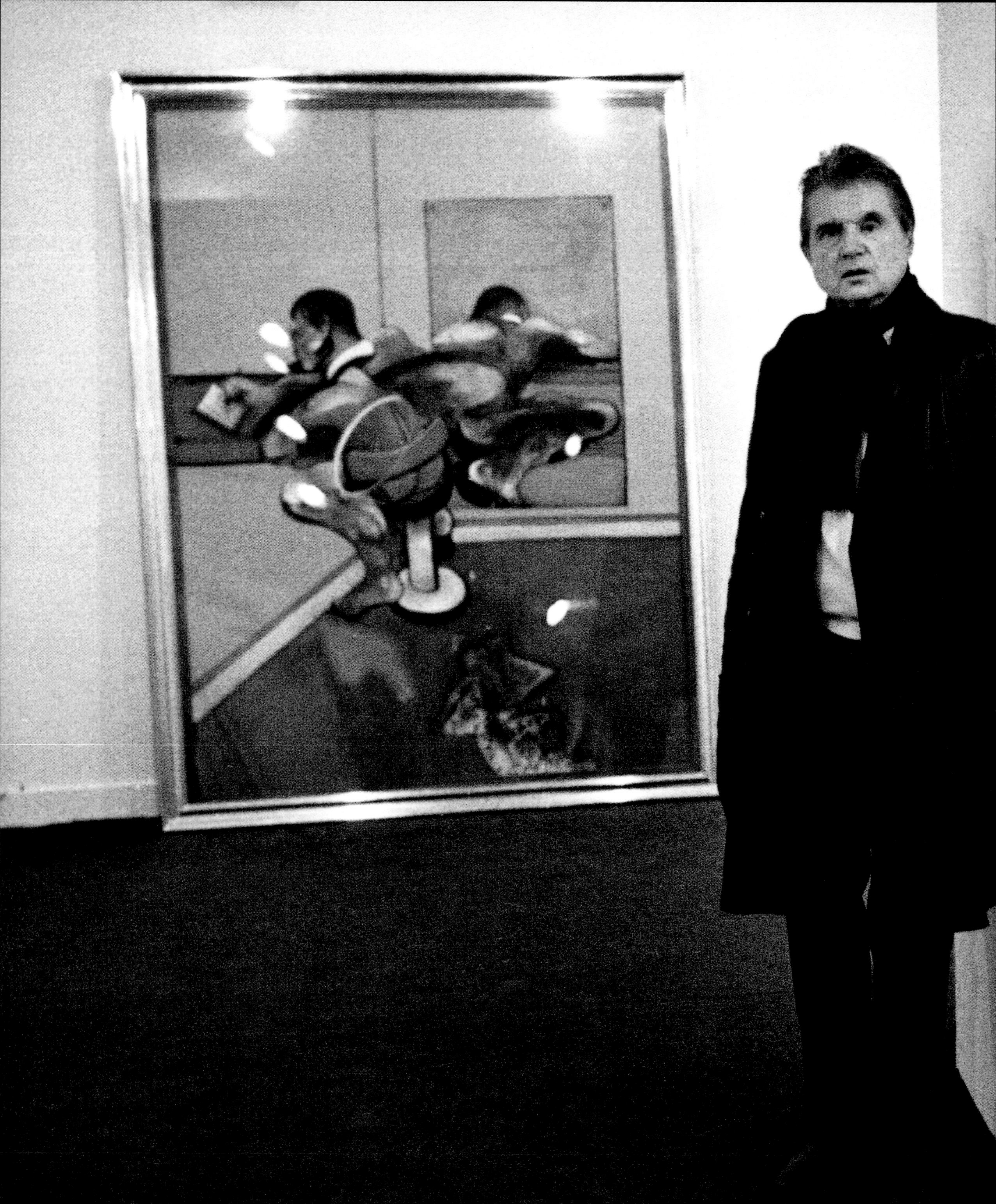

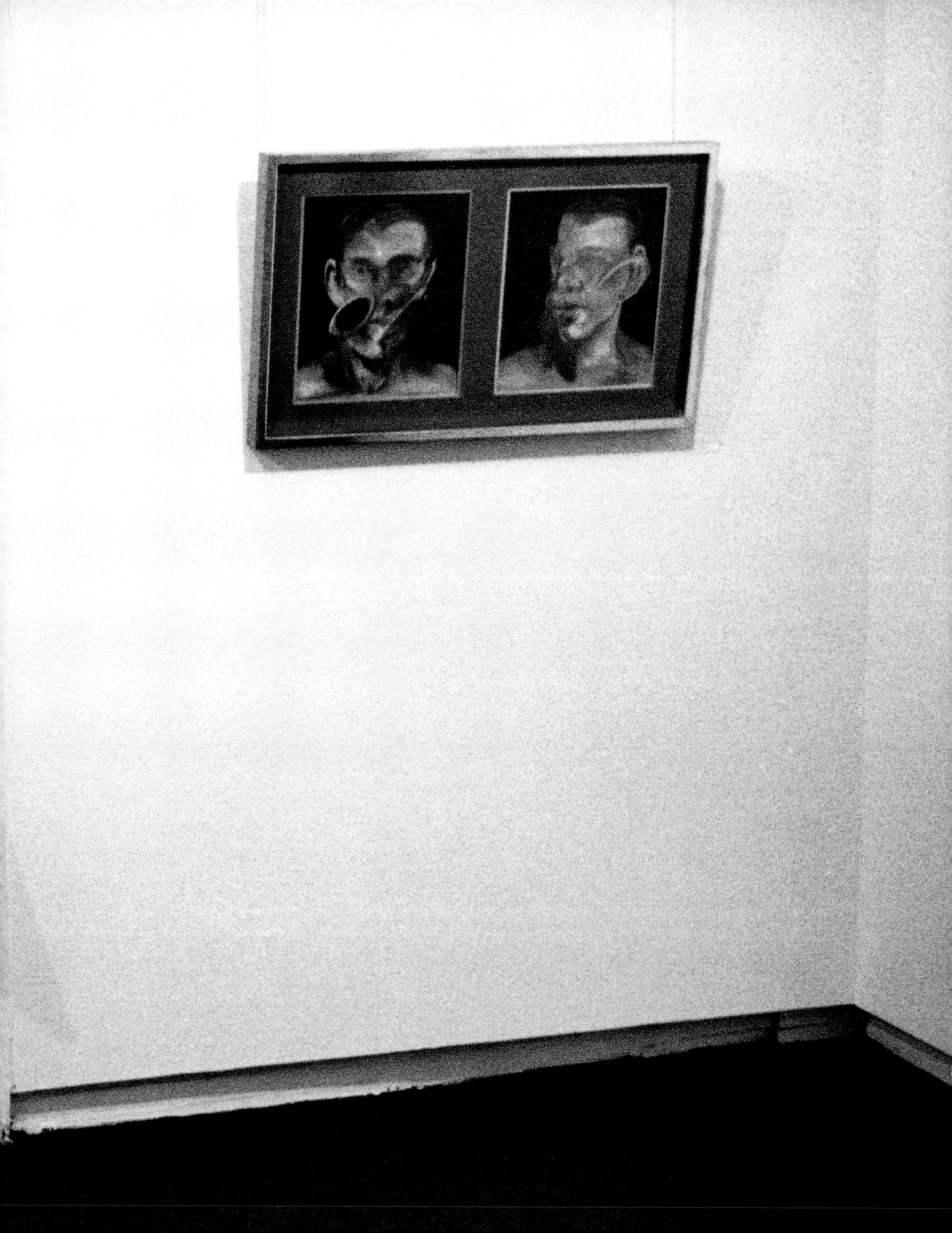

Picasso

David Douglas Duncan/1957

Picasso offered me many gifts out of pure friendship—and, I also think, because he liked the challenge of transforming an everyday object into something new and significant.

One of his presents was a self-portrait as an owl. He was inspired by a close-up I took of his eyes while I worked alongside him at the Villa Californie in Cannes in the summer of 1957. I enlarged the photograph and glued it onto a piece of white canvas, hoping he would sign it for me—he refused!

Ignoring me completely, he tore out a page from his sketchbook, found some scissors and charcoal, and began working. Once again I photographed creativity at its source.

As Picasso looked at me with his owl eyes, I looked back into the eyes of the artist who had recast our visual imagination, including that of the photographer to whom, with a shrug, eyes shining, and a perplexed smile, he later on gave his signed self-portrait.

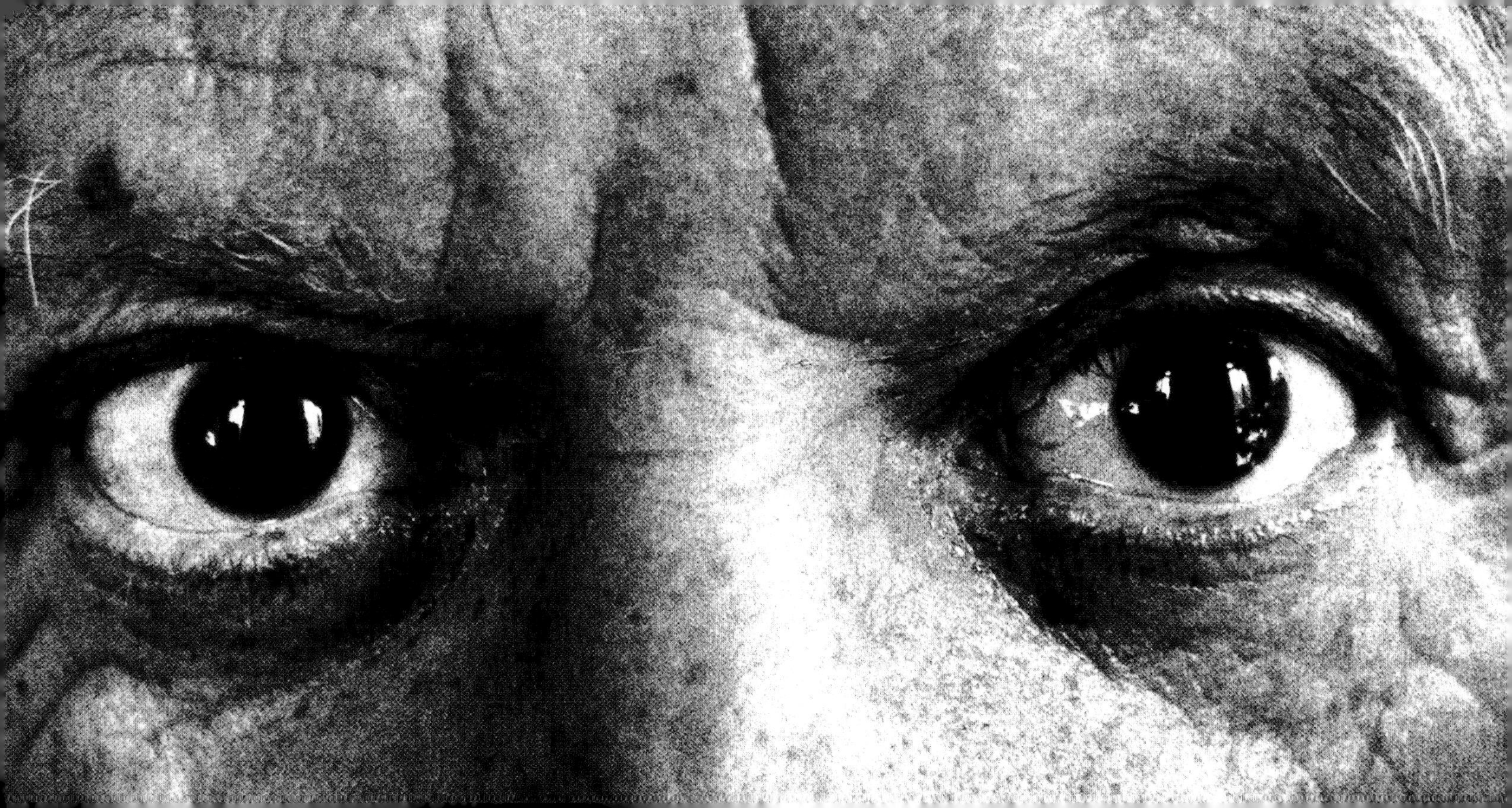

Picasso began painting before the onset of the twentieth century.

"Painting is far more powerful than I am. It makes me do what it wants."

"You can experiment with painting. You even have the right to; as long as you don't ever start over."

"If you know exactly what you're going to do, why do it? It holds no interest. It's better to do something else."

"We can make it terribly difficult for ourselves and all of a sudden torture ourselves over paintings without anyone making us. On the contrary, no one gives a damn whether you do one thing or another. We always choose the worst, even if we know people prefer a bouquet of flowers. In any case, they won't think it's any good. And even if they think it's good, you can be sure that it's in no way because of the painting. You, the painter, you've done some work; that's already something, you're happy. At that point, you go take a walk and you do a landscape or a fellow playing music. Why? Why that and not Notre-Dame? Or a portrait of my parrot? I'll tell you why. It's because at the moment you do it, it makes you feel better. And that's what's important."

To Edouard Pignon, the painter: "You, you paint divers, divers, always divers. But is there one that is a real diver? As he is? No. As for myself, I paint women, or heads. Women, women, women. Yet, is it a woman as a woman is? No. What I want is to convey a woman as she is, or your head as it is...That would be something..."

"I want to TELL the nude. I don't want to do a nude as a nude. I only want to TELL breast, TELL foot, TELL hand, stomach. Find the way to TELL it, and that's enough. I don't want to paint the nude from head to toe. But to be able to TELL. This is what I want. One word suffices when talking about it. In this case, one angle, and the nude tells you what it is, without sentences."

"Looking at a bicycle seat and handlebars in my studio, I decided to put them together. I made a bull's head, which was very clever, but I should have thrown out the bull's head right after; thrown it out into the street, into the gutter, wherever, but thrown it away. Then, a workman passes by. He picks it up. Maybe he thinks that out of this bull's head he could make a bicycle seat and handlebars, and he does it. That would have been wonderful. It's the gift of metamorphosis."

"What's terrible is that not one of these colors exists in a tube, ready to buy. They'll sell you thousands of greens, Verona green and emerald green and cadmium green and whatever, but this green here, never..."

"What I want is to make a bullfight as it is...I want to create it as I see it. I want the whole arena, the whole crowd, the whole sky; the bull as it is and the matador too; the entire *cuadrilla,* all the *banderilleros,* the music, and the paper hat merchant...a REAL bullfight...I would need a piece of canvas as big as the arena...It's terrible not to be able to do it, it would be great...Well, we're joking around, but I've been thinking about this painting for a long time, and nothing says that one day I won't find a way to do it."

"There's never a time when you can say, 'I've worked well and tomorrow is Sunday.' As soon as you stop, you start over."

"We talk about painting as if it were a contest. The winner is the one who can go the furthest. But what does this mean, the furthest?...We're talking about paint. What is the equivalent of breaking the sound barrier in a painting? Does it mean being van Gogh?"

"Nowadays we talk about painting like we do miniskirts. Tomorrow it will be longer, or it will have fringes. We need the never-before-seen event—a real mind blower. But when you look for it, you've already seen it, everywhere, with a pleat in the pants."

"What's unfortunate is that no one speaks badly about anyone. If you believe what people say then everything is good. In every exhibition, there is something meaningful. In any case, everything is worthwhile, or almost everything. People can be indifferent, or even a little mean. But no one kills anyone, everything is valid, nothing is thrown down on the floor, and nothing is raised like a flag. Everything is on the same level. Why? Surely not because it's true. And so? Because we don't think anymore? Or because we don't dare say it?"

"I try to understand. I try to put myself in Untel's place, for example. But what a life! What could he be thinking about in his studio, all alone in front of his easel? He's been working on the same painting for ten years! This question frustrates me. What in the world can he be thinking about? He is undoubtably bored! If I fall flat on my face, I often end up knowing why. Maybe I have learned something. Perhaps it's when I think that I've fallen flat on my face, I haven't at all. In any case, no one can say that I haven't tried. Untel paints—that's his business—and if he enjoys it, perhaps he's the one who's right. But in the end, it's a painting that's comparable to taking the subway every morning."

"The subject of a commission never scares me. When I'm given a commission, I do it. You can take fifty thousand abstract paintings, or Tachist studies, and even if the canvas is green, well, the subject is the green. There's always a subject."

"My interior self is necessarily going to be in the painting, since I am the one creating it. I don't have to agonize over it. Whatever I do, it's there. Too much, even. The problem is the rest!"

"You have to pay very close attention to what you do. It's when we think that we're the least free that we're sometimes the most. And not at all when we feel we have a giant's wings, which prevent us from walking."

"If there were one single truth, we wouldn't be able to make a hundred paintings on the same theme."

"Truth cannot exist. If I search for the truth in my painting, I can make a hundred paintings with this truth. Which one is the true one? And who is the truth? The one who acts as model or the one that I paint? No, it's the same as in all the rest. Truth doesn't exist."

"They tell you that you have to give freedom to children. In truth, we make them do children's drawings. We teach them to make them. We've even taught them to make children's drawings that are abstract. In truth, under the pretext of giving them freedom, and especially of not hindering them, we confine them to their genre, with their chains."

"It's funny, as a child I never drew like one—even when I was very young. I remember my first drawings. I was maybe six. In the hall of my father's house, there was a Hercules with his club. Well, I set myself down there in the hallway, and I drew the Hercules. But it wasn't a child's drawing. It was a real drawing of Hercules."

"What does it mean for a painter to do an Untel or imitate another? What's wrong with it? On the contrary, it's good. You have to attempt to imitate another. The thing is, we can't! We'd like to, we try, but the whole thing fails...and it's at the moment when we fail that we are ourselves."

"If Raphael came back today, with exactly the same paintings, no one would buy them and no one would consider him."

Picasso and I visit Matisse's chapel in Vence. At the end of a hall, an elderly nun is offering postcards. She is surly with Picasso, who buys catalogues from her. A visitor recognizes Picasso and cries, amazed, "What luck! We've come to see Matisse, and at the same time we meet Picasso!"

"This is Picasso?" the Sister exclaims. She quickly comes out of her booth, hunched over, and explains to Picasso, "I didn't recognize you because I'm so old! I'm delighted to meet you! I have something for you. It's something that Matisse said to me one day when he was showing me his paintings in the chapel. He said: "I don't know what one should think of them, but there is only one person who has the right to criticize me and that is Picasso."

"At the time of Cézanne, and during the Impressionist movement, one didn't see modern painting. When it was noticed, it was often thought scandalous. Today, provided that it doesn't look like painting, everything is modern, and it's very obvious, hardly conceived, and devoid of genius. All of a sudden people have become clairvoyant; they interpret everything the moment it is born. Whereas in reality, they see as they always have and even worse, but they think that they have learned to see."

"A painter, Tintoretto for example, begins his canvas and continues, and it's only at the end, when he has filled it up and worked it from all angles, that the painting is finished. Whereas if you take a Cézanne canvas, as soon as he lays down one stroke, the painting is already there. This is modern painting."

"Cézanne hasn't changed. As a result, it's always the same Cézanne. One day he will do something completely different. And, once again, no one will realize that it's Cézanne."

"The Impressionists worked in incredible solitude, which may have been both a grief and a blessing. What is more dangerous than comprehension? It doesn't exist. We will always misunderstand one another. We think we're not alone, but in reality, we are all the more."

—Hélène Parmelin

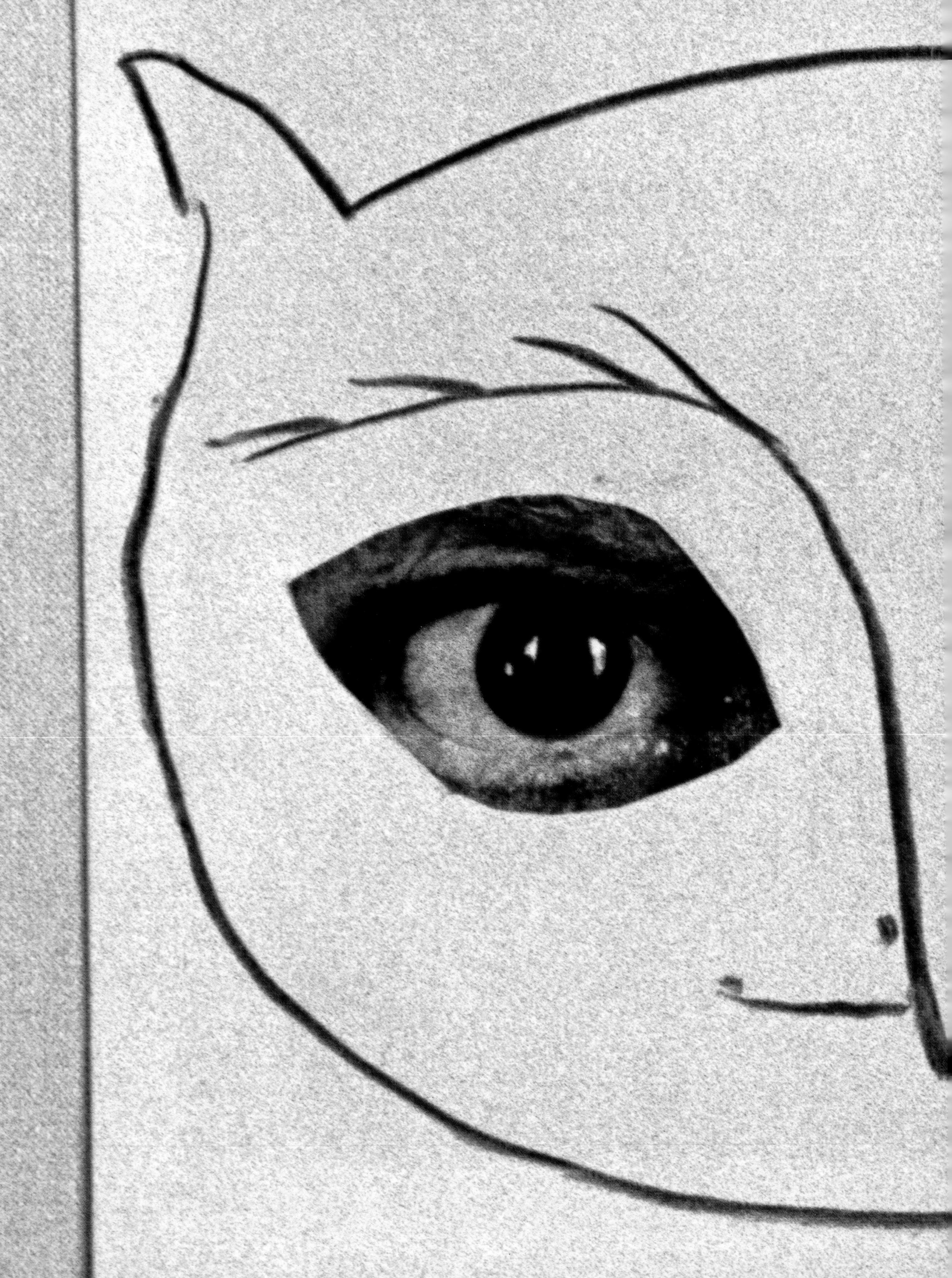

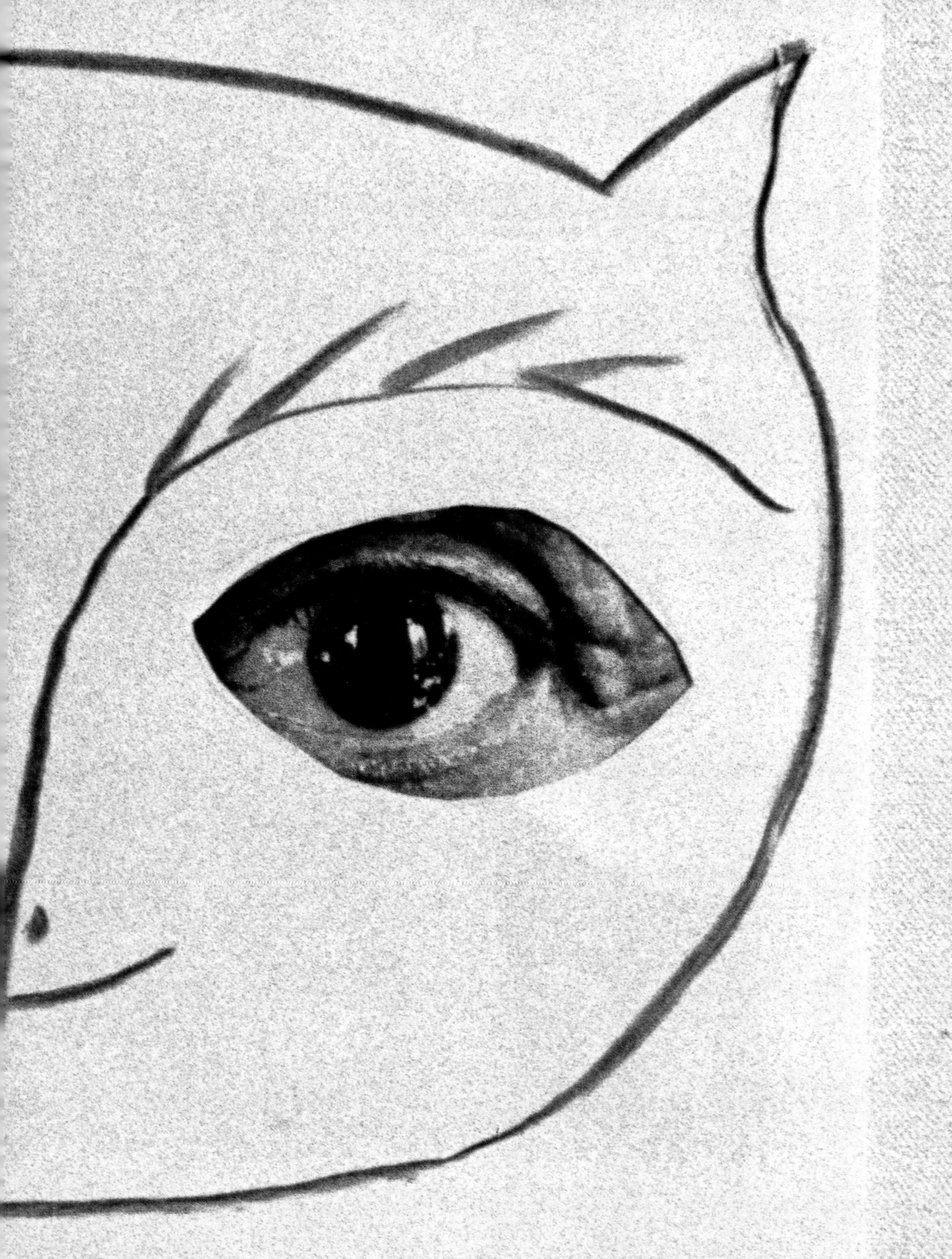

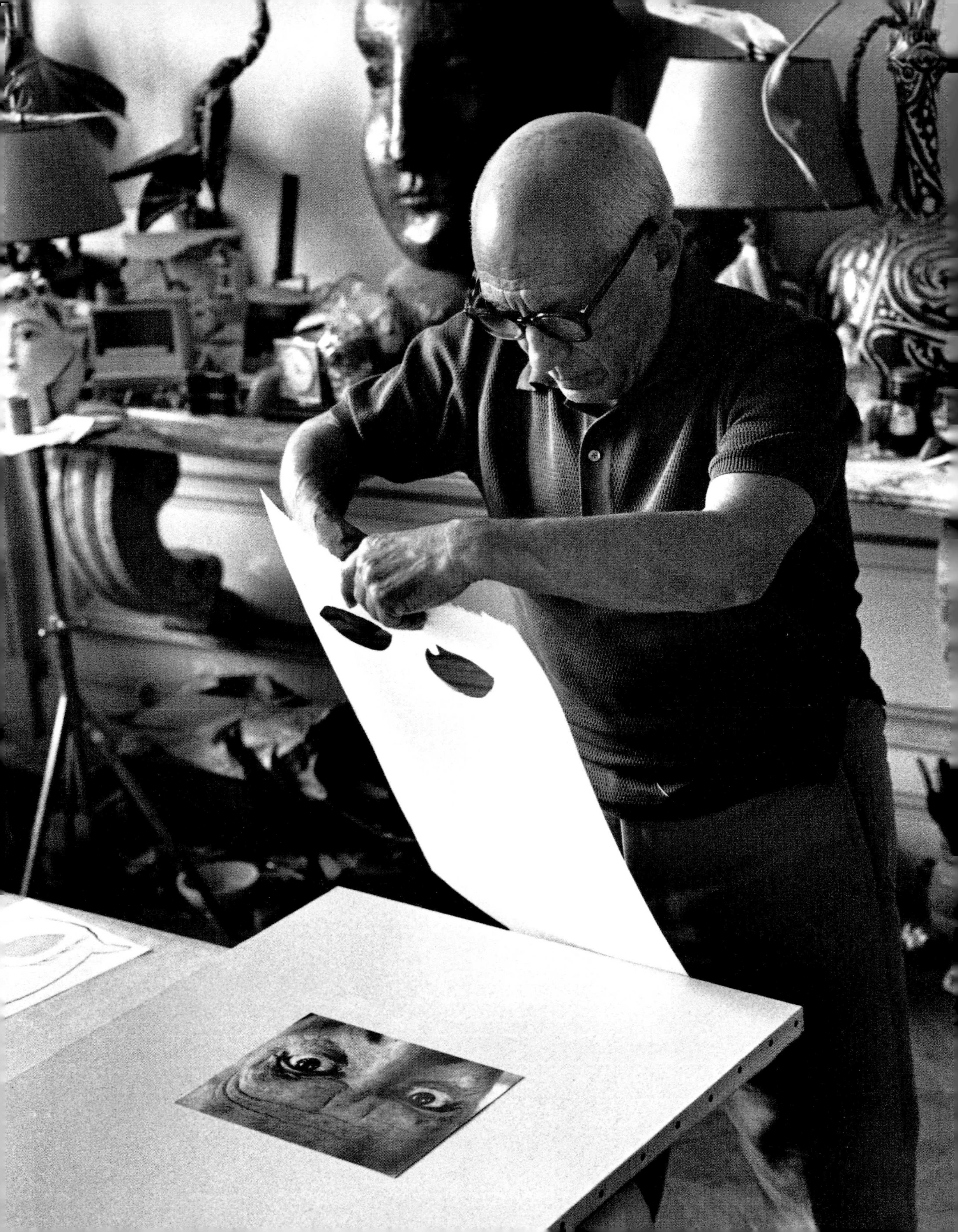

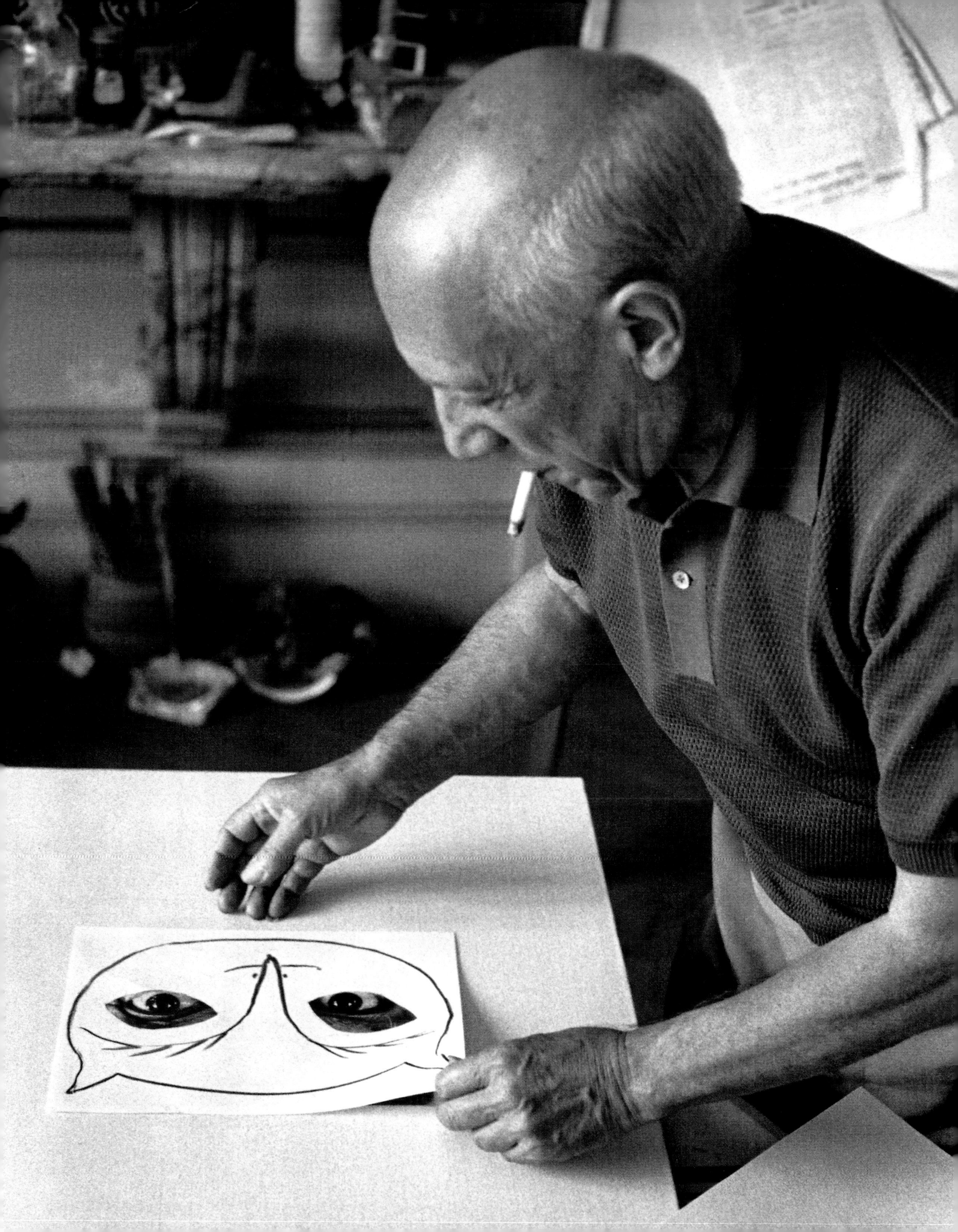

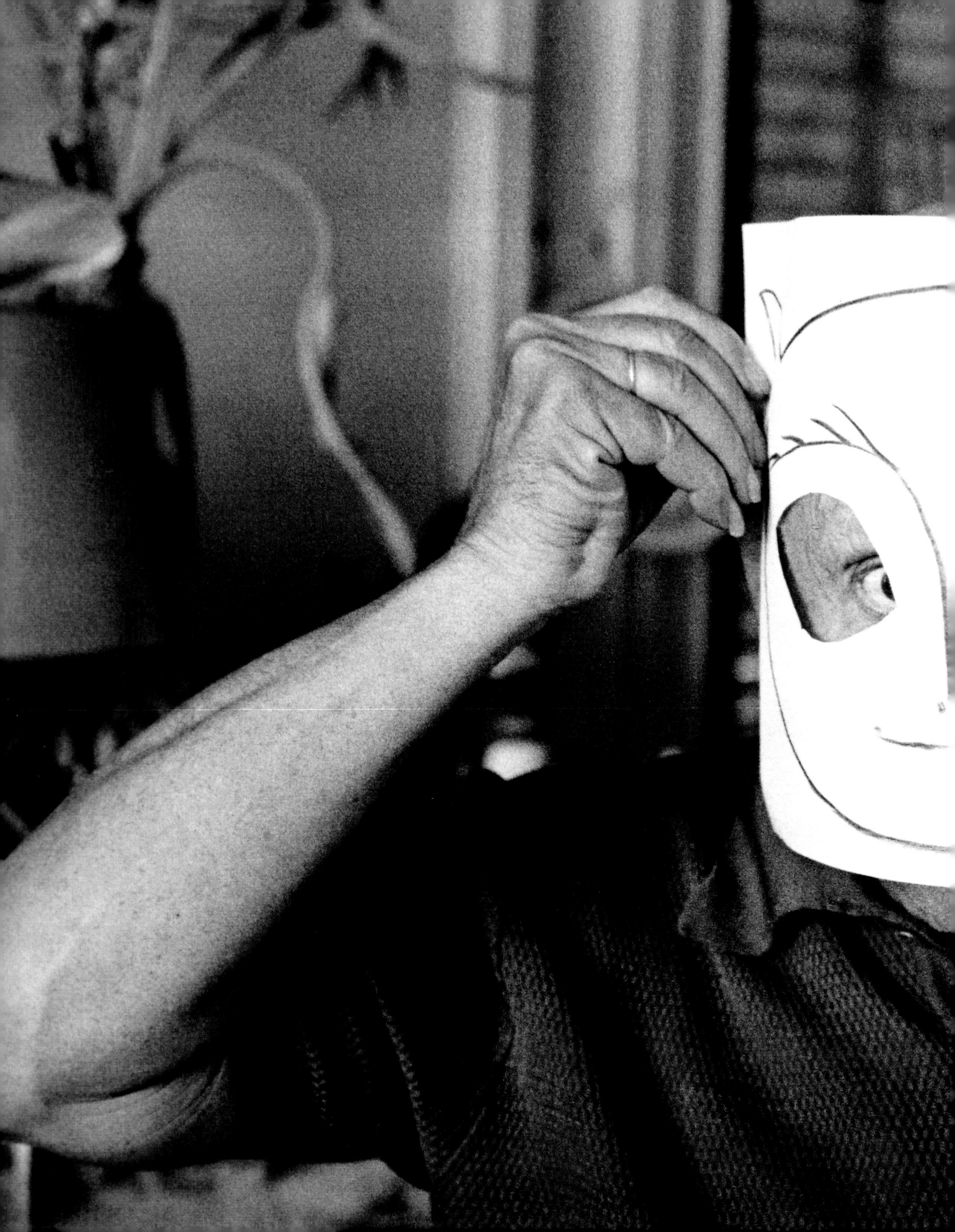

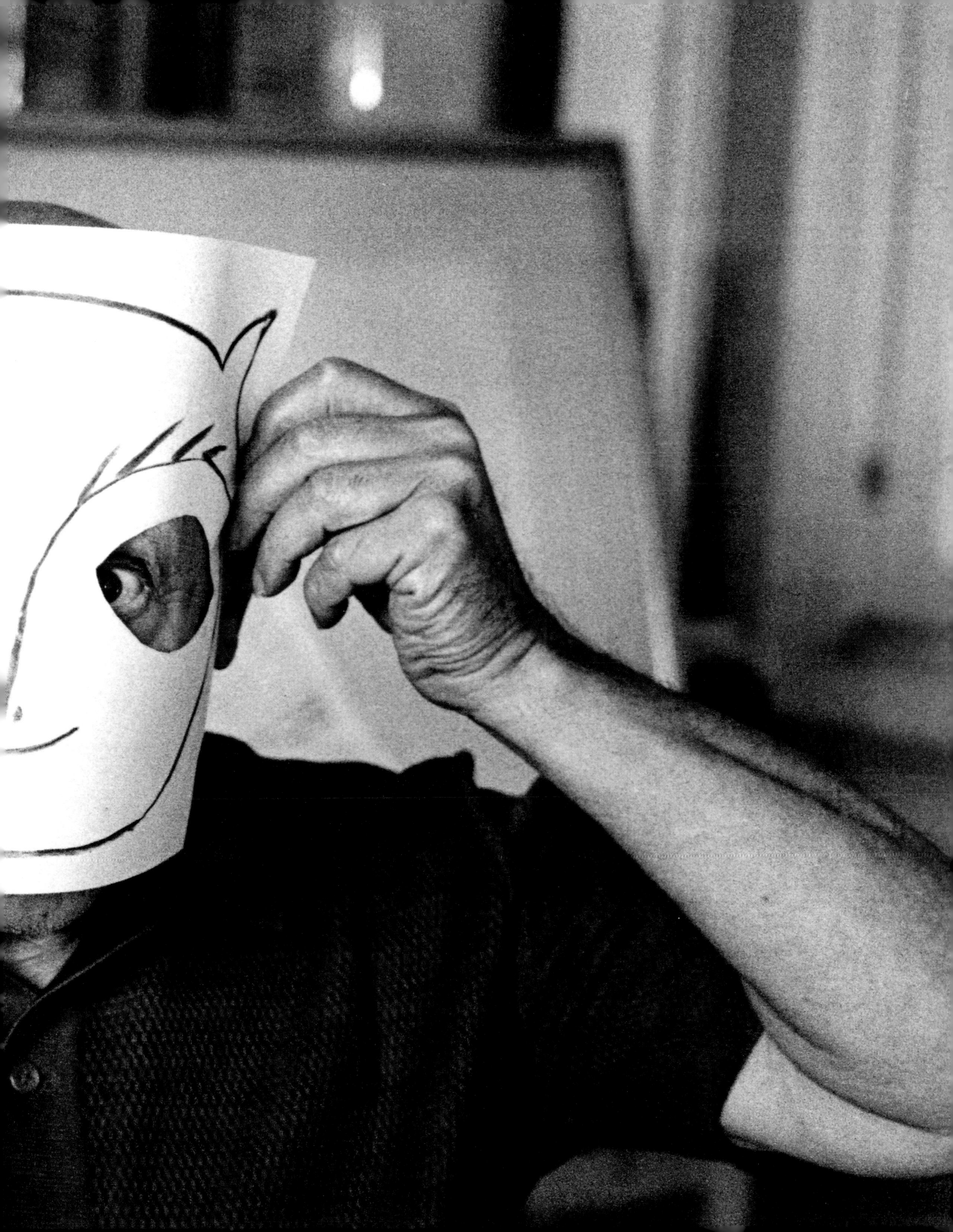

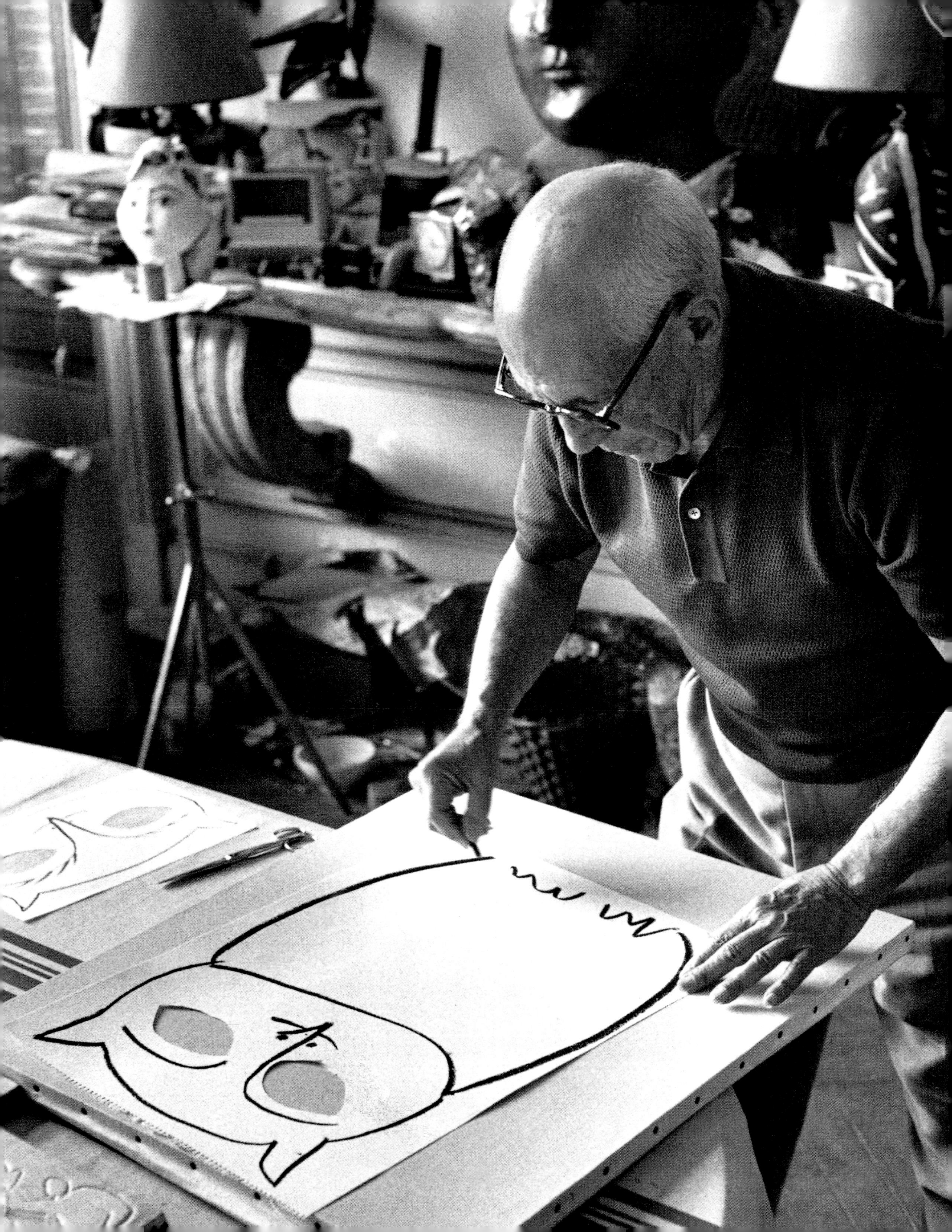

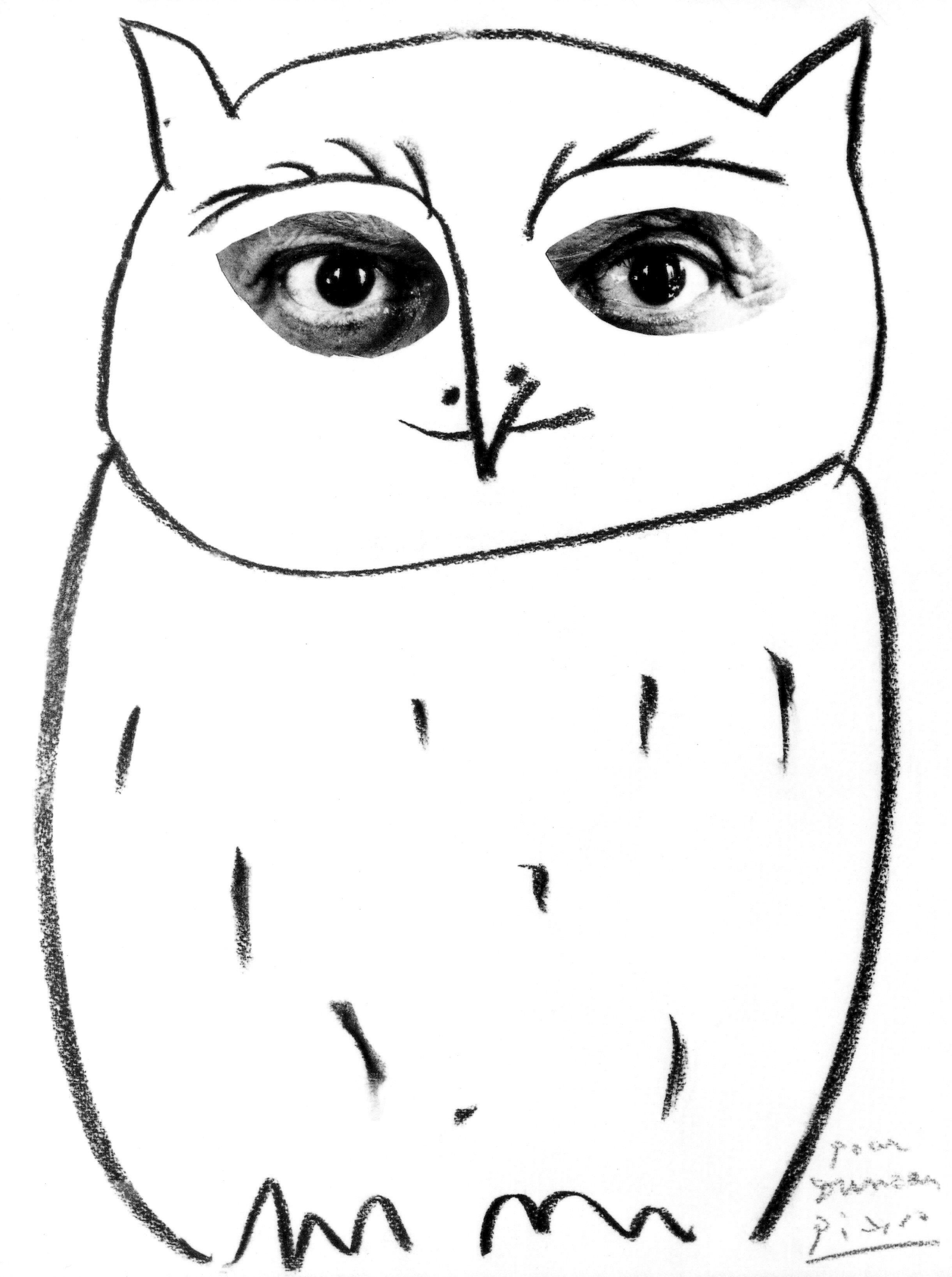
pour

Chagall

Izis
1964

Marc Chagall's ceiling decorations for the Paris Opéra are masterworks of flowers, music, and dance.

The pictures Chagall saw and the sounds he heard were, for him, Tchaikovsky's *Swan Lake*.

"Without the Bible, or without Mozart, life wouldn't be worth living," said Chagall while painting *Mozart's Angel*.

He unrolled his canvas, and with the help of eighty tubes of color, plus a demonic zeal for work, Chagall brought his figures to life.

On scaffolding, eighty feet above the ground, he skillfully disguised the joins linking twelve separate panels.

André Malraux: "There comes a moment in an artist's life when all his genius becomes focused on one masterpiece."

Even when Chagall's two granddaughters came to see him at the Paris Opéra, he hardly stopped working.

With his wife beside him, Chagall finally put his signature to two years of work—the labor of Hercules was complete.

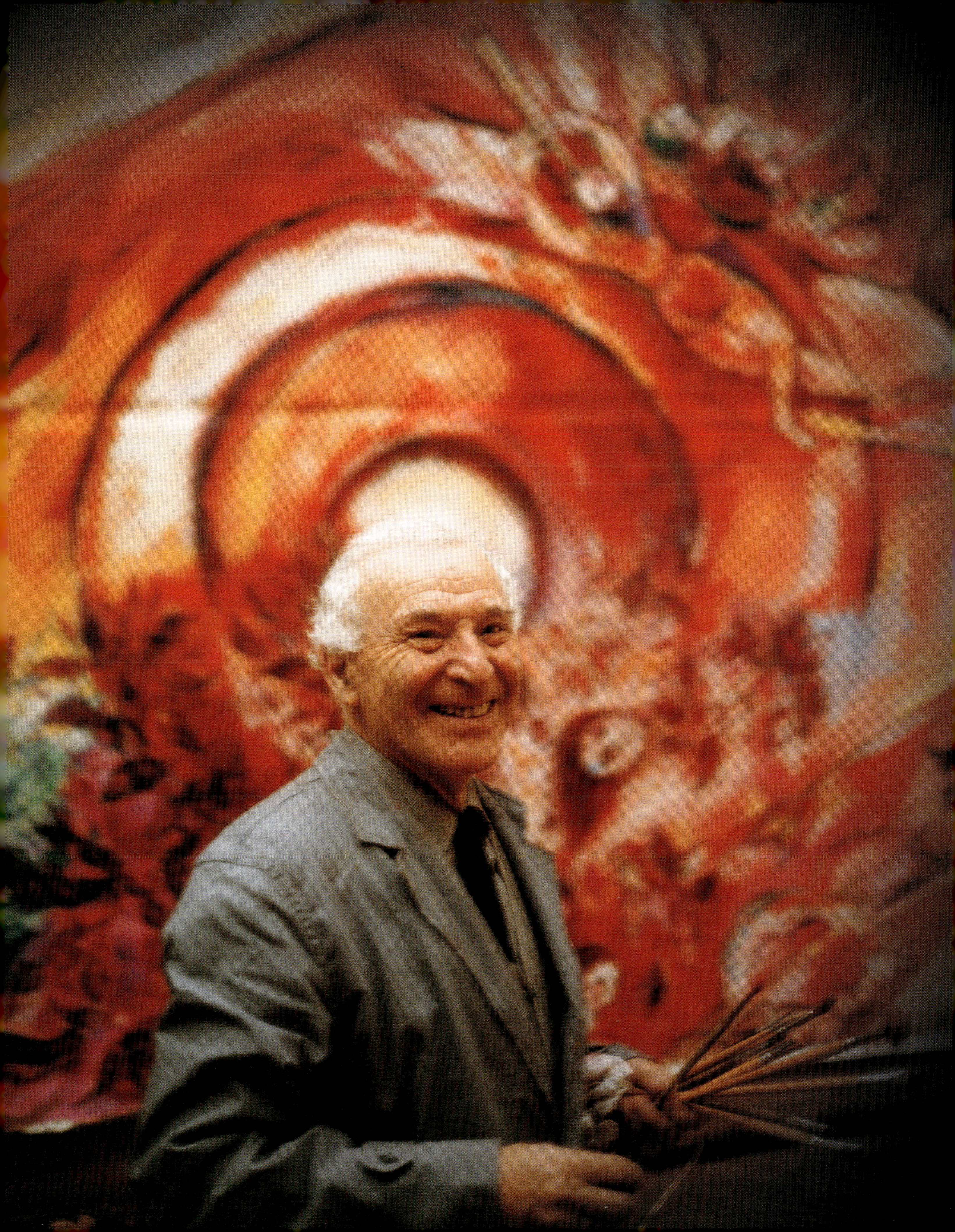

"This is paradise!" With an expansive gesture Marc Chagall points to the scene he has chosen to contemplate until the last day of his life: the colorful Mediterranean landscape that stretches from his house down to the sea covered by a morning mist.

Two bright-blue, malevolent eyes light up his face, which is topped by a halo of fine white hair. Each word, each gesture, expresses a sensitivity that seems to vibrate like the string of a musical instrument.

"Look at that wisteria, smell the jasmine, feel that leaf, soft as velvet. I could never paint this scene, but my love for it led me at last to understand the real language of the flowers. I've had to have a floral motif in my paintings ever since, even in the stained glass that the government commissioned for the Metz Cathedral. There will be flowers in the sets for *Daphnis and Chloe,* which I'm designing for the Paris Opera. The premiere will be in Brussels, but it's in my garden that I really hear the music of Ravel!"

Ever since his boyhood in the Russian town of Vitebsk (now Viciebsk), Chagall's mind continued to explore our world. He has become one of the most famous artists in the world, whose pictures change hands at fabulous prices, but his roots remain firmly in the Jewish ghetto of his childhood. He enjoys talking about those days, not to complain but to describe how even in the darkest days there was always a little flame of hope burning.

"Tired and anxious, my father would sit down in his chair and sip the scalding tea from the samovar without saying a word. My mother was still young in those days, but I can only remember her as always tired and worn out."

In the Chagall household, the family didn't just read the Bible, they lived by it. Around the table, barely big enough to seat the eight sisters and one brother, there was always an extra place setting—it was reserved for the prophet Isaiah. Chagall's grandfather spent only half of his day in his Lyozna butcher's shop, and the rest of the time in the synagogue. In one of his paintings, Chagall depicted him perched on the roof of his house enjoying the evening air while eating his dessert. Then there was his uncle Noah who belonged to the Russian Hasidim, a sect that was still widespread in those days. Opposed to the ascetic way of life, they taught the principles of an ever-flowing communication between God and man in a state of perpetual joy.

Sixty years later, Chagall has ceased to wait for the prophet Isaiah, but has managed to preserve intact the rich heritage of memory and legend, and has made it the lifeblood of his art.

His parents made great sacrifices to further his education. Marc Chagall was a good student: he wrote poems and, as he had a good voice, he earned extra rubles singing in the synagogue on feast days. In the evening, he spent his time drawing. He still remembers the first portrait he painted—it was of the Russian pianist Anton Rubinstein, which he copied from a magazine.

He gained admission to the Pen Academy at Vitebsk, and quickly realized that the art instruction there was closer to photography than to his own vision of painting. Accordingly he left for St. Petersburg, only to come to the conclusion there that, once again, he was wasting his time. Only by working alone and trusting his instincts could he hope to fulfill his vision. So he returned home to Vitebsk and there began to paint like a man possessed, discovering his personal sense of color and way of looking at the world. It was there that he met Bella Rosenfeld in 1908, and with her stepped back into his dream, into the old streets of Vitebsk, dancing to the music of his uncle Noah's violin and drawing her with him into his fantastic world peopled with goats, roosters, and the merry folk of the village. Bella agreed to pose nude for her fiancé, but her mother found the painting and asked Chagall to destroy it. On top of Bella's portrait, he painted *The Burial,* a fantasy in which a red horse is seen pulling a pauper's hearse through a snowy street in Vitebsk.

As Chagall fell asleep at night, a strange alchemy appeared to take place. The objects in his room seemed to dance: the towel hanging on the wall became Bella, the stove rose up to the ceiling, the samovar was transformed into a goat, and the palette of his dreams was already conjuring up the vision of the next day's painting. Life might have gone on like that forever, and the world might never have heard of a poor little Jewish painter called Chagall. But luck finally came his way early in the year 1910. Winawer, a member of the Russian duma who had already noticed Chagall in St. Petersburg, offered him a small income to go and paint in Paris. The Diaghilev Ballet was then enjoying a huge success in the French capital at the Théâtre du Châtelet, and Russian culture was all the rage. Consequently, Chagall found himself taken up straight away by the artists of Montparnasse. He moved into the bohemian community known as La Ruche (the beehive) in the Passage Danzig, next door to the Vaugirard slaughterhouses. La Ruche is a curious round building which an old sculptor known as Le Père Dubois had turned into a commune for impoverished artists. Chagall was given the studio next to the sculptor Amadeo Modigliani's, while two doors down the painters Chaim Soutine and Fernand Léger were at work.

"Stretchers, eggshells, and dirty tin saucepans littered the floor. The lamp shone and I too burned with enthusiasm. I couldn't stop painting. It was there, within those four grubby walls, that the scales finally fell from my eyes and

I became a painter." Occasionally the French poet Blaise Cendrars dropped by to take him out and feed him a proper meal in a nearby bistro, but he had to wait at the door! "I'm getting dressed," Chagall would shout, because for comfort and for economy he used to paint naked—he only had one set of clothes.

There Chagall found kindred spirits in the Futurist poet Riciotto Canudo, and the artists Max Jacob, Roger de La Fresnaye, André Dunoyer de Segonzac, Robert Delaunay, and Modigliani. He invited the poet Guillaume Apollinaire back to his studio, having met him one day on the boulevard Montparnasse, and one by one, showed all of his paintings to this key figure of Cubism. Apollinaire sat on the only chair in the artist's studio, gazed intently, took a deep breath, roared, smiled, and pronounced Chagall's panels "supernatural."

"Supernatural!" For Chagall, reality always included unexpected visions of the past and the future. His paintings existed on several levels. His figures and objects became weightless, floating in space and revealing their intrinsic beauty.

"Supernatural!" A label like that didn't sell paintings, which were gradually accumulating in the artist's studio.

Apollinaire and Cendrars, however, did manage to organize an exhibition of their friend's paintings in Berlin. Before going to the opening, Chagall wanted to return to Vitebsk to see Bella, who had been waiting for him for four years. But this was the summer of 1914, and war broke out the day after the painter arrived home, and the government's first official recognition of his genius was to put Chagall in uniform.

The next year, Marc and Bella were married. For the following thirty years, the couple remained united through their love of art and of each other. Bella, a talented poet in her own right, was the Chagall's constant inspiration, his model, and also his most important critic.

With the onset of the Russian revolution in 1917, Chagall was appointed director of the Institute of Fine Arts in Vitebsk, thanks to the intervention of the Russian author and politician Anatoly Vasilyevich Lunacharsky, who had met him in Paris in 1912. For a short time, the new regime supported modern art, but soon the government's official attitude reverted to a strict and narrow formalism. There was no place for Chagall in such a reactionary environment and he accordingly resigned to face poverty once again. He fled to Moscow, where he painted frescoes and designed sets and costumes for the Jewish theater.

Chagall was now waiting for a glimmer of hope to relieve his present life of hardship and misery. One morning in 1922 he found it. A letter came from the poet Rubiner in Berlin:

"Did you know that you are famous here? Your paintings have inspired our Expressionism, and they sell for a lot of money. But don't expect so much as one penny from the dealer Walden. He thinks fame alone is payment enough." When Chagall finally returned to Paris in 1923, he rediscovered his creative imagination. His pictures began to sell, he discovered the beauty of flowers and the vivid colors of the south of France, and he was happy once again. It was at this time that Ambroise Vollard suggested that Chagall begin doing illustrations. Chagall learned the art of engraving and completed ninety-six illustrations for Nikolai Gogol's novel *Dead Souls.* He also illustrated the seventeenth-century writer Jean de La Fontaine's *Fables* with a hundred etchings, and from there began work on the greatest project of his life, illustrating the Bible. "I know of only two great mystic painters alive today," said Vollard, "Rouault and Chagall."

Although he had taken up engraving, Chagall still continued to paint his dreamworld; with fiddlers and bouquets of flowers floating in the sky, blue-winged clocks and flying goats. It was all as surprising as ever, but was poetic metaphor out of place in painting? Was there not something ridiculous about painting a clock with wings as a metaphor for *tempus fugit?* Yet Chagall's continuing success as a painter defied such criticism. Museums all over the world were paying top prices to acquire his paintings, when in 1935 the hideous shadow of racial persecution began to envelop Europe. Deeply disturbed, Chagall began to incorporate social and religious elements into his work. In 1941 he received an invitation from the Museum of Modern Art in New York, and decided to go to America and escape his pursuers, who had already tracked him to the little Provençal village of Gordes, where he had taken refuge.

When Bella died in 1944, Chagall's work took on a new depth. His imagery was charged with a sharper meaning. In a flood of reminiscence he completed a huge painting begun in 1937, *Autour d'elle.* After this, peace returned to him and he went back to France to settle permanently in Vence. There he has remained, in his sunny whitewashed studio, while his paintings resumed their travels around the world in a series of important exhibitions.

—Jean Diwo

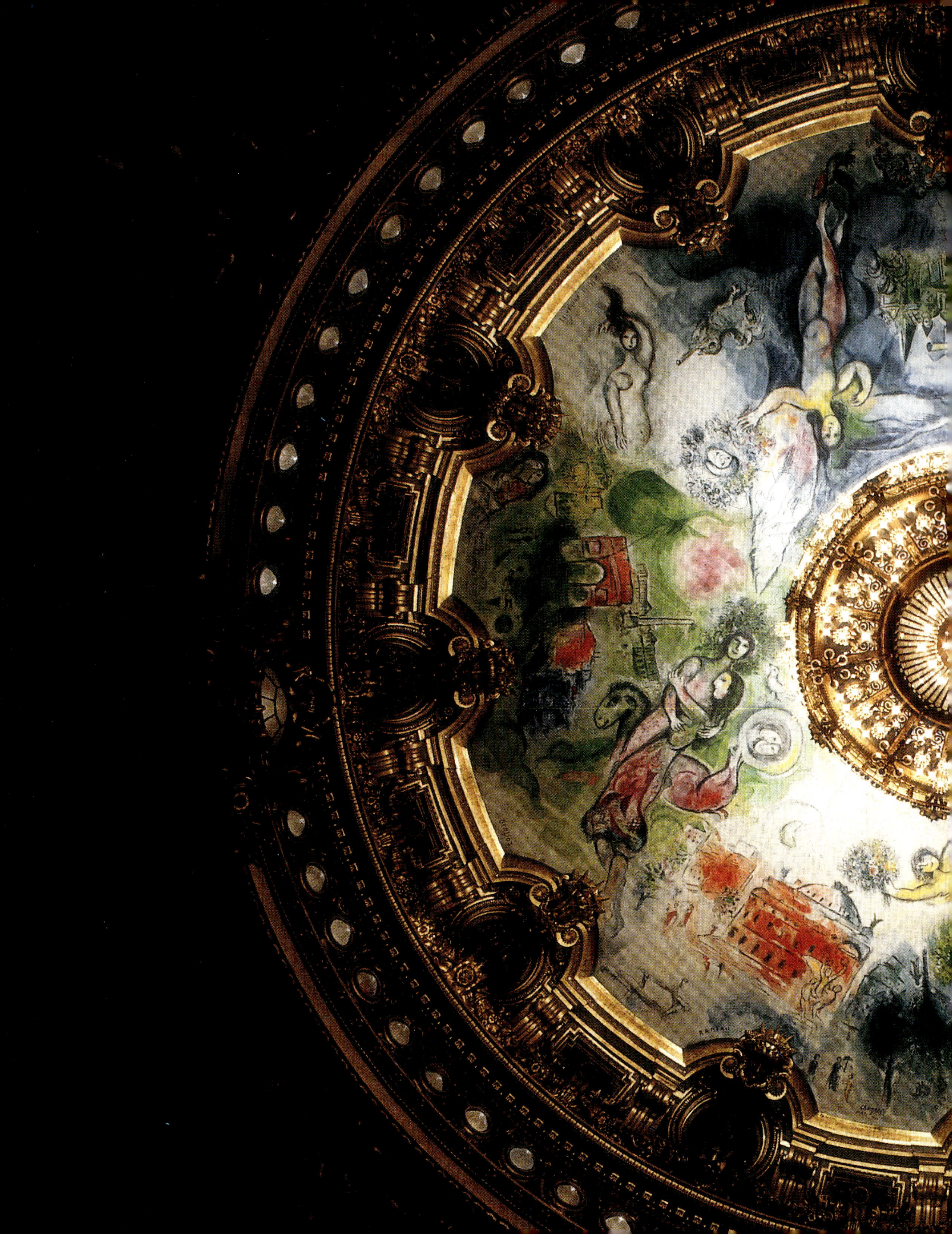

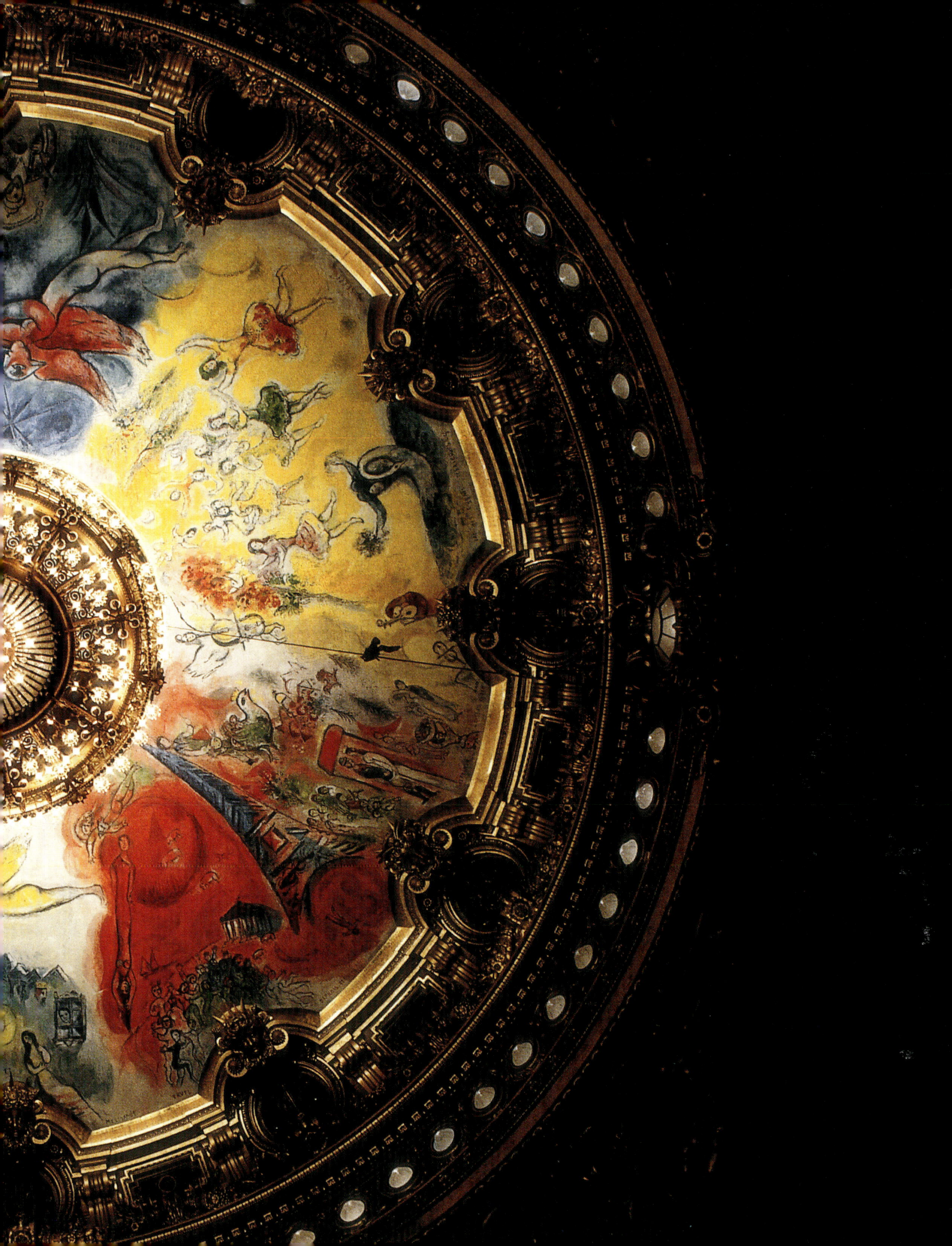

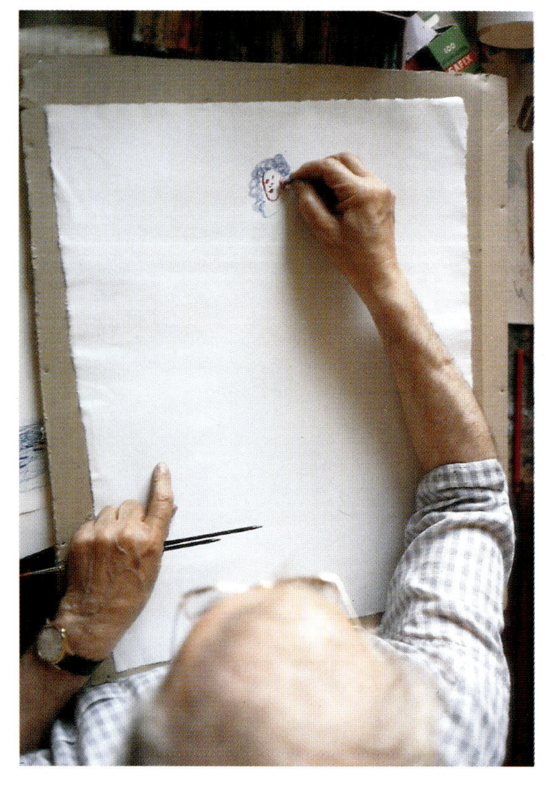
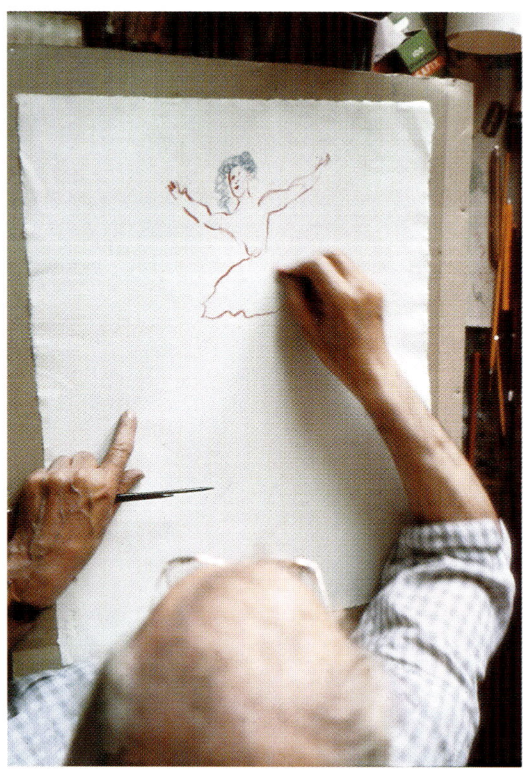
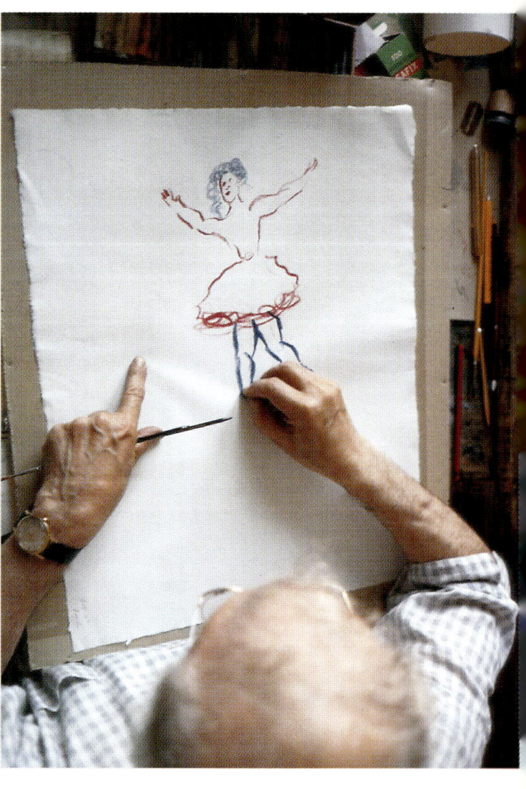
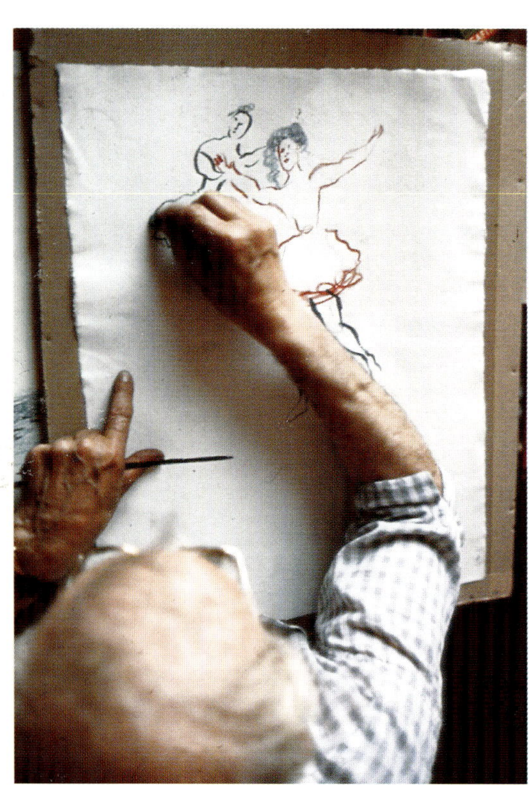
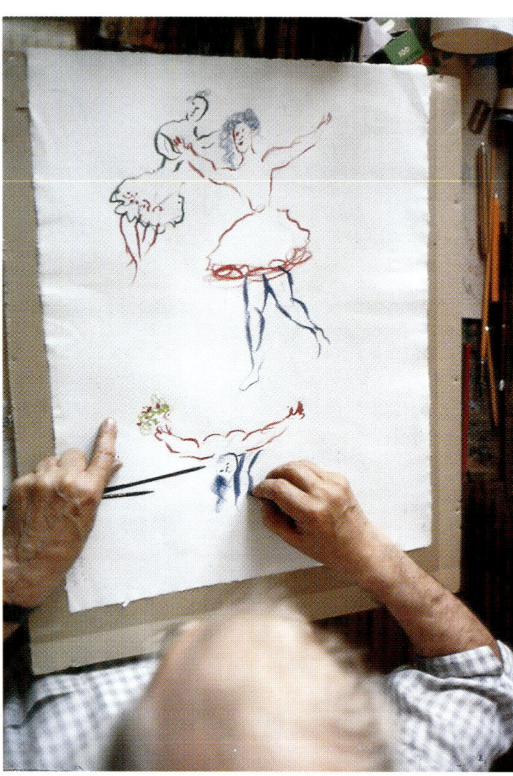
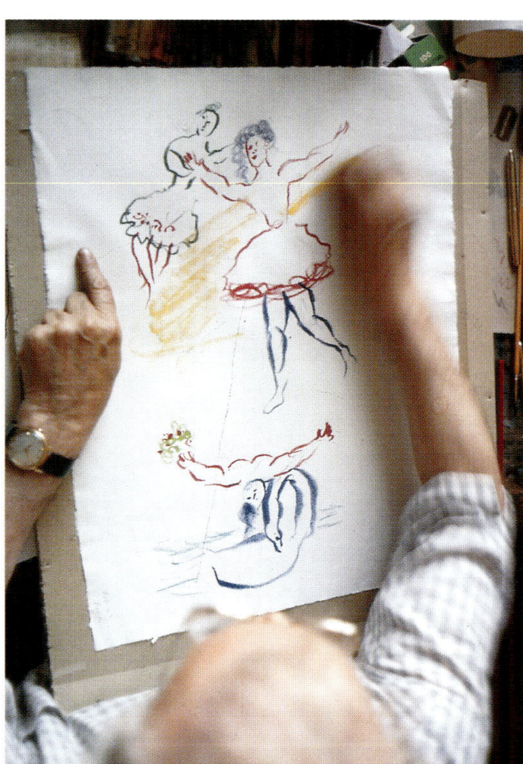

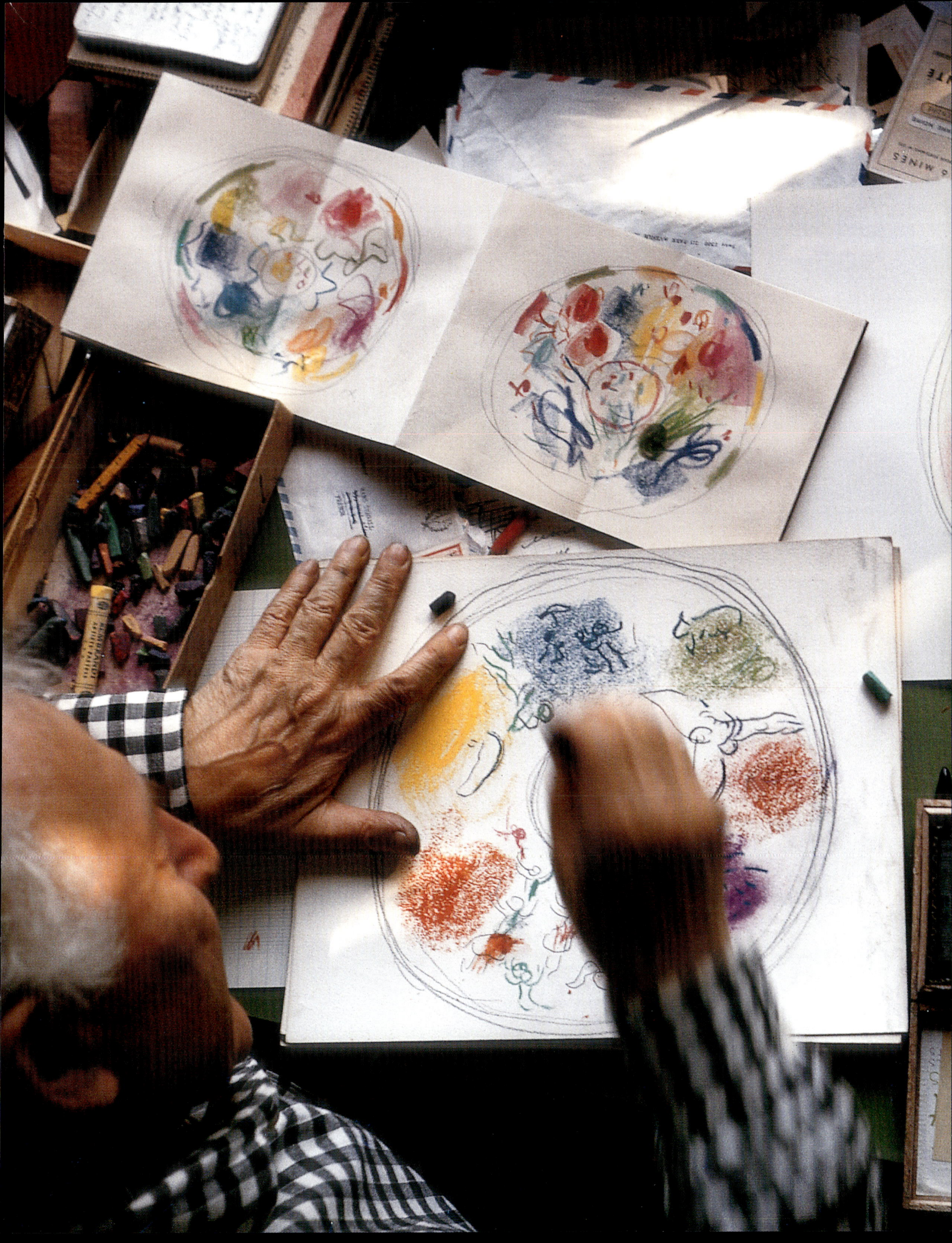

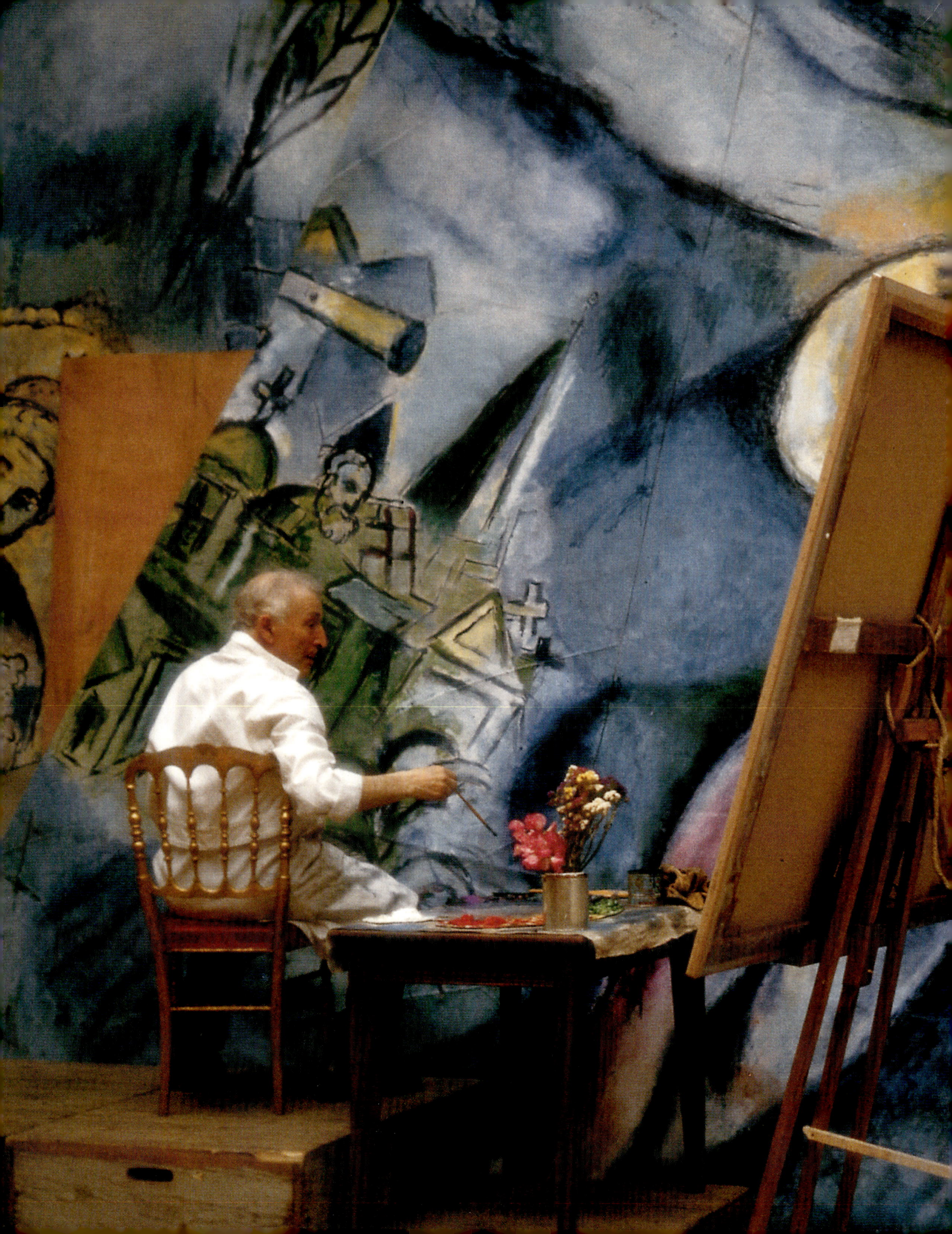

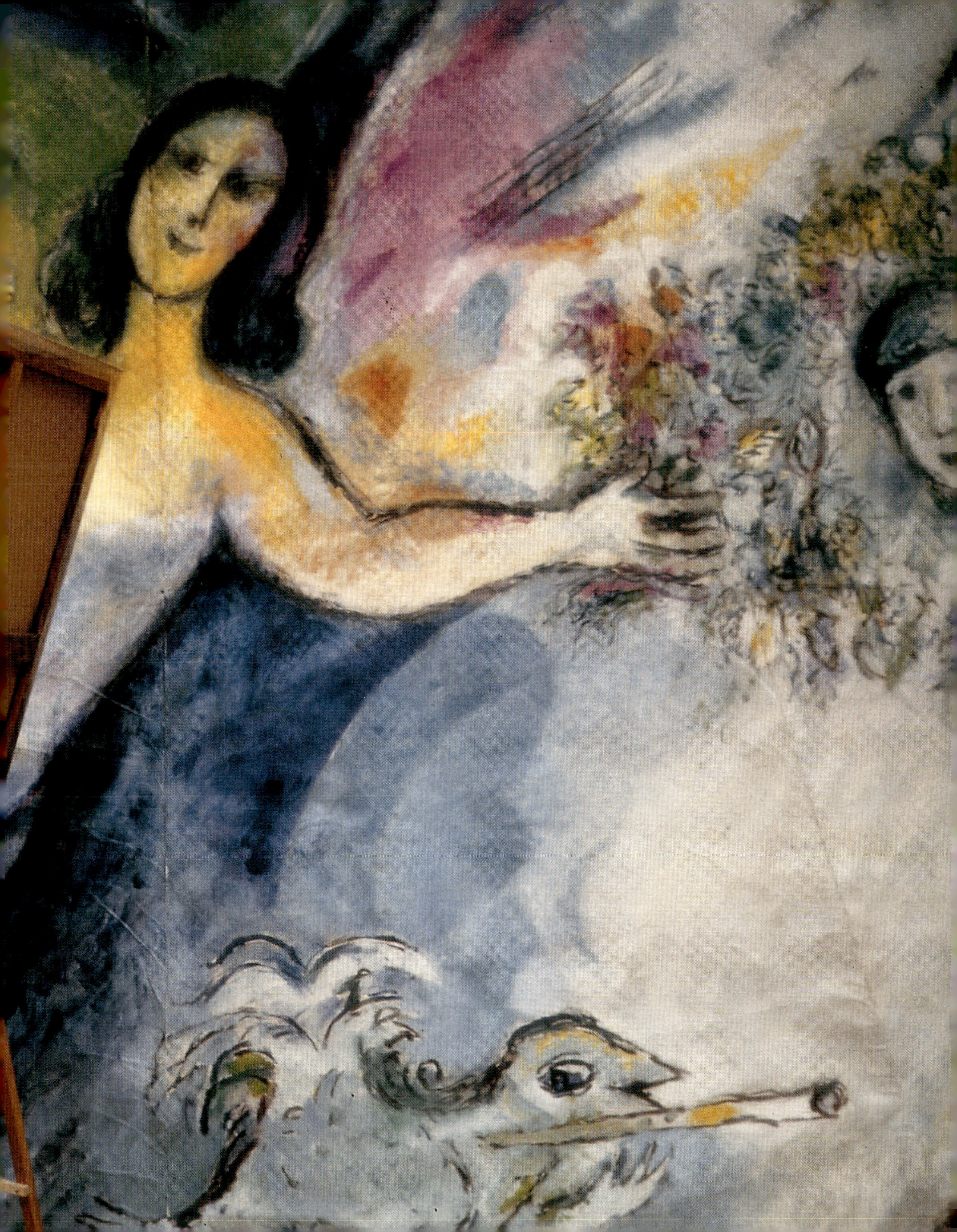

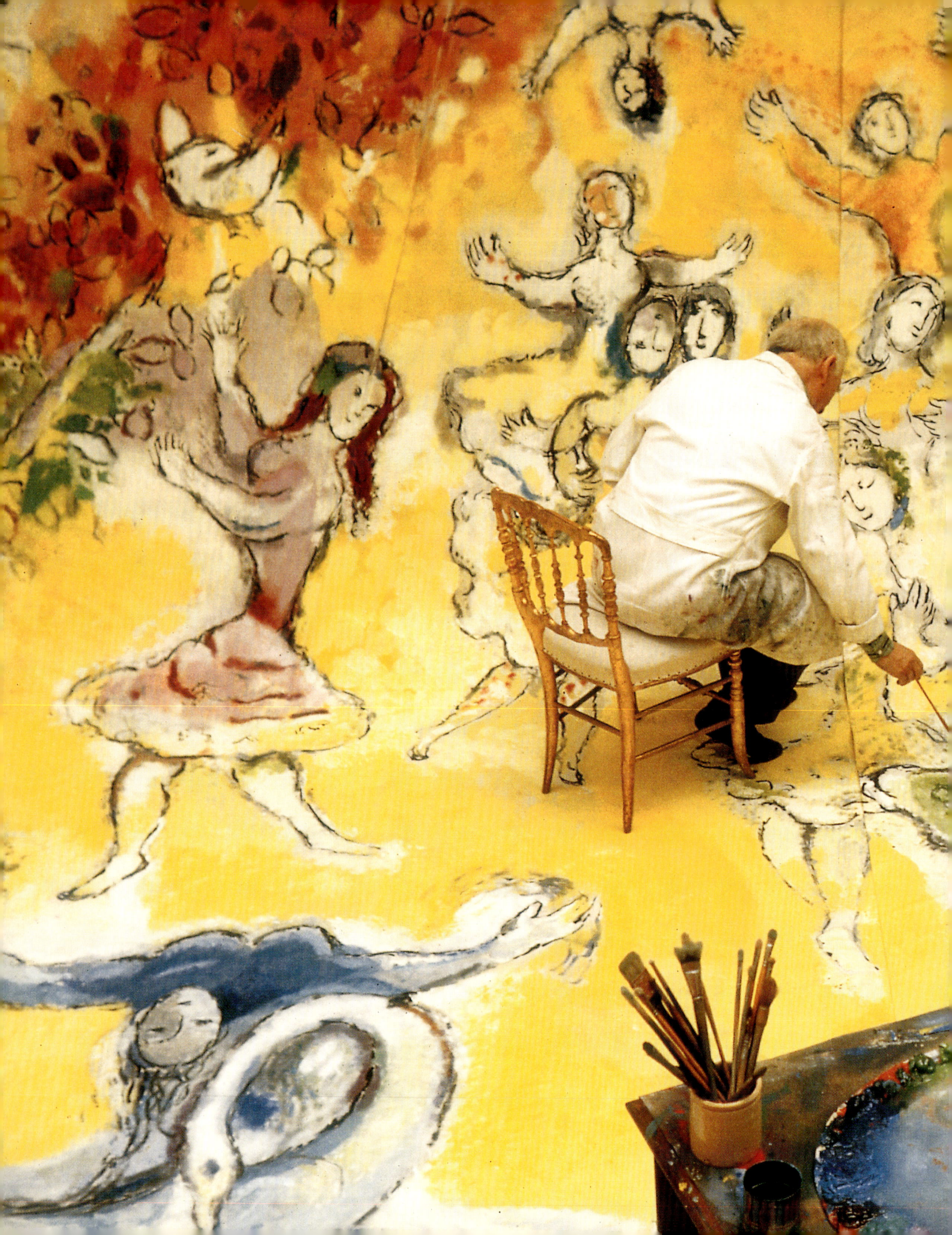

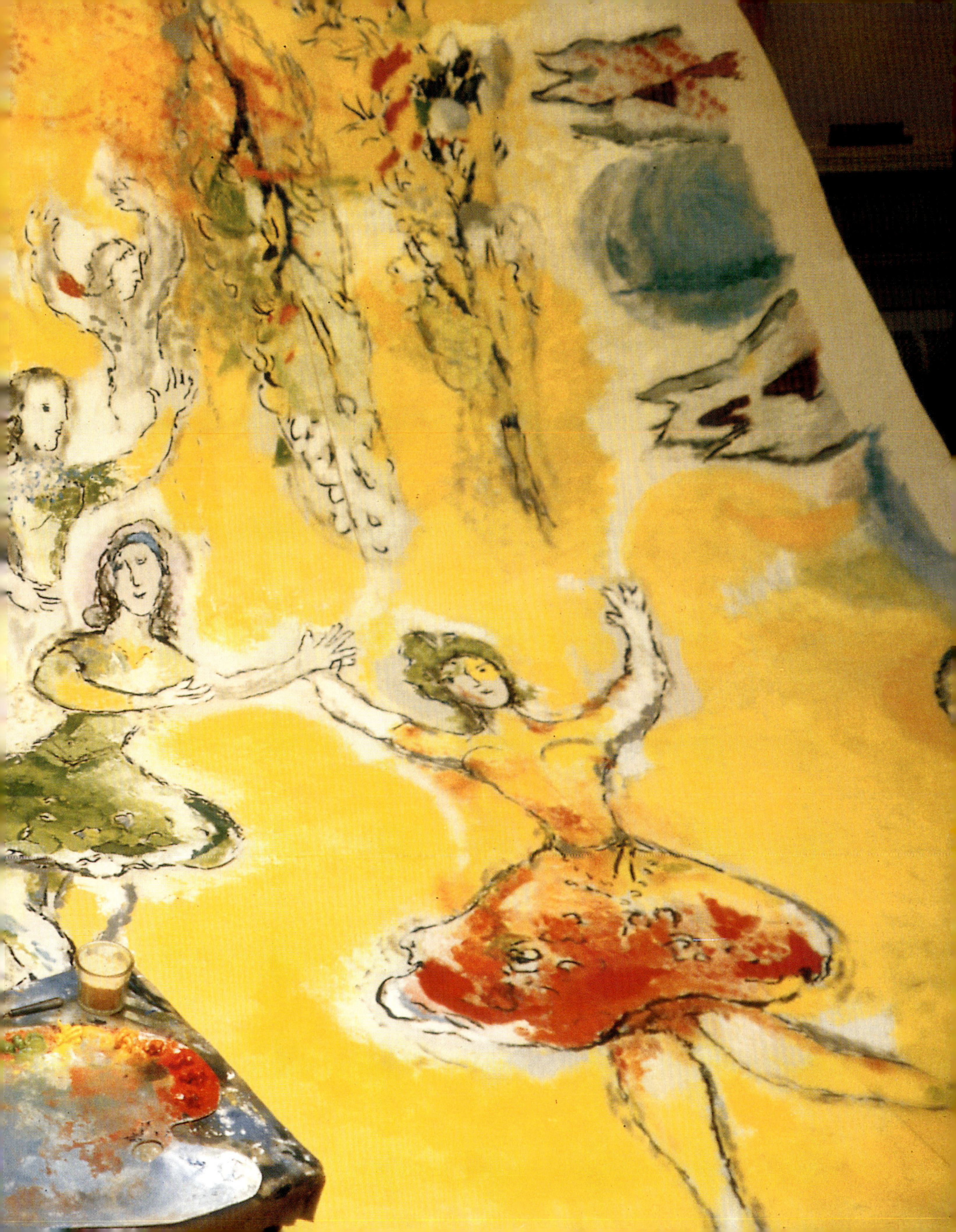

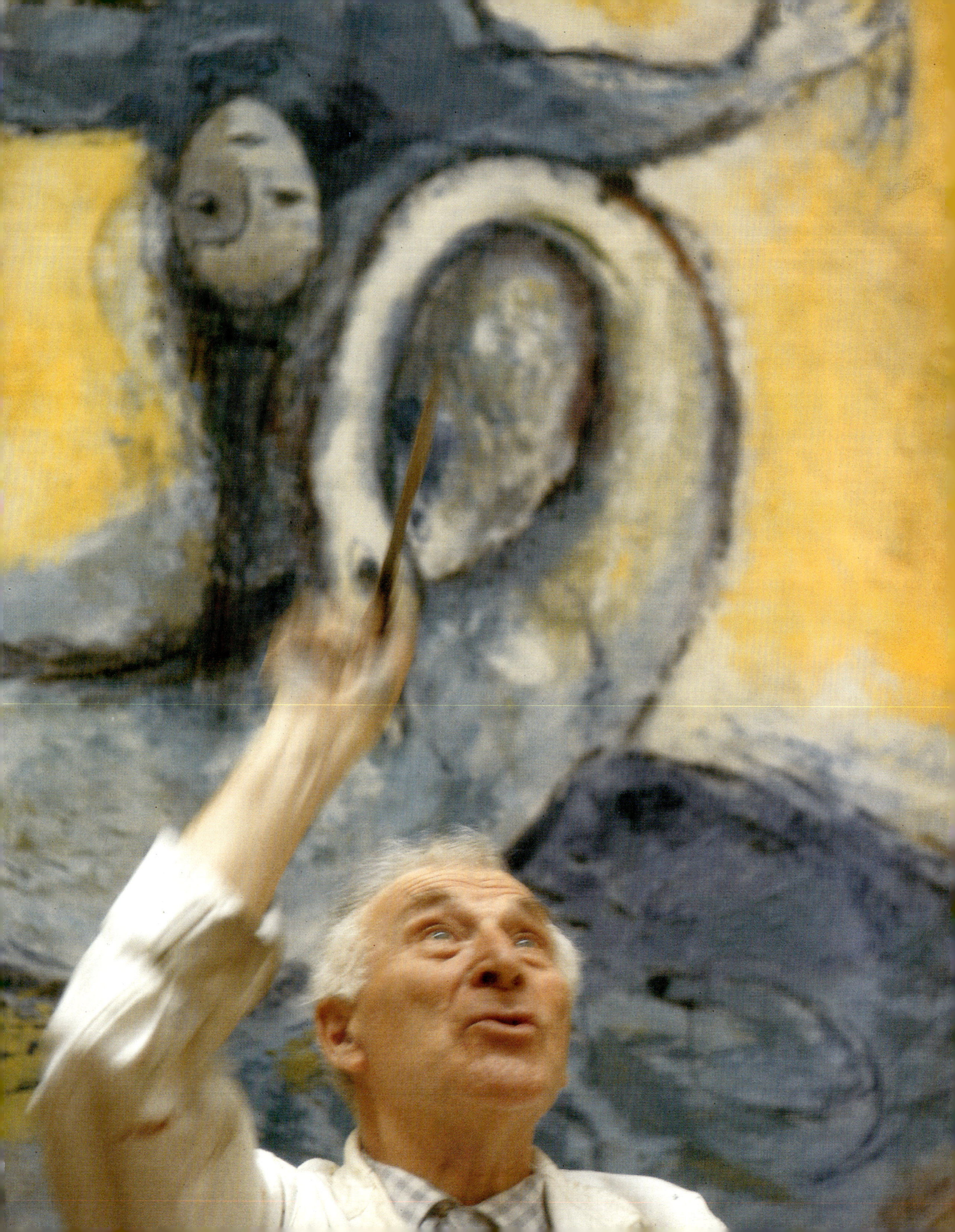

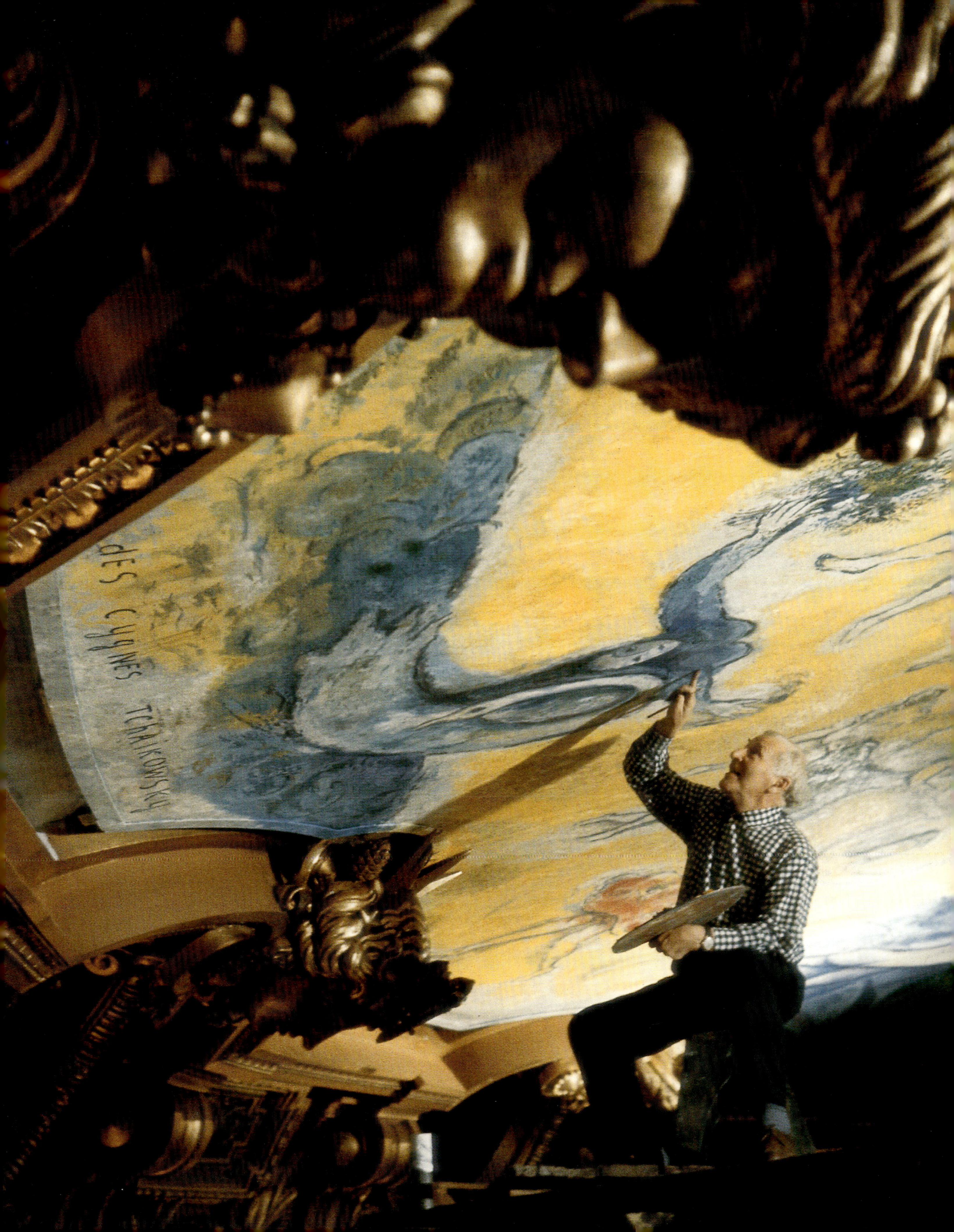
des Cygnes Tchaikowsky

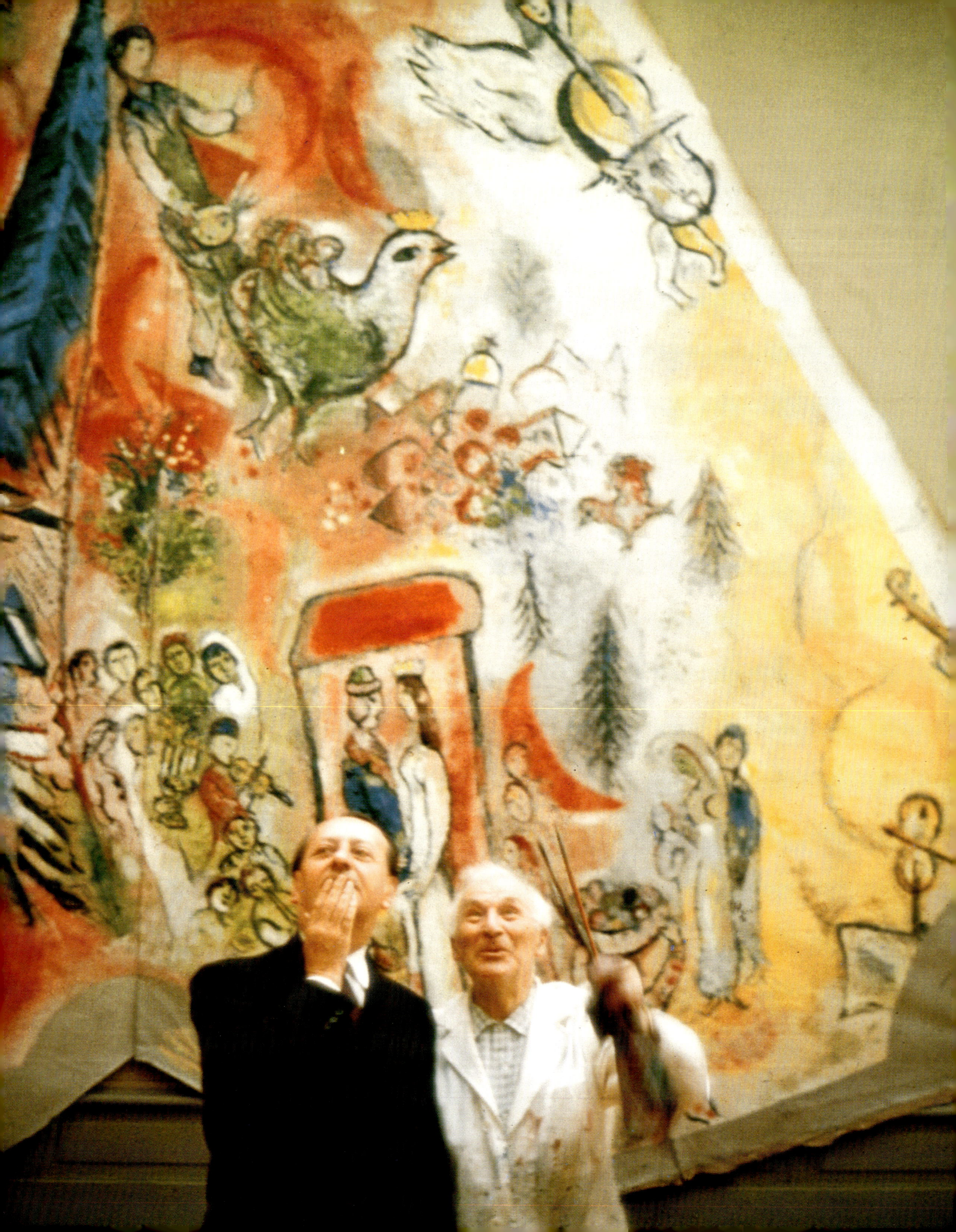

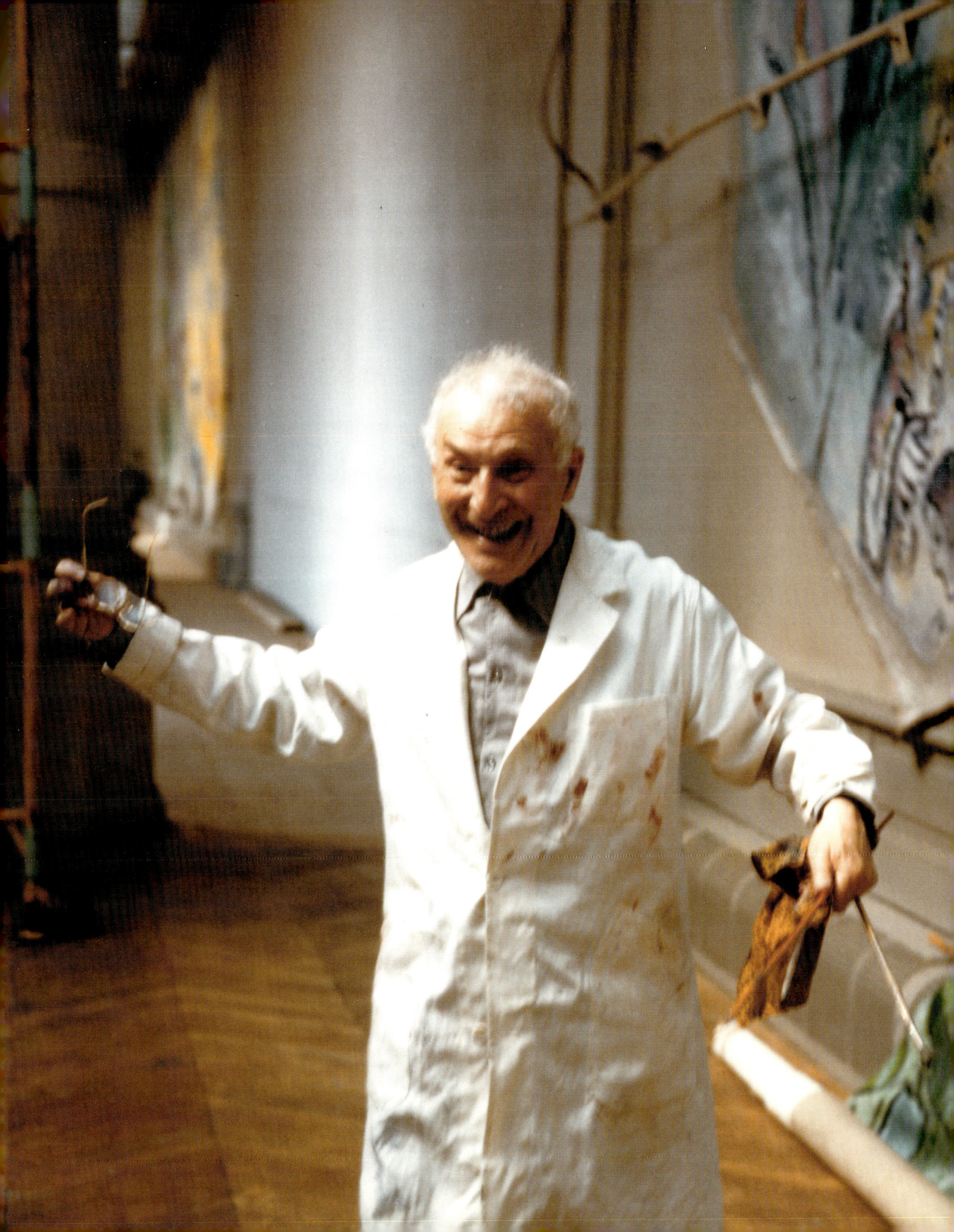

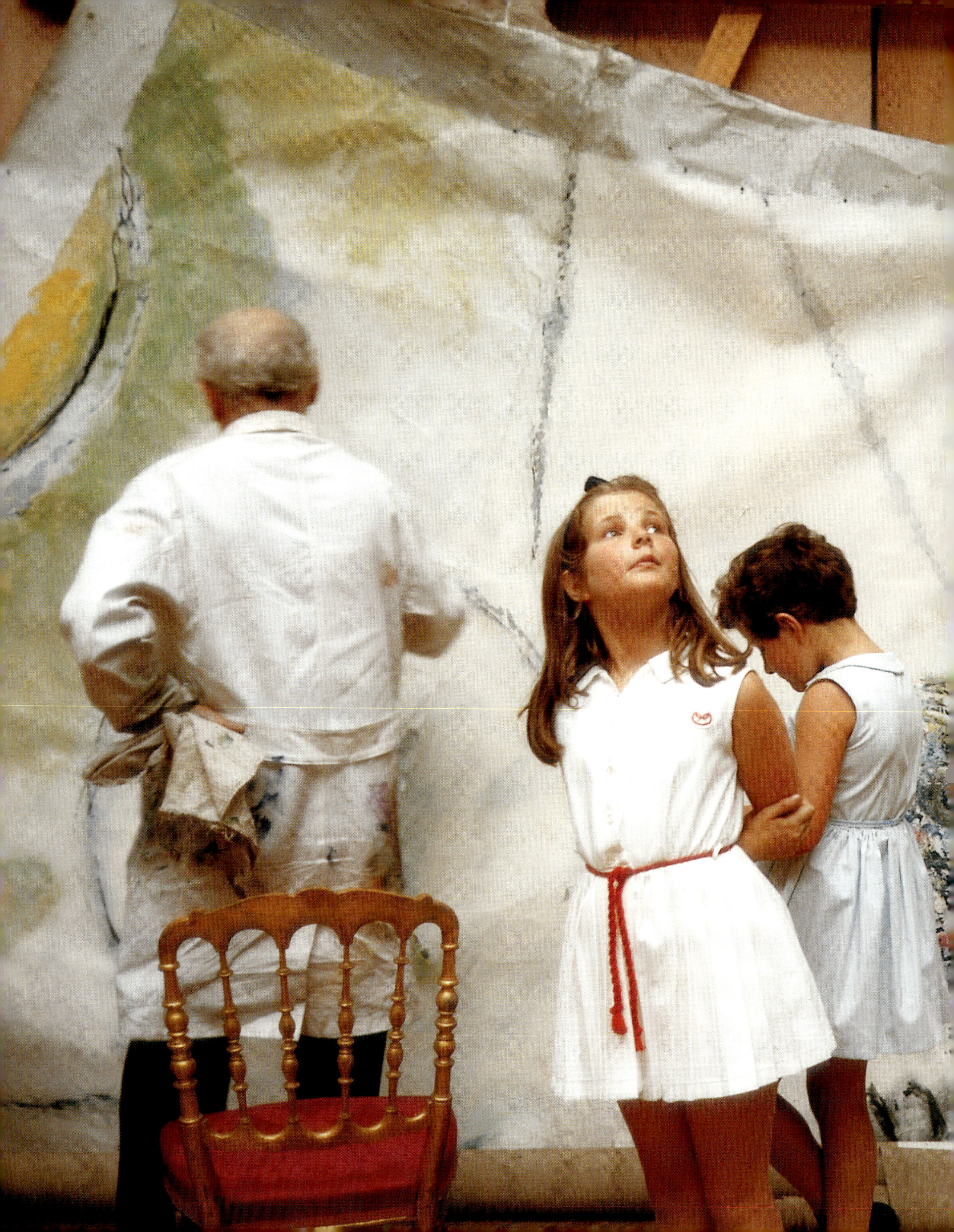

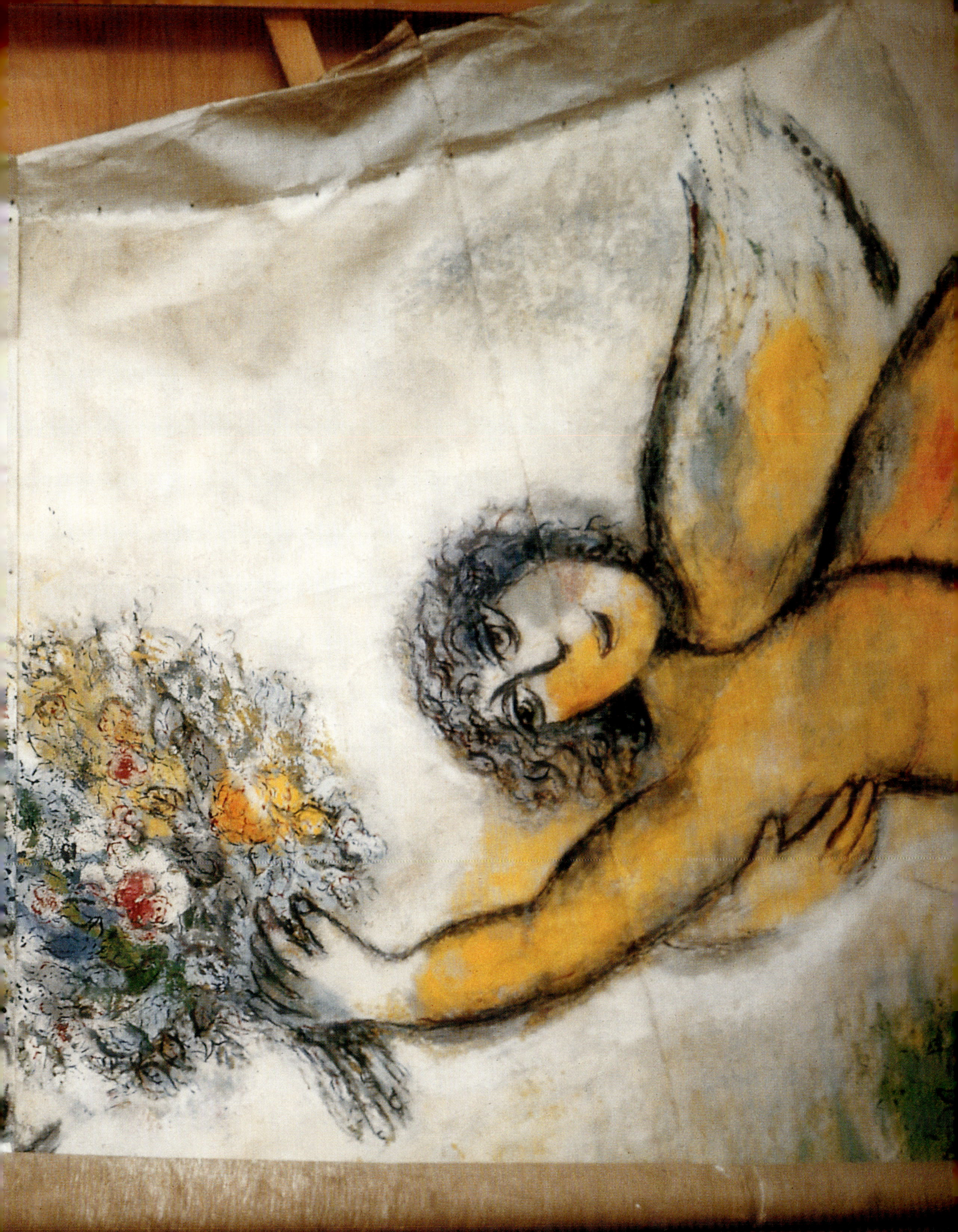

We're all a bit disappointed. At his great age Marc Chagall appeared to have already achieved immortality. God was apparently impressed by the vast numbers of "Christs in Glory" and "Rabbis at Prayer" that he painted in his long life, all surrounded by hosts of fluttering angels.

My last visit to the master took place ten years ago. I found him as lively as ever, still interested in all that was being said about him, roaring with laughter from time to time, and enjoying any compliments that came his way as a cat laps up milk. No fool for all that! Wearing a cashmere jersey knitted in typical Chagall colors, he appeared quite at home in a rather austerely furnished house that is in current fashion with the smart set on the Côte d'Azur (a house that was built, incidentally, seventy-five years ago for Edouard Bourdet). His welcome was as warm as ever, and when he talked of his paintings, he was never less than modest but at the same time quite objective; his words seemed to scatter color about the rather spartan setting. His head bent toward me, Chagall listened, smiling. Sitting next to a carefully arranged bouquet of roses, dahlias, and calla lilies, the master seemed to be waiting politely for me to leave so that he could capture them on canvas before they withered.

It was a delight to be in the company of this old and gentle man, whose wide and innocent eyes lent him the look of an angel. Instead of seeming elderly and feeble, Chagall had kept an eternal childlike innocence of expression. In the mornings he sometimes looked like the venerable pianist Anton Rubinstein, while in the afternoons he resembled Harpo Marx. It would have been fantastic to have captured these three figures together in a photograph, the first of them playing piano duets with Chopin, the second plucking away at his harp while mounted on an airborne donkey, the third pointed toward the heavens.

Having rejected the ever-shifting fashions of Paris, Chagall preferred to stay within the boundaries of his universe of poetic symbols. Much like Guillaume Apollinaire, who became his friend, he dreamt and created as the inspiration took hold of him; for his marvelous picture *To Russia, Asses, and Others,* Chagall borrowed the title from Blaise Cendrars, whose intellect he admired.

"I should so much like to know Picasso," said Chagall to Apollinaire. "Do introduce me."

"Do you want to kill yourself?" replied the poet.

Chagall lived on instead in the dreamworld of his childhood, its stable doors forever half opened. The beasts of the farmyard were his models: the red-faced donkey is perhaps Russia, at times incomprehensible and evil; the gentle cow with a green muzzle has a soft motherly look in its eye, while the butcher draws near to kiss its nose before slitting its throat.

Such images, along with snatches of folklore told him by his mother, remained in the forefront of his mind. Sometimes the presence of these images became overpowering, these ghosts from the past, and almost subconsciously Chagall's paintbrush recreated a Slavic universe that lived inside his head.

Time passed and war came upon Chagall's life. He returned to Russia, where the Revolution of 1917 transformed him into an official member of the new establishment in the guise of a minor minister of culture for the Vitebsk region. It was a constraint that was soon to prove intolerable: "My eyes," he wrote, "now burn with the flame of administration."

In 1922 he bade the Revolution goodbye and left for Paris with his wife, Bella, and his delightful little daughter, Ida. Later Chagall was to say that he took all he had to Paris, and that there the City of Light shone upon it. Strictly speaking, this may not be entirely true, for up until 1925 or 1926 the lambent Slavic fire continued to burn, rekindling the lost world of the old Russia. His *Self-Portrait with Seven Fingers,* 1912–13, and *Bride with a Fan* are two significant examples of this.

Again time passed, and life improved each day. Dealers were quick to snap up whatever Chagall produced. Then came the war, followed in turn by the Occupation—and, once again, Chagall was forced into exile. To the Americans, in whose country he made his home, he seemed the brightest flower of the immigration. Chagall designed the sets and costumes for a production of Igor Stravinsky's ballet *Firebird,* with Bella at his side to encourage him. The show took New York by storm. But this opportunity for further glory proved too much for Chagall. It may have been his age. In 1944, when Bella died, he found nothing else to enjoy but his new-found prosperity, and he searched in vain for new ideas.

The avant-garde was not for him. He stood center-stage, bowing again and again, but delighting his audiences with the same old repertory. "You're still the greatest of them all," André Malraux assured him, as a commission to paint the ceiling of the Paris Opera and three important retrospectives in less than one year bore witness. Who could resist all that?

Chagall was one of the great masters of color, but two others survive him: Picasso and Matisse. "I'm only a little *maître,*" joked Picasso, imitating the Russian describing his achievement.

"Not even a centi-*maître,*" responded Chagall with a laugh.

—Maurice Rheims
Académie Française

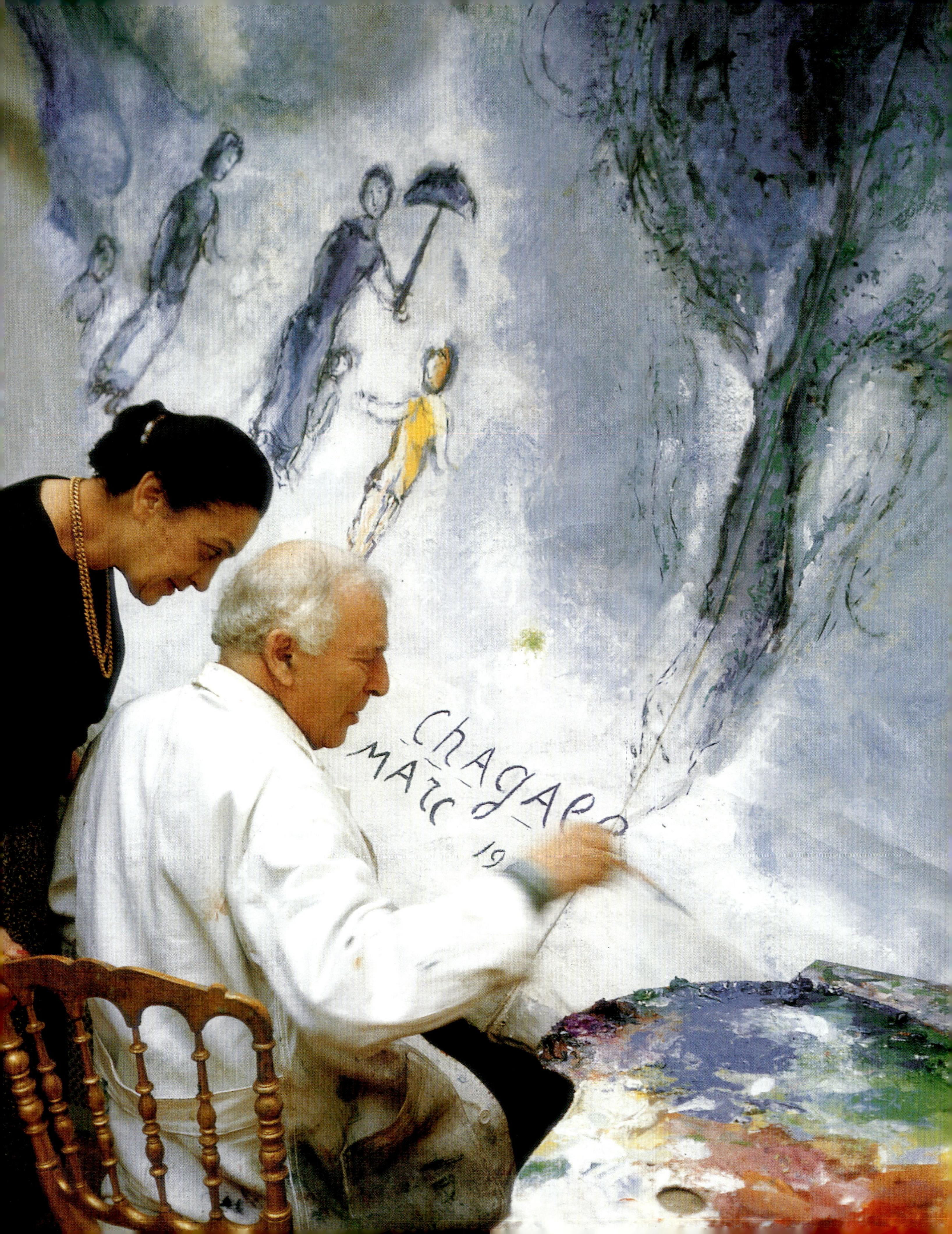
Chagall
Marc
19

Braque

Hubert de Segonzac 1955

Georges Braque, the quiet cubist in the heart of his universe: the bird, the guitar, the jar, and *L'Atelier* in progress.

Braque examines his evolving canvas with a studious expression. He works on twelve or more paintings at once. For Braque, paintings are never finished.

The strong hands of an artist combined with the fragile harmony of a palette.

At seven in the morning Braque finds his studio silent.

As soon as he touches it with his hands, an object belongs to him: he engraves the stone he finds; the wood he saws frames his paintings.

He drops anchor in Varengeville-sur-Mer. Here, he is together with friends from the village, including the parish priest, and his night companions, the birds from the pond, which accompany him while he paints.

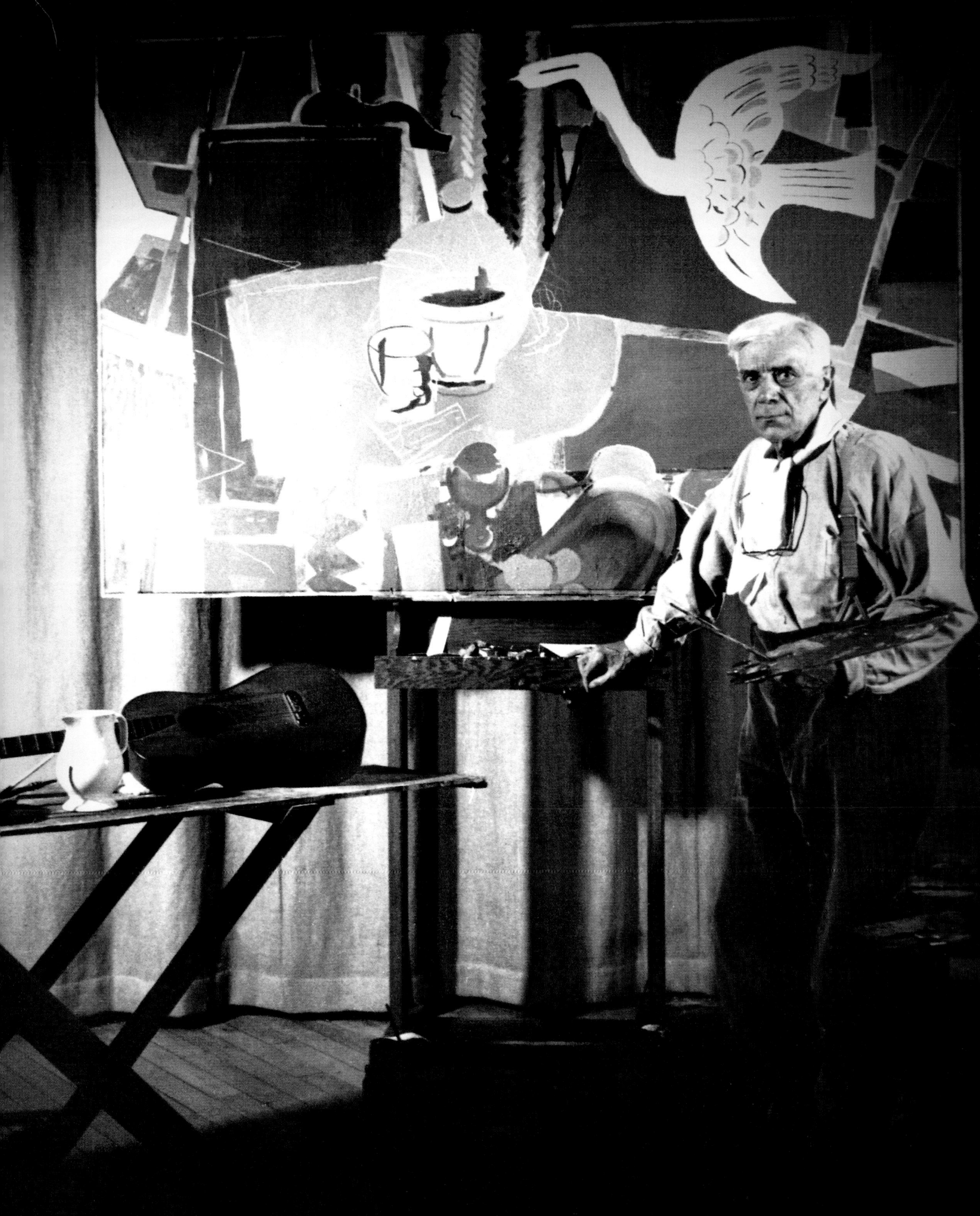

Georges Braque is and will always remain a painter. He devoted himself to painting as one does to religion. Except for his love for his wife, nothing else in this world competed for his attention. In Braque's calm, ordered, uncomplicated, and solitary world, everything happens on the inside. At the age of twelve, with his first savings, he bought an easel and a box of oil paints, which he carried with him on his bicycle. Throughout his entire life he rode through the streets, searching for motifs to paint in the natural landscapes and existing structures of his environment.

He stands in the back of his studio at Varengeville-sur-Mer on the Normandy coast, in front of an impressive gray, black, and white sketch he began two years ago. He speaks in a slightly muffled voice and says little, but briefly offers: "There is the painting and the painter; there is what it wants, there is what I want. Nothing matters except the relationships between objects. There is nothing that exists in and of itself. It is a bitter struggle towards harmony. When it gets to me, I go to work. But I don't know what will become of it."

Braque discovered Rimbaud's visionary poem *Le Bâteau ivre* (*The Drunken Boat,* 1871), which revealed to him the subtle and suggestive possibilities of language. He studied the drawings of Théophile-Alexandre Steinlen published in journals such as *Chat Noir,* and admired Henri de Toulouse-Lautrec's lithographs for poster advertisements and Armand Guillaumin's seascapes and Parisian cityscapes. As an exercise, he practiced imitating the formal composition and personal styles of many of his contemporaries. "I've never learned so much," he says to this day. Braque's canvases reveal a picture space that has been liberated from classical perspective and deliberate pictorial calculation. His obsessive and repetitious depictions of objects convey a process composed of layered facets and multiple views of the physical world. "Things happened without involving my direct control. I've never wanted anything in life and I've never made any decisions. Everything came together on its own." While working in Le Havre, he attended classes at the Ecole des Beaux-Arts.

Braque lived in a one-room flat in Paris on the rue des Trois-Frères, surrounded by the bohemian culture of Montmartre. During the day he worked for Laberthe, his father's decorator, while at night, he attended painting classes at the Batignolles public school taught by an M. Quignolet. Saturday evenings, Braque went dancing at the Moulin de la Galette, where he proved to be an excellent waltzer. His athletic build, lively expressions, and fashionable wardrobe caught the attention of many.

When Braque completed his service in the army he didn't face the problem of choosing a profession. A portrait of his cousin Johannet, convinced his family that his talents should be directed towards a career in painting. His father provided him with a small allowance and he was able to move to a flat on the rue Lepic in Paris. After the Ecole des Beaux-Arts in Le Havre, and the studio course at the Batignolles school, he took up painting classes at the Académie Humbert on the rue Rochechouart. He was dismayed by the rampant conformity of the students and instructors at the Humbert, but discovered companionship with the French painters Marie Laurencin and Francis Picabia, as well as the Spanish sculptor Manolo, the young critic Maurice Raynal, and, in the seaport town of Honfleur, Raoul and Jean Dufy. He socialized with these friends often, but ultimately chose to remain a distant acquaintance. He disliked the bohemian life, drank little, kept his finances in order, spent in accordance with what he had, and carefully balanced his budget. On winter Sundays he enjoyed staying at home to practice the flute and accordion. This is how he came upon the music of Bach and was hit by a flash of inspiration.

The painter had been searching for a visual language to express the mental picture of a world he sensed forming inside, one which seemed immediately congruent with that of the Baroque master's musical compositions. Examining Bach's fugues, counterpoint rhythms and keys, led Braque on a path to exploiting the range of expressions color possessed. Color escapes from form to become his counterpoint, a free element in space, independent of a linear program. In 1912, he marked this revelation by painting *Hommage à J.S. Bach,* which spearheaded his oeuvre.

The epiphany brought on by Bach's music influenced Braque's decision to sever his ties to academicism and the notion of an official career. From this point on he planned to work alone. He rented a studio on the rue d'Orsel, where he hired models, paying them seven francs an hour to sketch their poses. The view from his window inspired paintings of urban vistas while his interior still lifes gathered dimension and weight. He soon followed in the footsteps of Cézanne to the south of France where, in L'Estaque, he experimented with color and the sensual gradations of warm southern light. The sun-drenched landscapes and earthy clay colors of southern France transformed Braque into a Fauve, but a Fauve who looked to Cézanne and his voluminous constructions, who had mastered the process of drawing, and who had studied the structures of his subjects in the manner of a craftsmen.

The new, initiated Braque triumphed at once with his first entry in the Salon des Indépendants in 1907. The success dispelled his doubts: "I understood at that moment," he says, "that I was a painter. Until then, I didn't believe it."

Upon his return from L'Estaque, Braque abandoned the vivid colors of the Fauvist palette in favor of a more monotone, ocher and brown color program. He painted canvases in which forms were simplified to the extreme. The result was immediate, but the jury for the 1907 Salon d'Automne was less impressed and rejected his paintings. Some art historians believe that it was Matisse, who, as a member of the jury at the Salon that year, exclaimed upon seeing Braques paintings, "What cubes! What cubes!," thus coining a moniker for the new school of painting called Cubism. A young art dealer Daniel-Henry Kahnweiler, proposed to buy all of Braque's work. Kahnweiler had already purchased Picasso's primitive period canvases from Horta de Ebro, and Braque's paintings from L'Estaque added to the theme of nature subjected to a rigorous pictorial treatment. Braque and Picasso did not yet know each other. It was Kahnweiler the art dealer, who initiated their friendship from the beginning and was responsible for forging their intimate working relationship and close camaraderie, which developed over the ensuing years before World War I. Picasso is said to have declared: "Braque is my wife," conveying with wit his friend's mannerisms and the finesse of his colorful personality. The two masters worked together and in such a similar pictorial style that it was sometimes necessary to look at the signature on the back of a canvas to decipher the artist.

It was the height of Cubism's popularity, the battles at the Salon d'Automne and the Salon des Indépendants, the invention of Max Jacob's famous Bateau-Lavoir, the house next to his at 13, rue Ravignan, where Picasso and another emerging Cubist painter Juan Gris, each rented a studio. He broke from his solitude, dined with his new friends at restaurants, went to roar at the Medrano clowns, and finished the night at the Closerie des Lilas, where poetic discussion often ended in a brawl.

But, rather than partaking in drinking binges and brawls, Braque preferred bicycling to nearby Sorgues, just outside of Marseilles. It was during this time that he renounced all painting that treated its subject as "pictorial fact,"or the representation of an object, place, or thing, by its specific physical symbol. In its place, he instituted "anecdotal fact," and parted from traditional, visual descriptions of reality in order to emphasize the nuanced qualities of pure form and color. Yet he was only able to do so in stages. One day, in Avignon, he bought a roll of wallpaper that resembled an oak wood grain. With charcoal, he drew a still life of grapes, a cup, and a fruit bowl resting on a table. A strip of wallpaper suggested a drawer, another went around the bowl—the concept of the collage had just been born.

World War I came upon Braque at the age of thirty-three, while he was in Sorgues living with his wife. On May 11, 1915, he was wounded in combat by a piece of shrapnel. His orderly took him for dead, gathered his papers, and sent them to his family. A few weeks later, a note from a nurse informed Braque's wife, Marcelle, that her husband was regaining his health. Braque continued to paint mostly still lifes in which the objects are but the pretext of colors, without a third dimension. He experimented with media, sometimes mixing sand and ashes from the stove into his pigments. He limited his color range to browns, blacks, whites, and light yellow tones to successfully achieve subtle expressions of atmosphere through simplified forms and a diminished palette. It was shortly after working on the Ballets Russes's production of *Zephyr and Flore* that Braque returned to the south of France to revisit the Normandy of his youth. While on vacation visiting friends, Braque and his wife discovered a fair-sized plot for sale with a pond and a view of the horizon. The painter bought it immediately and had an extensive farmhouse built with a large studio attached. He built everything for the house including the frame, decorative ornaments, and furniture. He had special tables made by artisans, with a beautiful wood that was accented with stones, starfish, and guitar motifs. Braque's art evolved with the rhythm of a period fraught with anguish, and brings forth his shining and hazy forms from a deep darkness. Serenity escaped but moderation and balance remained—his moderation, his balance—and the finesse that defines the mark of a perfect artist, or the perfection of an art.

—Henriette Chandet

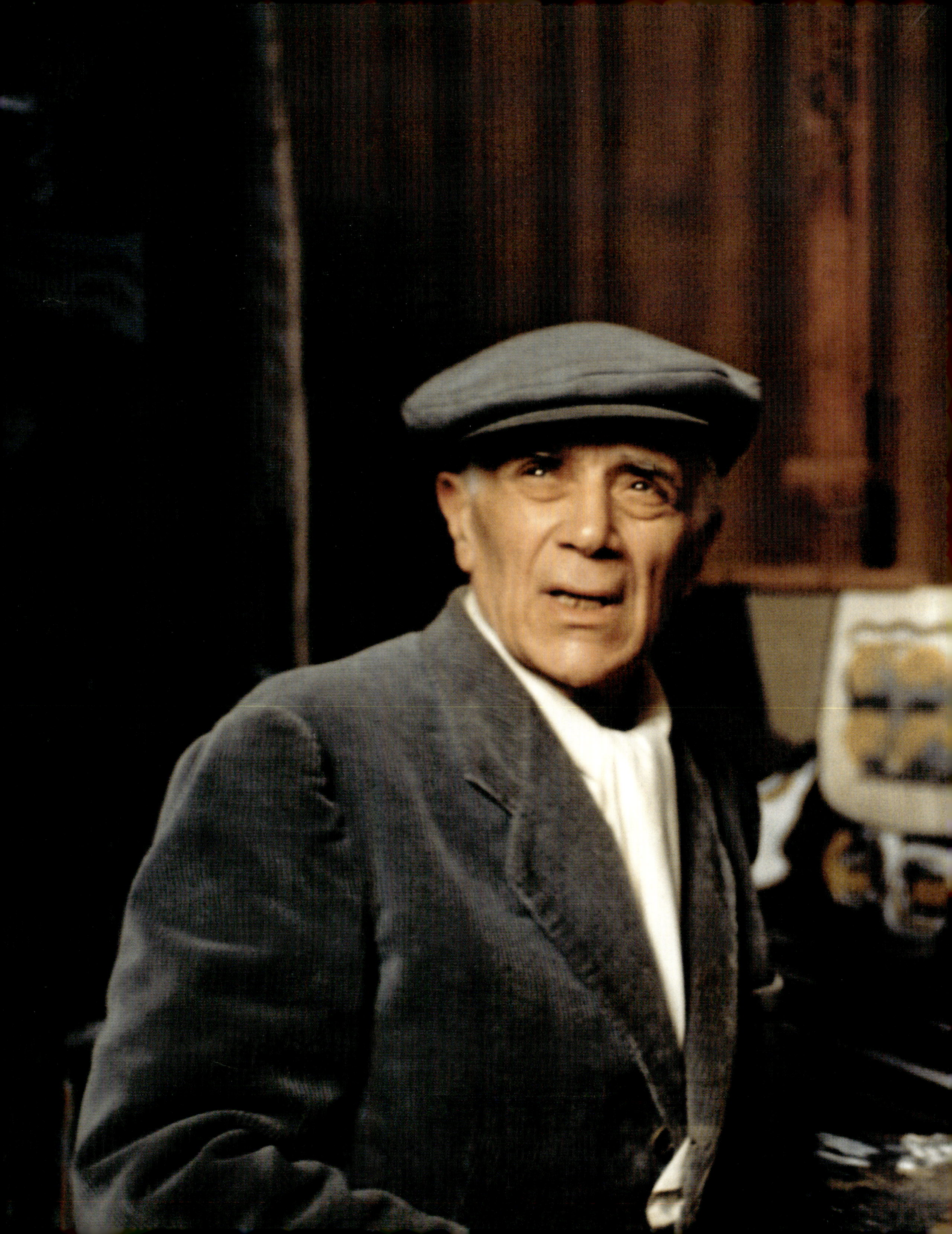

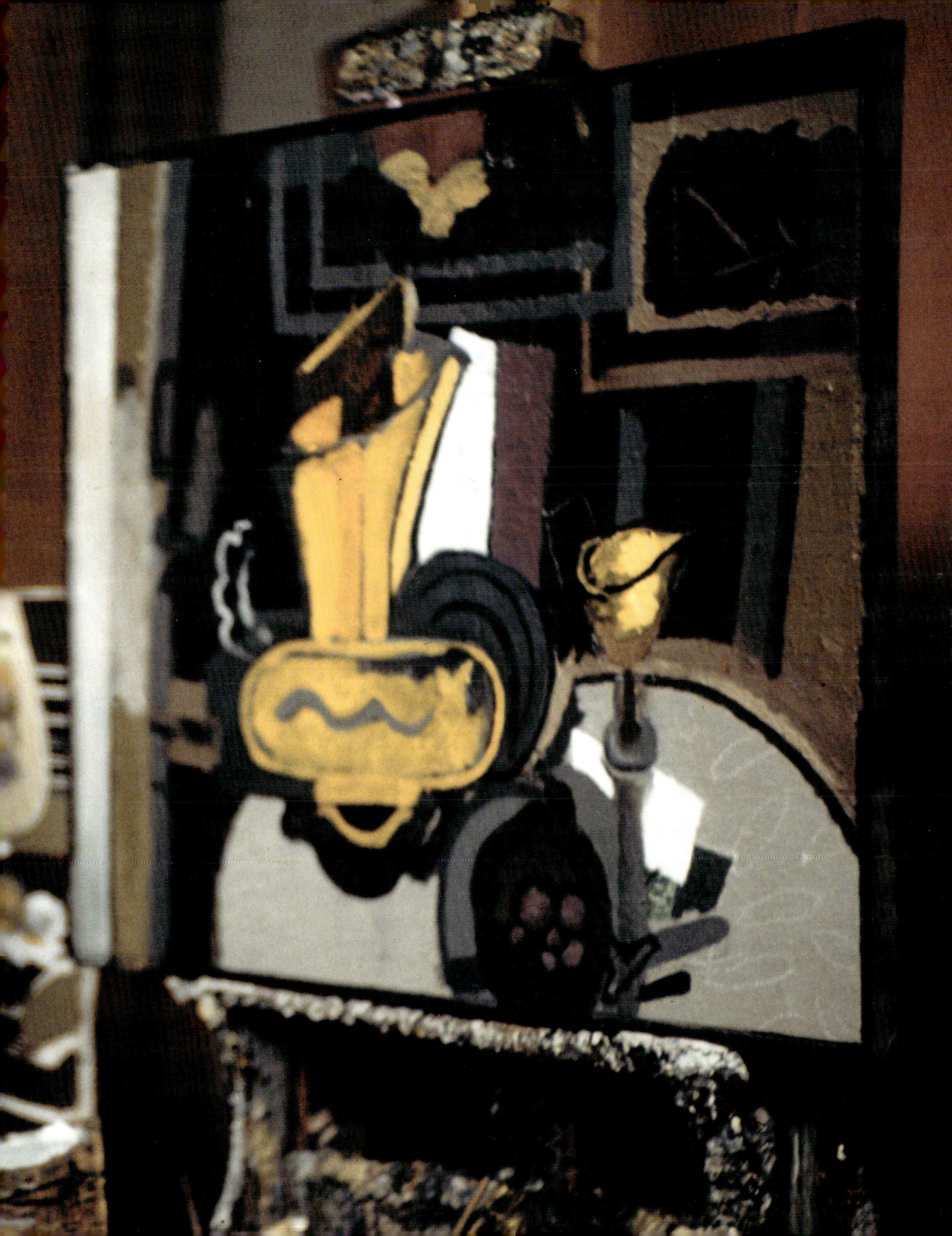

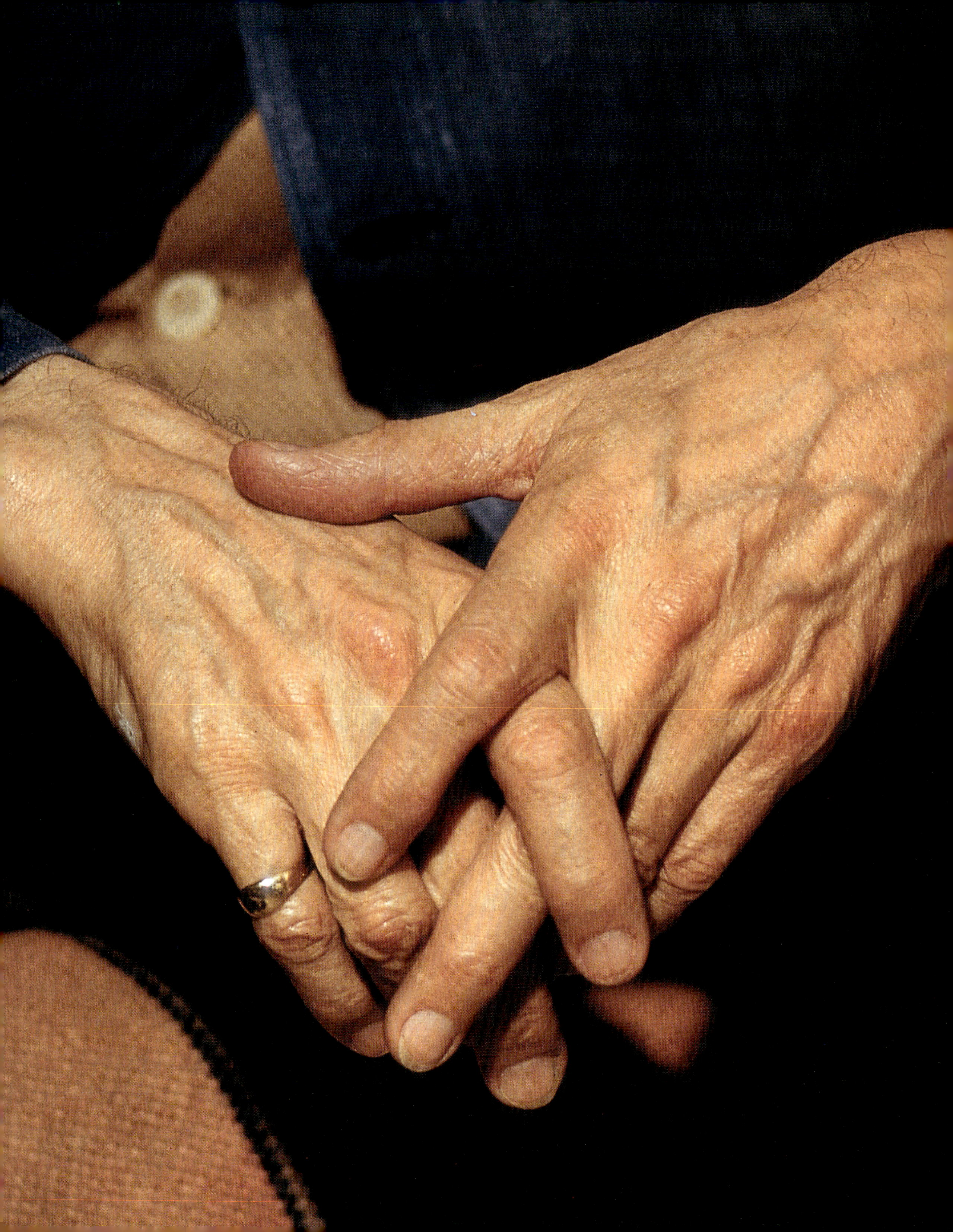

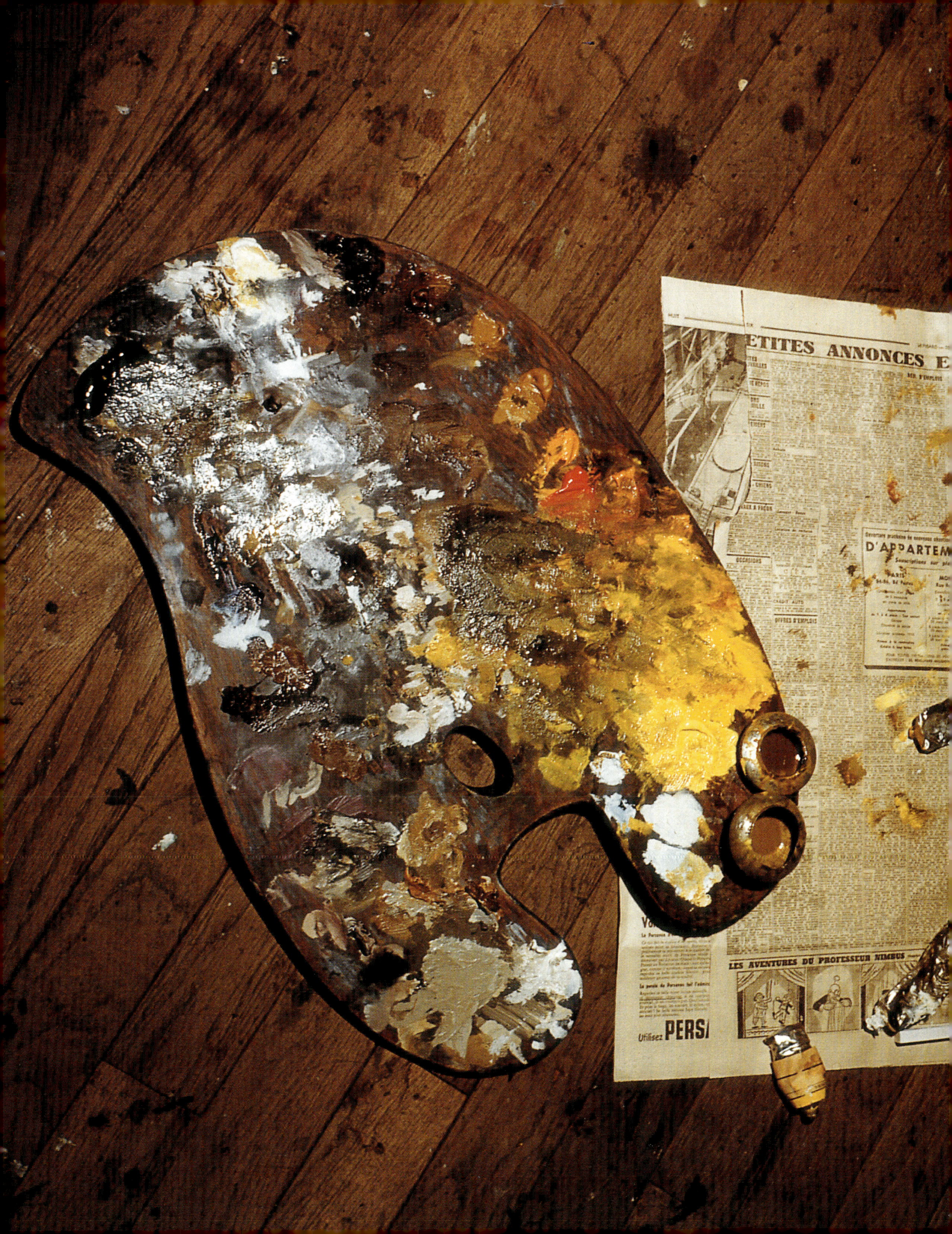
ETITES ANNONCES E
D'APPARTEM
LES AVENTURES DU PROFESSEUR NIMBUS
Utilisez PERS

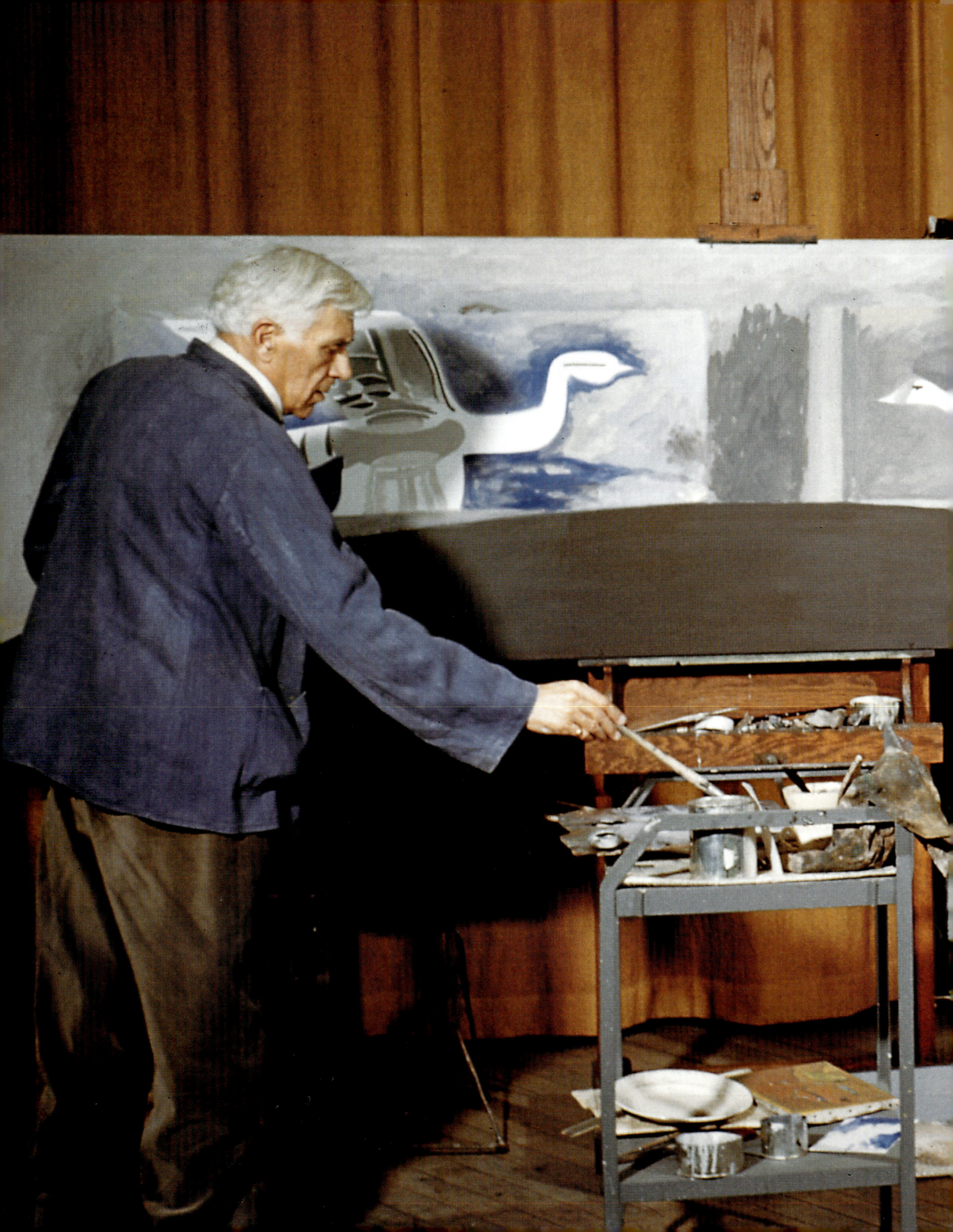

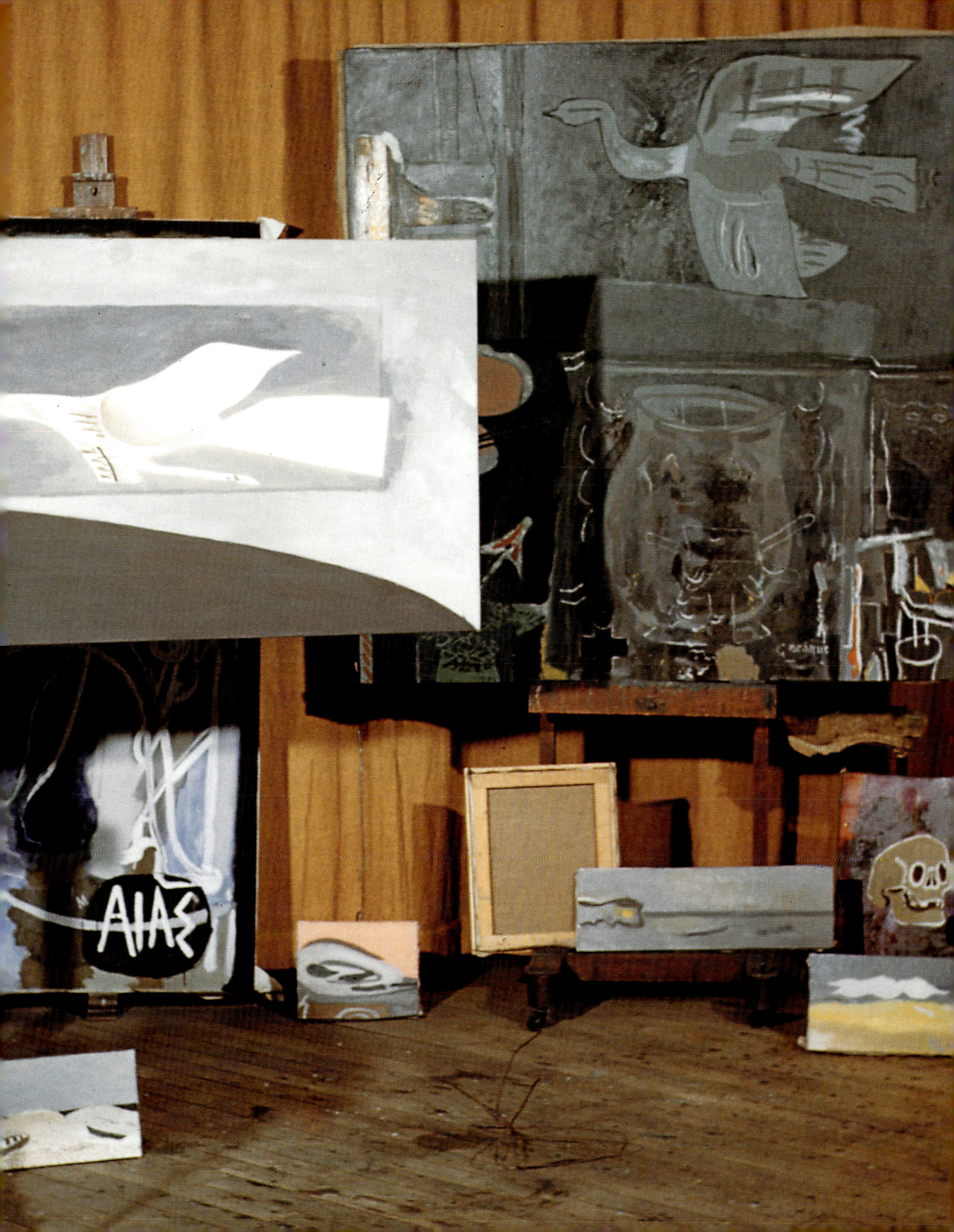
ΑΙΑΣ

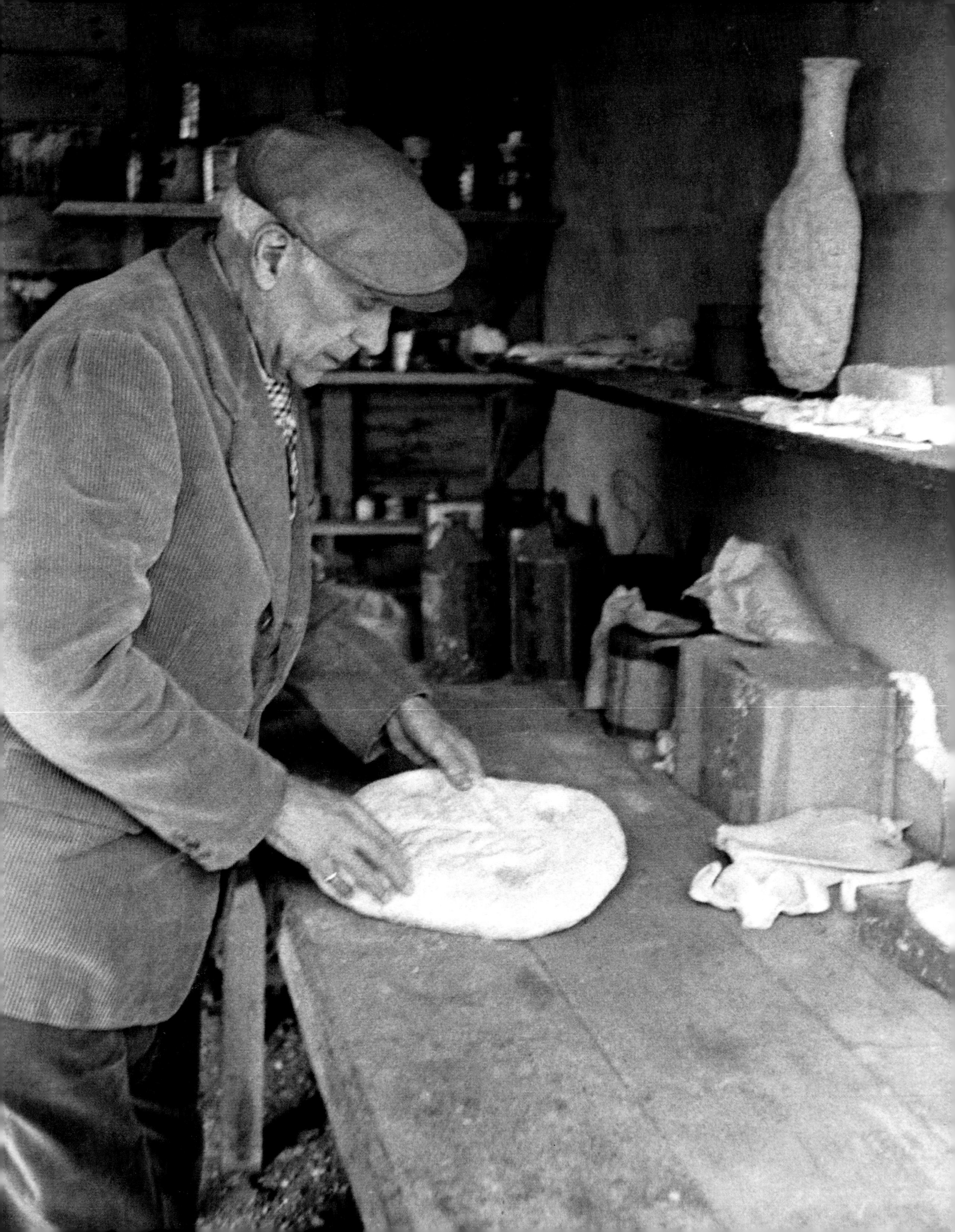

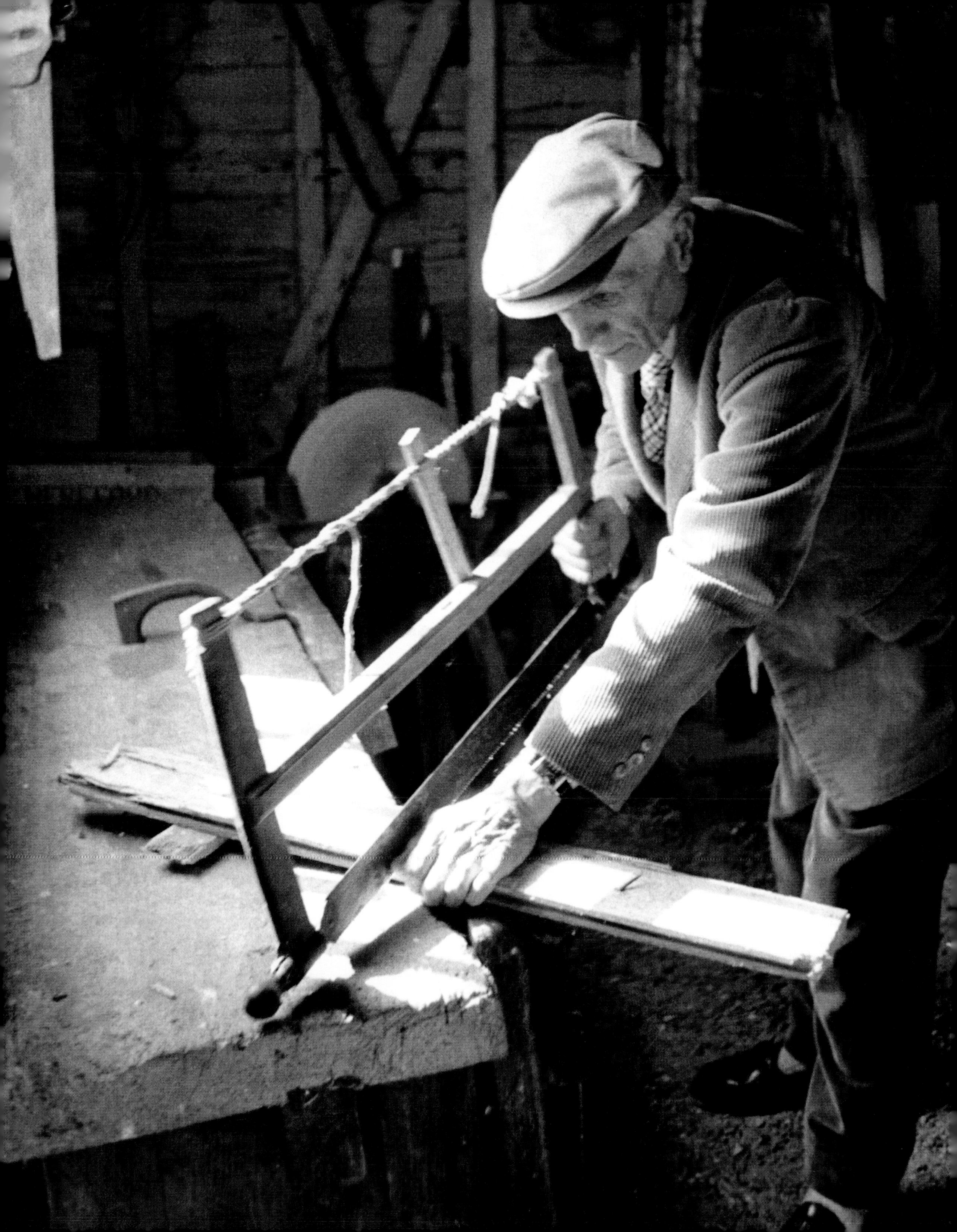

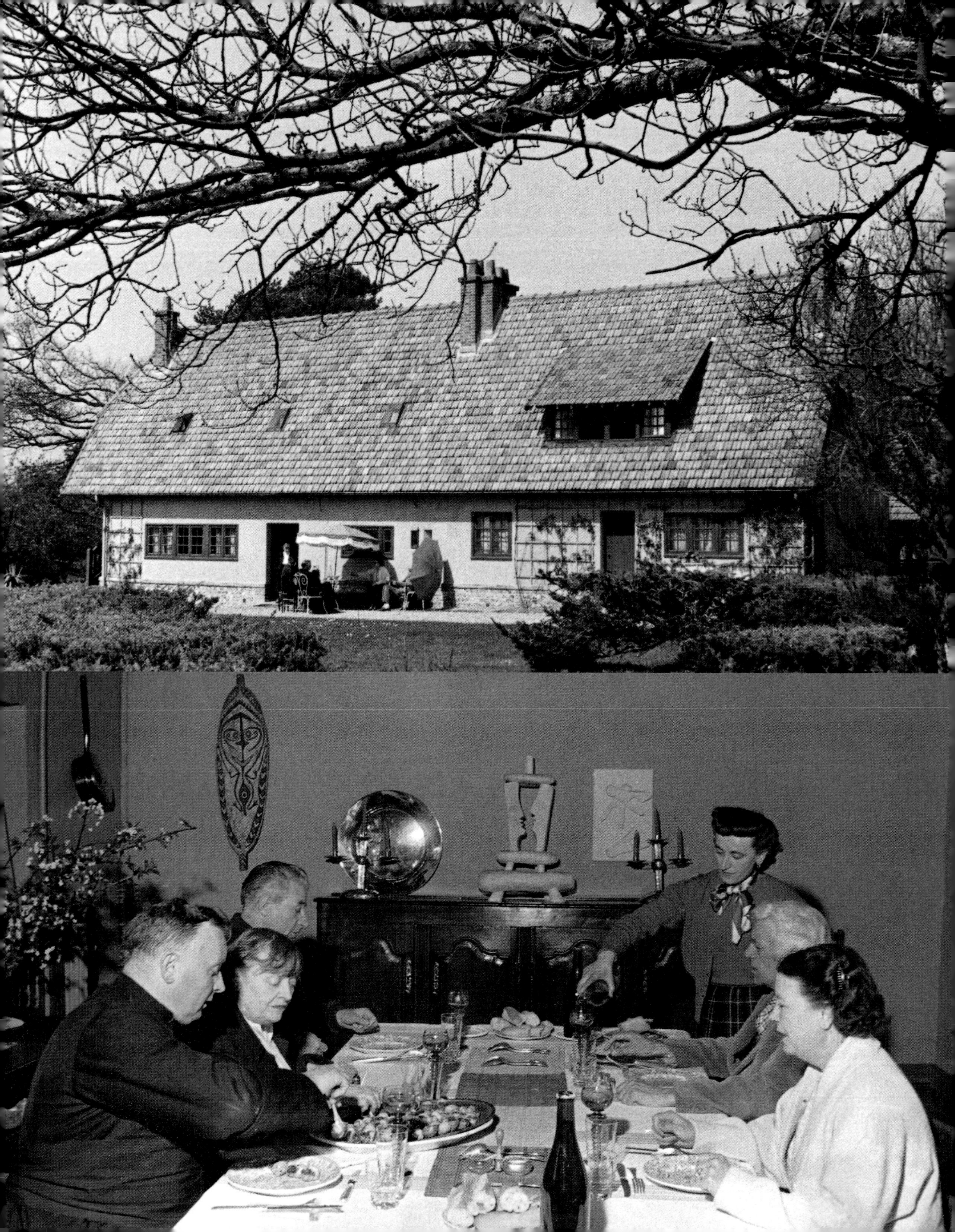

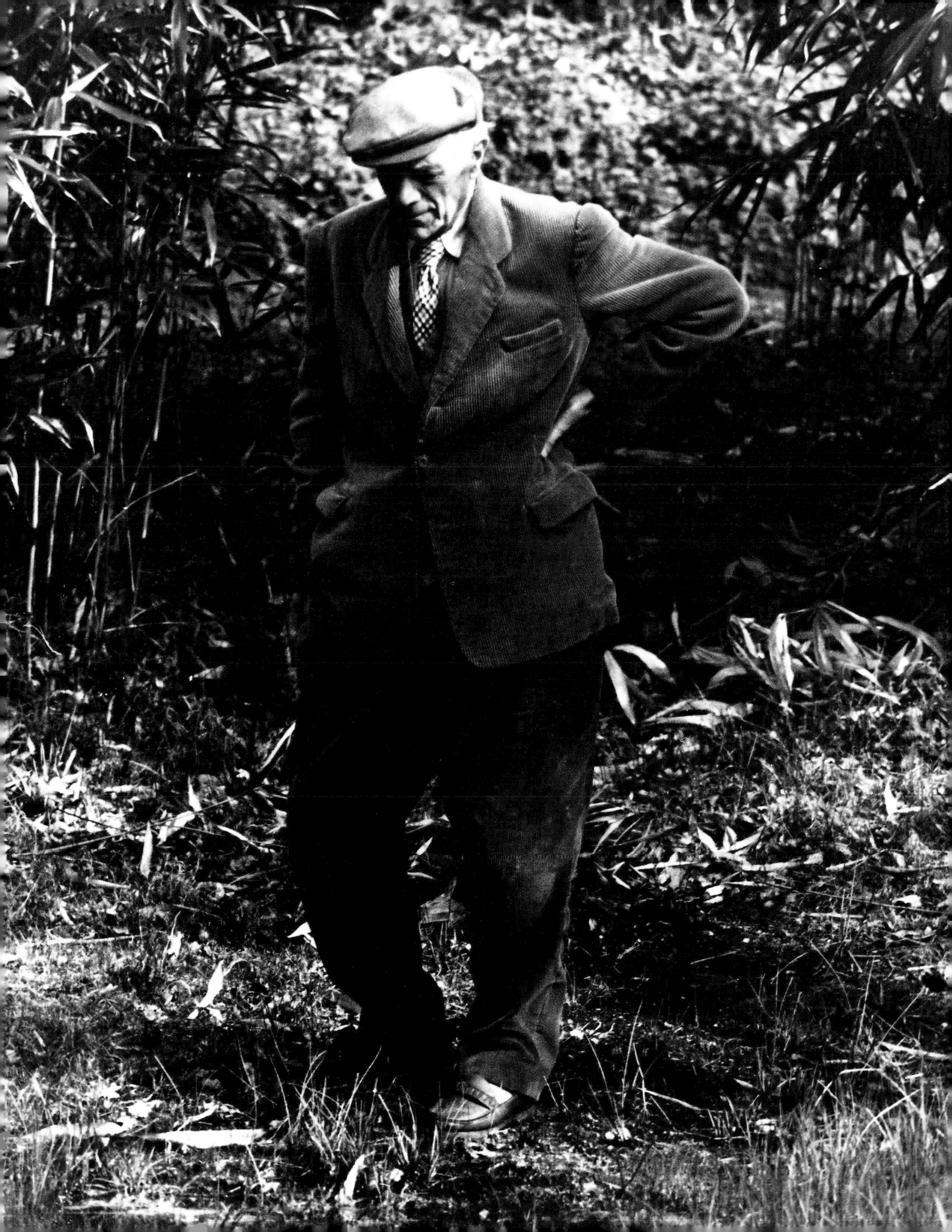

Van Dongen

Izis/
René
Vital
1959

The Dutch master and prince of Paris, Kees van Dongen, in his studio at 75, rue de Courcelles, with his vibrant, fresh palette—a touch of happiness.

Surrounded by his women, his truculence inspired by Rembrandt in the heavy atmosphere and density of a Dutch composition.

Paris has taught him freedom. He has become the most colorful of the Fauves and the most cultured of the intellectuals. The more contempt he has for his "subjects," the more we love him.

His perspective on painting: "I have to paint in order to make up for the time I lost playing with life."

Brigitte Bardot posed for van Dongen when she was an unknown actress. He meets with her again five years later and sees her as the perfect "van Dongen," long, thin, heavily made-up—she even looks like her portrait!

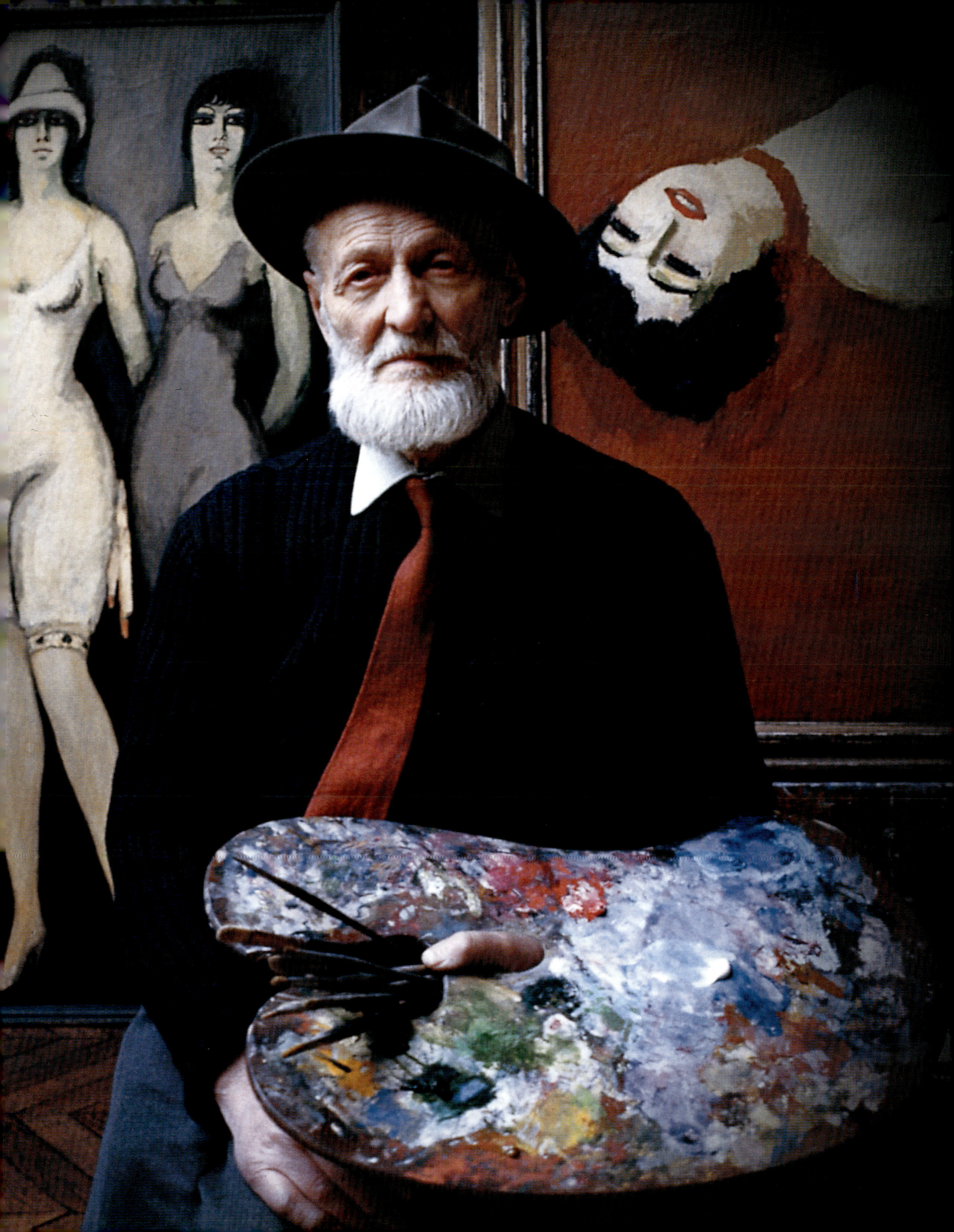

In the shadows of an Orthodox church in Paris, beneath its neo-Byzantine domes, surrounded by the ornamented facades of the Franco-Russian rue Daru, an American call seems out of place—"Hello, Van!"

The thin, erect outline of a young man brusquely comes to a stop on the sidewalk. This is no ordinary silhouette, but one of a man upon whom glory and fortune were cast like furies during the mad era between the wars, when this artist made his mark.

He turns his head to reveal a face adorned by a beard that has been carefully trimmed along the line of the jaw. Impeccably white hairs wrapping around the cheek and head frame his eyes, the blue eyes of a heron, which stare at the person who hails him.

"I'm sorry, I don't think we know each other." His answer is completely natural and in English, which he speaks among so many other languages—including French—with the mocking slowness indigenous to the countries of northern Europe.

The American is not discouraged: "I know you well, Van, and have seen your picture in the magazines, come on..."

"Van" is rather flattered. For if the American recognized him so easily in 1959, it meant that, even at eighty-two years of age, it hadn't been such a long time since he presided, almost by law, over the juries for the most beautiful thigh or the "wittiest" bathing suit in Cannes or Deauville between 1920 and 1939; nor since the time, about 1905, when Picasso, his partner in poverty at the Bateau-Lavoir in Montmartre, painted his portrait. His hollowed cheeks and beard made him look like van Gogh, the prince of light and his compatriot, and Russia's Kropotkin, prince of anarchy, his heart's compatriot.

"Van," is Cornelis Theodorus Maria van Dongen. "Kees," or "Keesy," to his friends, "Kiki," to the cloche hats and hobble skirts of society women.

"Goodbye, Van!"

A half hour later, the American leaves a bourgeois building at the corner of the rue Daru and the rue de Courcelles. Under his arm he carries a small painting for which he paid one million francs.

Time has stopped on the rue de Courcelles—time always stops when a painter captures on canvas the smile on a face or the trembling of grass. Alone in his cathedral-esque studio, van Dongen dons his favorite outfit: a gray wool toque and overalls spotted with multicolored stains. At eighty-two years old he continues to work standing at his easel, without glasses.

"I'm not good for much other than work," he says.

He repeats this sentence now to himself, joyfully, confidently, as he had uttered it before to answer his visitor's question.

He searches for a particular color blue that was running through his head. He needs just another touch, near the enormous lashes of Brigitte Bardot, whose image reigns, unfinished, over the large canvas. He has always enjoyed painting fashionable women and has never felt disoriented or intimidated around them. The twentieth-century stylish woman, lanky, with heavy make-up, was partly his creation, just as François Boucher had painted women of the eighteenth century, wearing blush, smiling and plump. A final brushstroke on the side of the easel prevents rust from one day rotting the nails holding down the canvas. At a restaurant he eats a lunch of grilled meat, vegetables, a salad he seasons himself, and no wine or coffee.

Night falls and van Dongen prepares his dinner, which consists of rice pudding, prunes, yogurt, and a glass of water. He won't put on his dinner jacket tonight. Perhaps he'll sleep fully clothed on the cot hidden in a tiny shed adjacent to the studio.

This quintessential high-society painter lives like a poor man and speaks with the wisdom of a sage—judging from a random look through the dictionary of van Dongen-esque opinions, a rather non-conformist sage:

PAINTING: "Me, I'm like a cow. I look. I do as I see."

PARIS: "Paris draws me in as a lighthouse does. There are splendid grays, like in Holland."

WOMAN: "The most beautiful woman I have known? I hope to meet her tomorrow."

THE ORIENT: "Luckily we live in a country that is not too beautiful...I went to the Orient and I understood why, in those blessed countries, there were no painters. Nature there is too beautiful. Over there, I only wanted one thing, like everyone, to sleep, to look...Painting was invented by people from the North."

WORK: "Life is a big mess. You have to work constantly so as not to work, just like you have to wage war to live in peace."

BUSINESS: "When I paint, I don't spend a moment thinking about the price I might get for it. But oh, when it's done..."

In contrast to most painters, van Dongen never kept sketchbooks for his preparatory drawings. Nor did he ever belong to any movement or specific school.

At the age of twenty he had only one thing on his mind and that was to travel to Paris. On July 14, 1897, he arrived in Paris and had hardly settled when the memory of Delfshaven, where he was born, began to haunt him. It was in Delfshaven, a suburb of Rotterdam, that he was educated, where he used to paint, at the age of fifteen, like Rembrandt and Turner, and where, in the old house built in 1602, his father, already accustomed to Kees disappearing, began to seriously think that Kees could no longer be relied upon to inherit the family malt business. It wasn't life in Delfshaven that van Dongen missed, it was its dazzling sky, the barge sails skimming the surface of invisible canals, nostalgia for a country where the ground seemed to have been flattened in order to give its expanse the splendor of the sky. In Paris, van Dongen painted light, vast spaces vibrant with color. "Madness," the critics cried, "it depicts nothing, it's Tachism!" But Ambroise Vollard, the art dealer and financier of almost all the major painters today, was impressed by van Dongen's work and organized the painter's first exhibition at his gallery in 1904. From this point onward, van Dongen was recognized. A minister Louis Barthou, made him famous. At the Salon d'Automne of 1913, he ordered that a painting depicting a naked woman be removed. "And for once," the artist sighed, "it wasn't one of the girls that usually modeled, it was my wife!"

Thirty-six years later, on June 14, 1949, during his first large exhibition in Rotterdam, a dozen or so paintings were censored and removed from the view of his fellow countrymen. Dr. Oudkerk, a Calvinist city councilman, declared: "I went to see these paintings. Then I observed the public's reaction. Believe me if you will, but there was an erotic glow in the eyes of the visitors." Dr. Oudkerk asked a guard how many "licentious" reproductions, sold for about three-hundred francs apiece, had been purchased. The guard answered: "They're selling like hot cakes." Dr. Oudkerk gravely replied, "Look at how evil is spreading."

"Evil" had indeed been widespread since 1913. In 1920 there was his "scandalous" portrait of the aging Anatole France. Snobbism came into play: anyone who was any one in the high society of the roaring twenties, Anatole France included, wanted their portrait done by van Dongen. Yet, relatively speaking, van Dongen was scarcely more tender with his clients than Goya, who painted with naïve insolence the aristocratic families of Spain as a catalogue of human degeneration.

If a woman only sparkled through her jewels, then her jewels were the subject of the painting. Thick brushstrokes indicated brilliance—the painter rarely sketched a head he found empty.

"Once I did the portrait of an important critic X," he said. "The poor man was suffering from stomach problems that made his face green and his nose very red. Since then, I'm not sure I'm considered his friend."

All of Paris high society courted van Dongen. Strangers. His old friends, those from the maze of Montmartre, and from the first "Van Dongen Balls," his companions from home were no longer present. They rejected this kind of social world and—legitimately—criticized his dark and somber painting style. To justify himself in their eyes—and perhaps in his own as well—van Dongen wrote, in 1927, *Life of Rembrandt,* in which van Dongen himself is implied: "Soon, the painter's friends began to turn their backs on him. They didn't understand. They believed that an artist had to create and not subjugate himself in order to please the powerful bourgeois class. He let it be said, for he knew just how much the rich and powerful were poor and just how much he loved them. This great painter was as moved by the conceit of the nouveaux riches as he was by the submission and misery of the poor."

Van Dongen occupied himself by admiring women, but there were only three who really counted: Augusta, his first wife, a Dutch woman; Jasmy, who modeled for him in 1916 and who graced many of his canvases until 1934; and Marie-Claire, his current wife, lanky and exquisite. Augusta shared the enthusiasm of his beginnings, Jasmy, his glory; Marie-Claire gave him a son, Jean-Marie. Today, this very young, old man, who dreams alone in his studio filled with ghosts in color, no longer thinks about glory. On a return trip from Deauville, he says, "It suits me. My clientele is there, and it reminds me of Holland because of the gray light and the rain over the ocean."

—Jean-François Chabrun

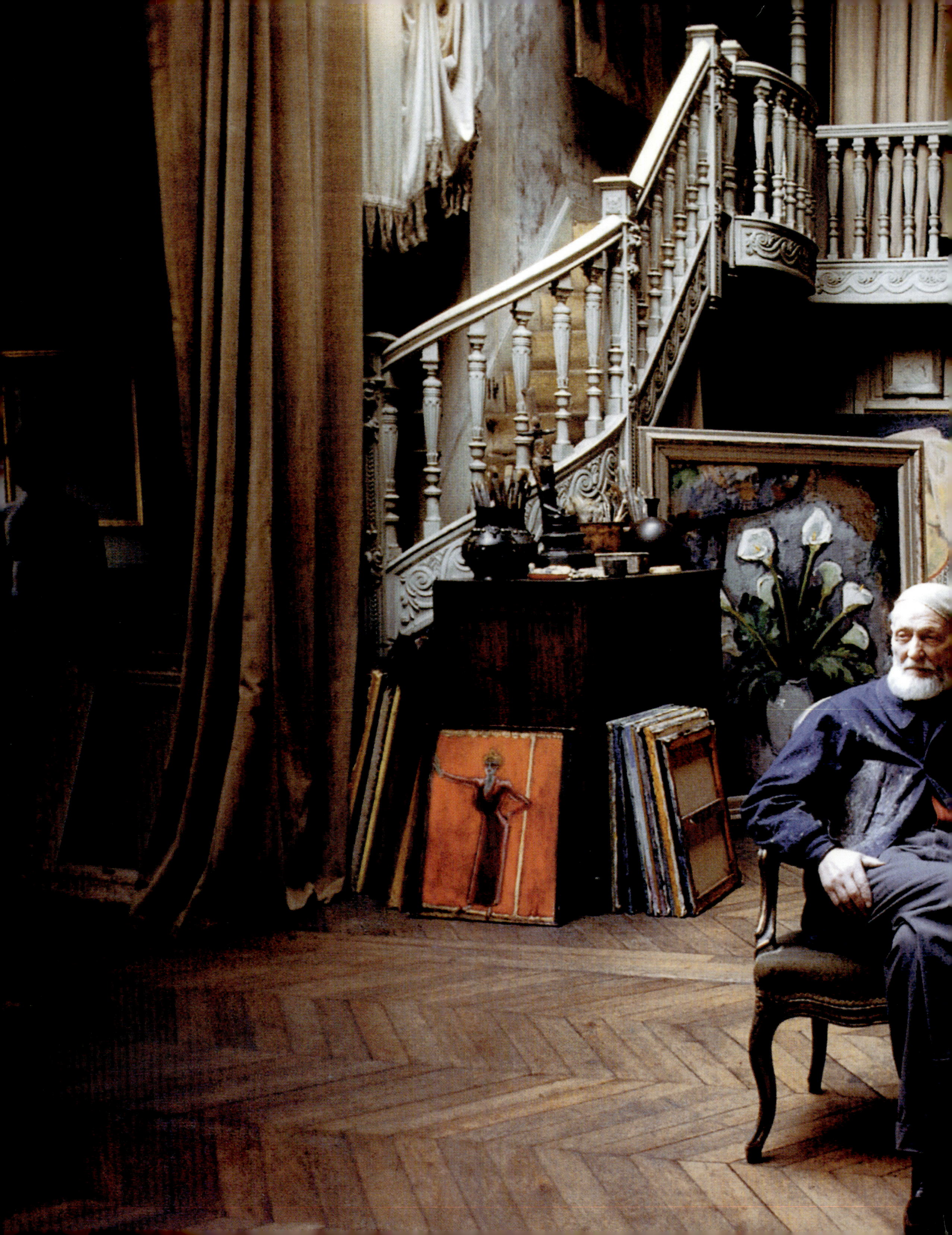

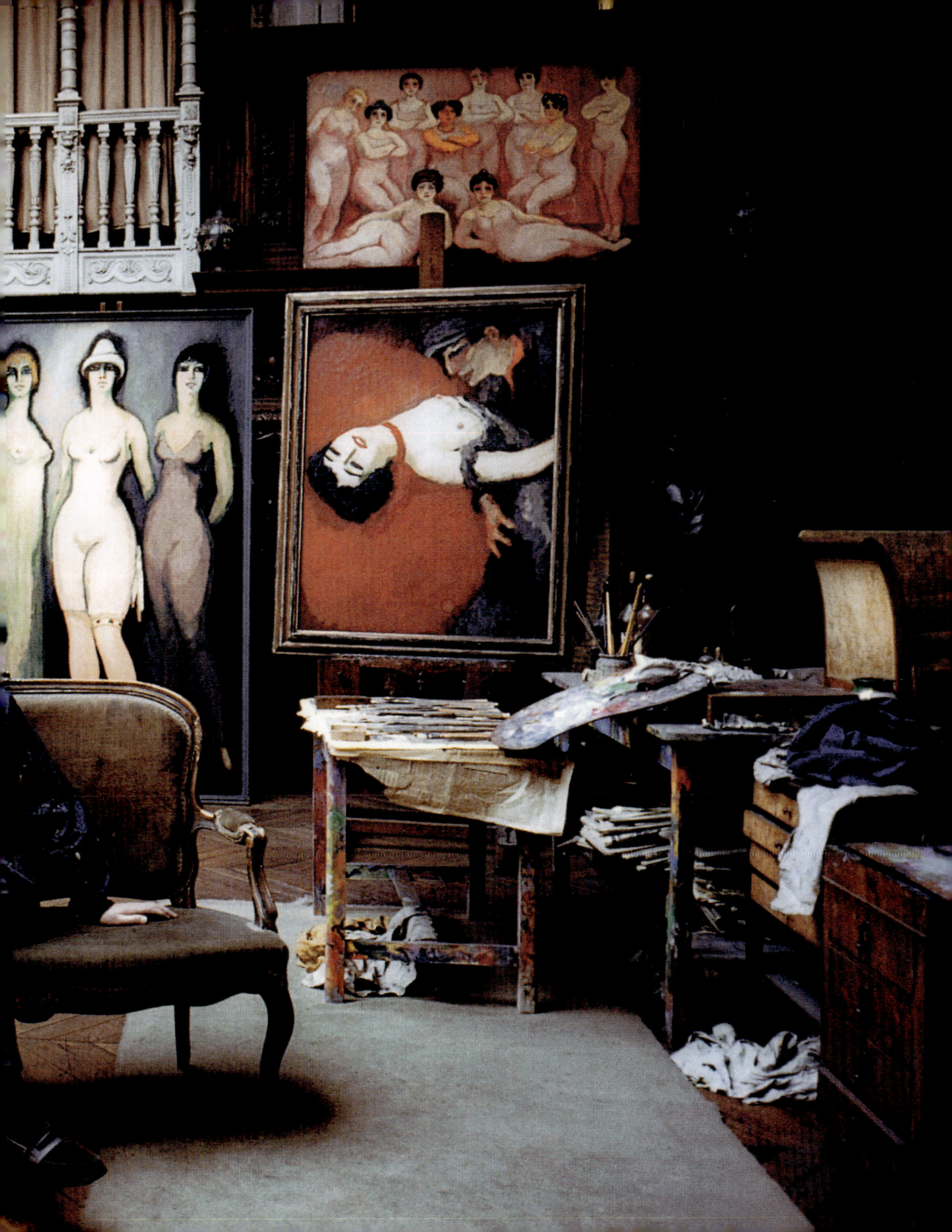

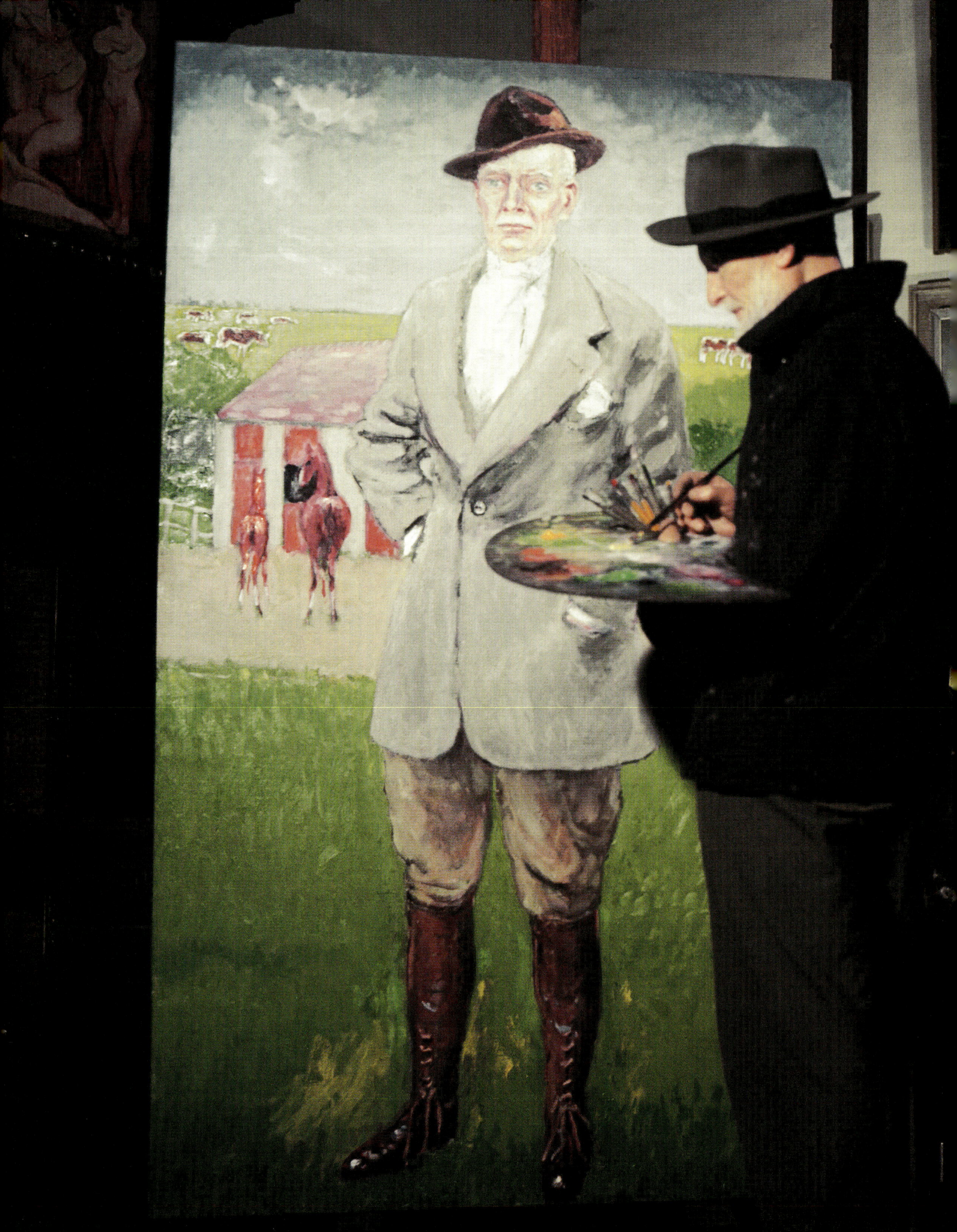

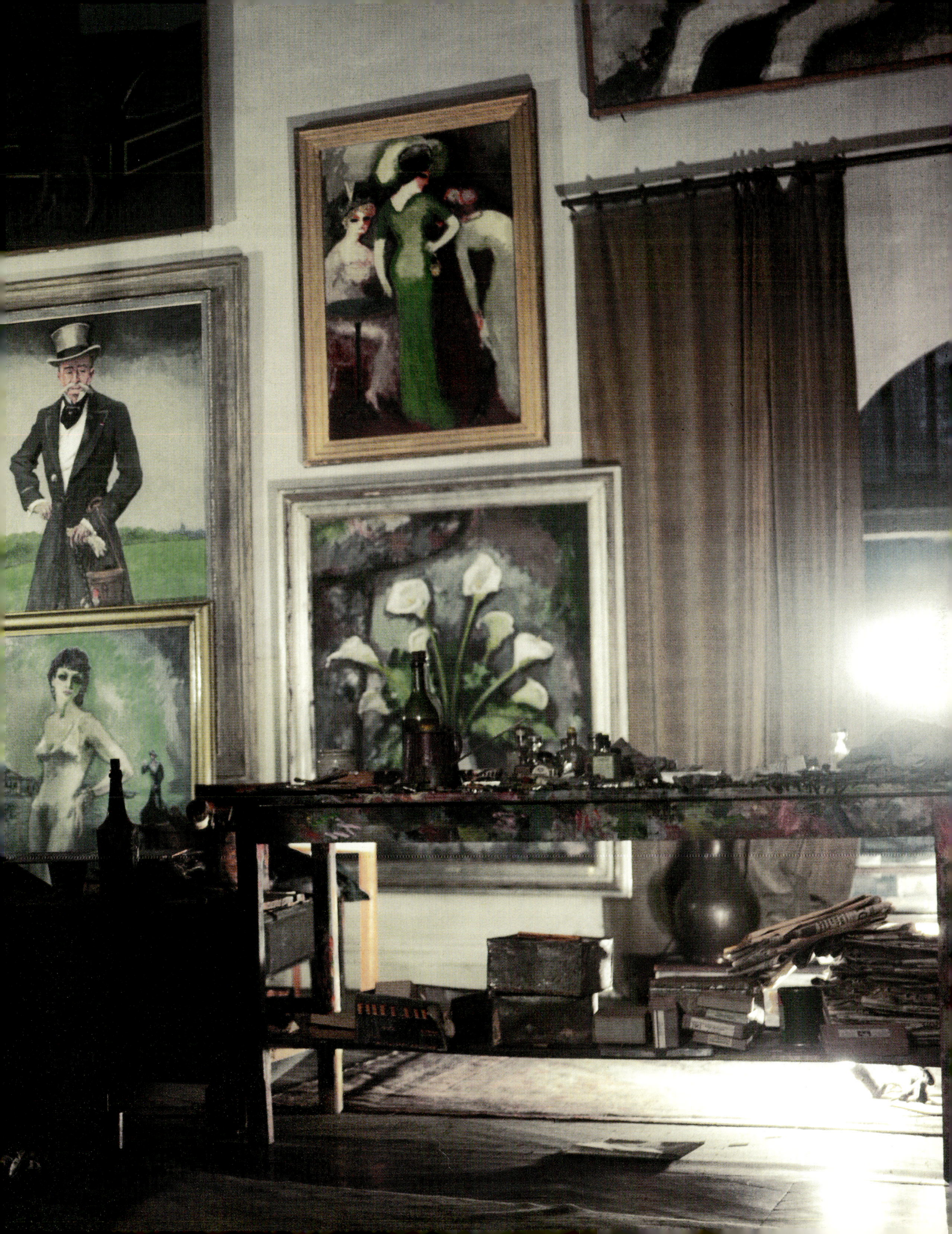

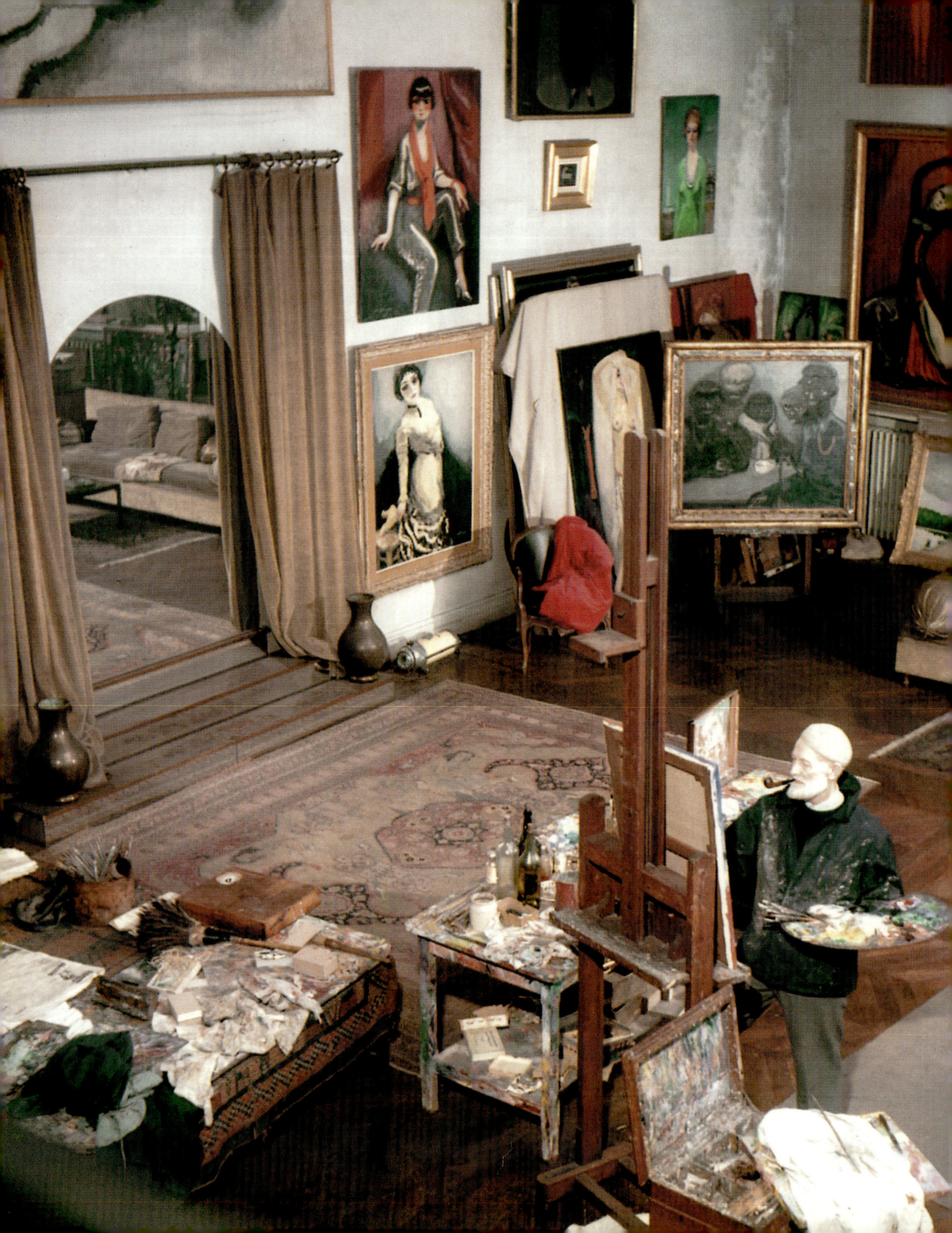

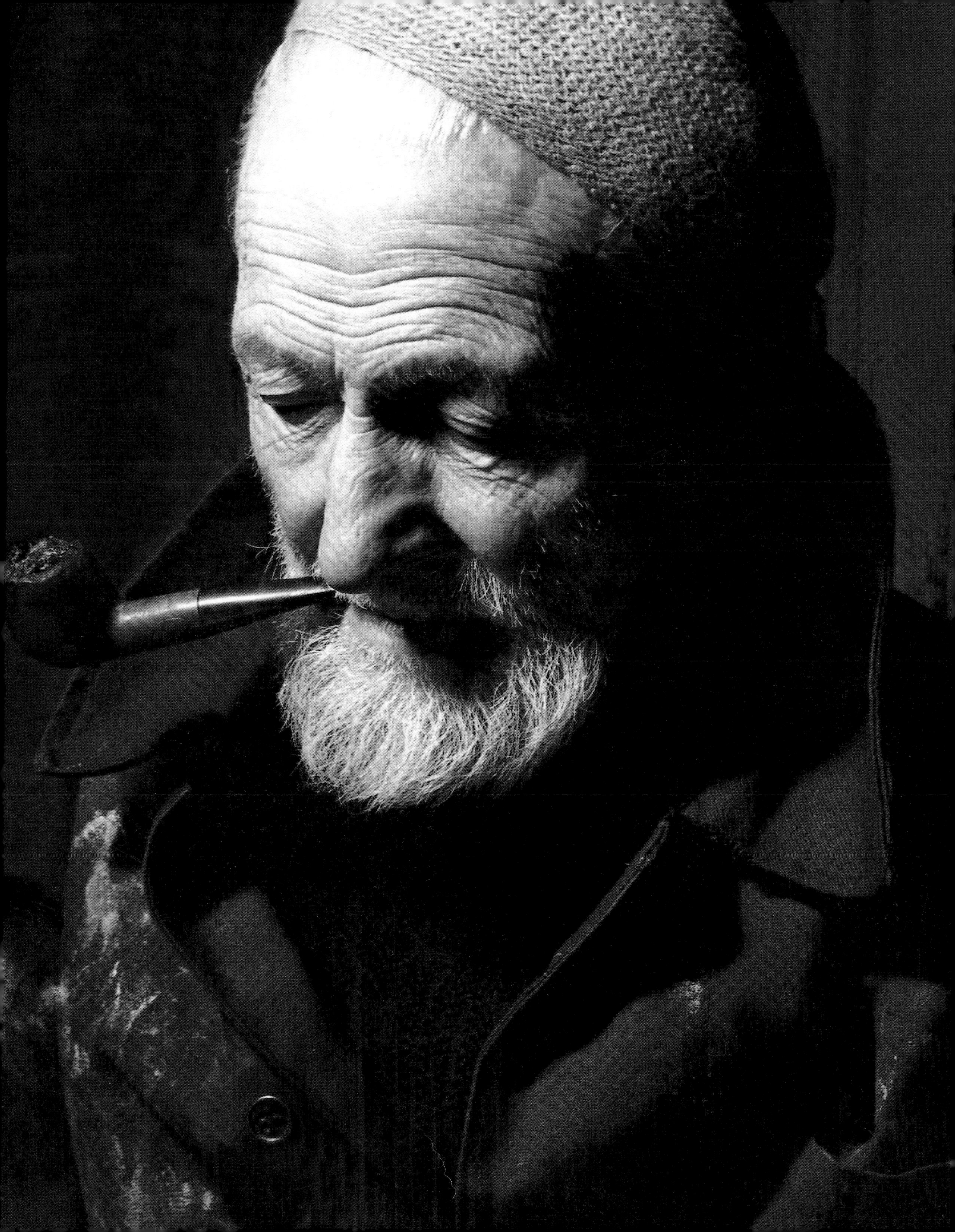

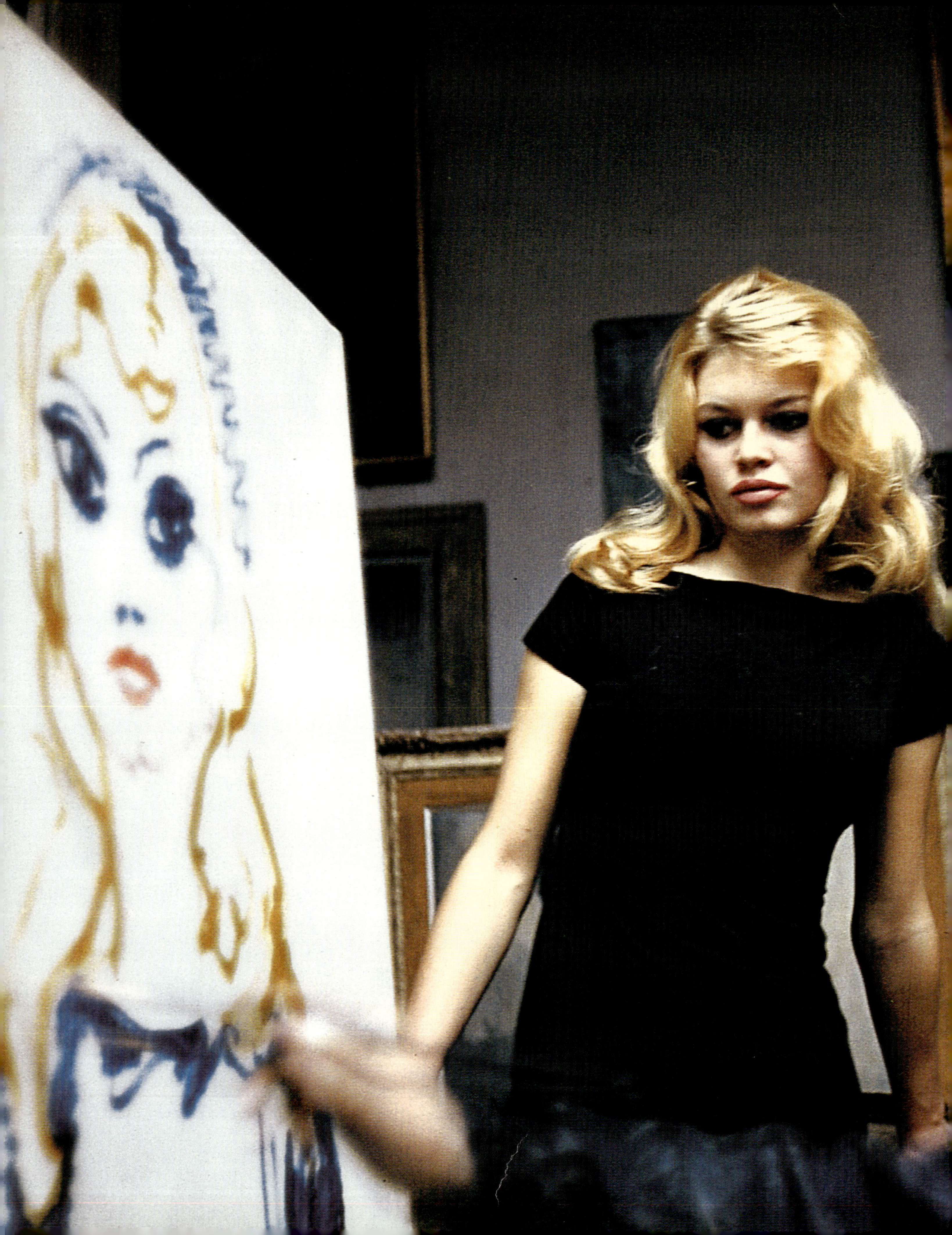

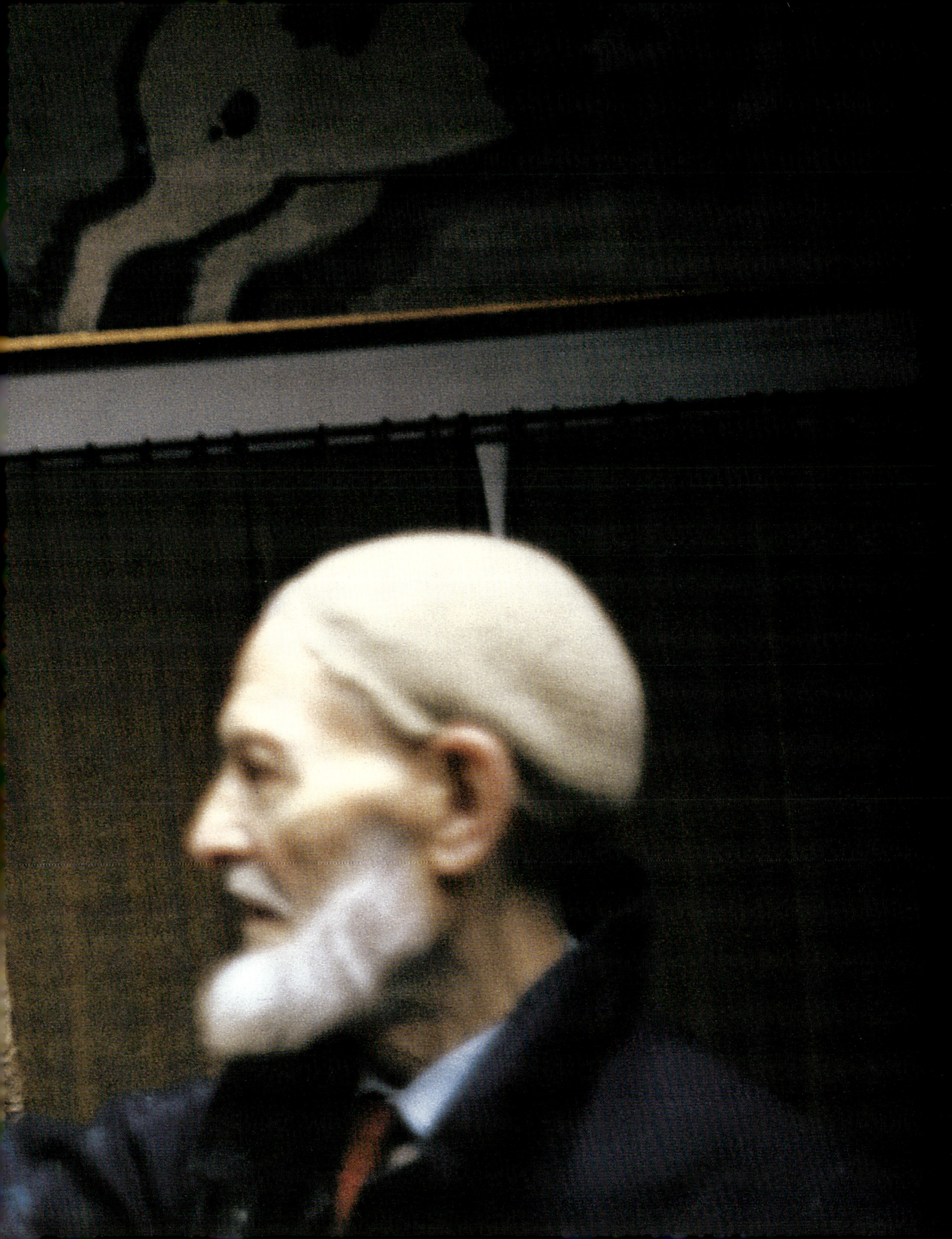

Miró

Tony
Saulnier
1961

"There is a mirror in Miró," Prévert said. It's through symbols that he reveals his timid face and his work.

Joan Miró's studio is meticulously organized. The brushes are aligned for his personal ritual. He paints according to how he feels. The sun, made of woven palms, hangs in his studio and provides the light of Majorca, his beloved homeland.

At night, he lights his sculptures. Nature's modest materials take on a surrealist dimension.

Miró locks himself into his disciplined world in order to find a new, living, lyrical language.

Miró has the freedom to create what he wants, when he wants. He squeezes a tube of gouache onto moistened paper and spreads the color by hand.

Displaying a selection of his work from between 1919 and 1961 he says, "I am not an abstract painter, but a lover of nature."

His house faces the ocean and on the terrace a gathering of friends and neighbors takes place. Island life guides his inspiration.

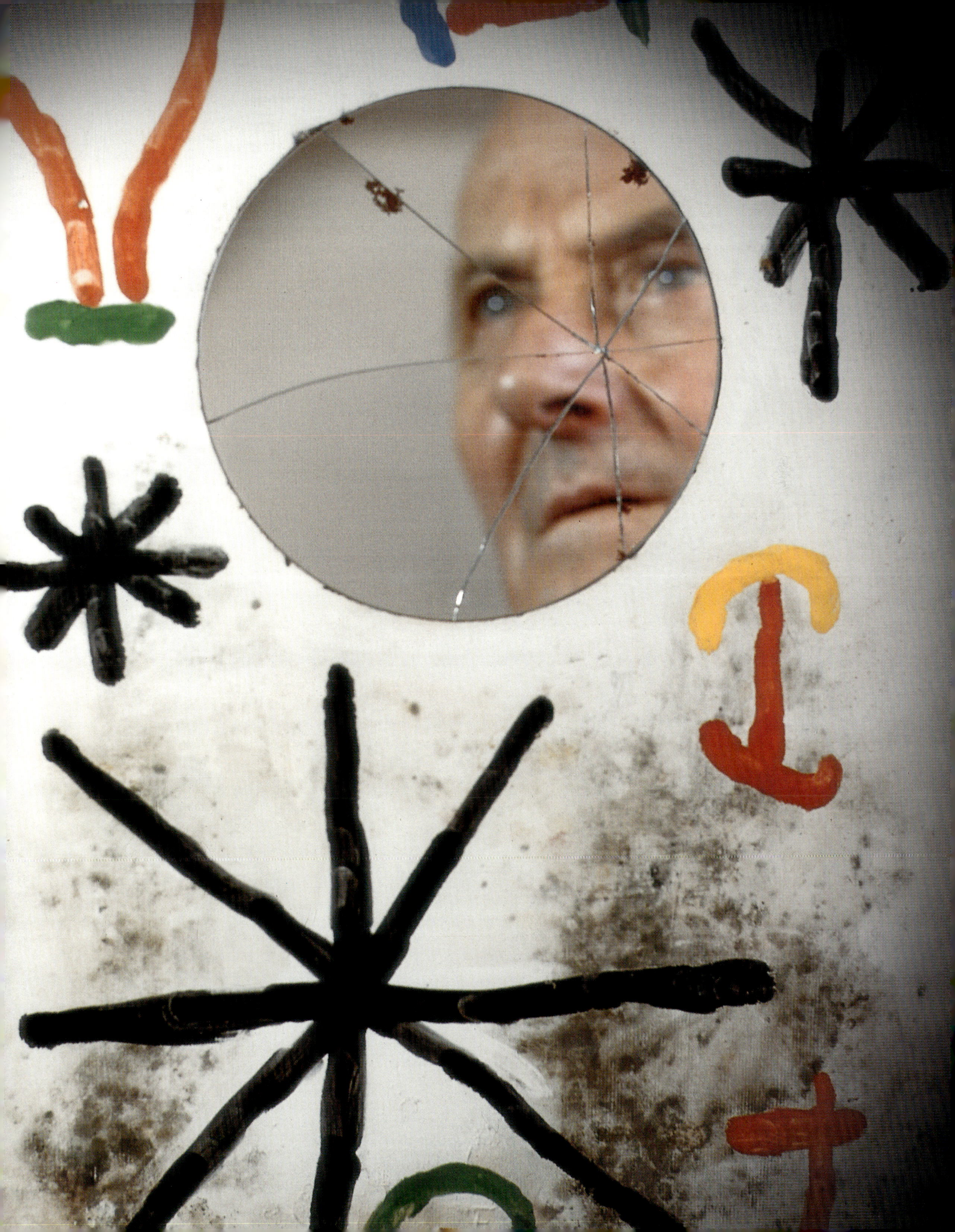

Pépita Dupont: After fifty-five years of marriage, your mother only criticized Miró for one thing: never painting a portrait of her.

Dolorès Miró: Yes, nor of me! My father only made one self-portrait, and it was Picasso who bought it. After that, he gave up figuration for good.

PD: What happened when the Spanish Civil War broke out?

DM: I had just turned six and we had taken refuge in Paris. On Sunday mornings, my father and I went to the Louvre, and then in the afternoon, to the Café de Flore on the boulevard Saint-Germain.

PD: When the Second World War came, you went to Normandy...

DM: My parents moved to a small house in Varengeville called 'Le Clos des Sansonnets.' Georges Braque was our neighbor. He was a frequent visitor and we often ate together. As for my father, he was working on his series of gouaches, *Constellations*. This was his only baggage when we returned to Spain. We were very poor then, for he was selling hardly anything.

PD: Jacques Dupin, a friend of Miró who wrote an extensive book on him, said, "Miró found that he had an inordinate love of solitude—his periods of silence were legendary."

DM: My father was introverted, and it was very difficult for him to express his feelings. When he was a teenager, my grandfather made him work as a bookkeeper in a hardware store in Barcelona. He had a nervous breakdown while working here, followed by typhoid fever. His father objected to his vocation; he didn't like the idea of having a son who was a painter. In the family, the life of an artist was considered immoral. My father often said to me, 'How I would love to see my parents' faces, now that my paintings are in museums across the world.' He was deprived of love and understanding in his youth, and he never recovered from it.

PD: When Miró arrived in Paris for the first time in March 1920, he immediately went to visit Picasso.

DM: It's a funny story. My grandmother was a friend of Picasso's mother, who always spoke proudly of her son who was living in Paris. When she learned that my father was going to Paris as well, she gave him a cake. Miró was overjoyed to have an excuse to meet Picasso. Picasso kept *La Danseuse espagnole* for his entire life. He bought it in the 1920s, along with my father's only self-portrait.

PD: Ernest Hemingway was also taken by *The Farm*, a painting that many dealers rejected.

DM: Yes, Hemingway was taking boxing lessons with my father at the American Center in Paris; he liked this painting right away and paid for it in installments by winning fights.

PD: What was a typical day in Miró's life like?

DM: A little like that of an employee. He woke up at seven, washed, and ate breakfast with my mother. Then, he worked in his studio until two in the afternoon. After a break for lunch, he sometimes went swimming or did some other form of exercise. Then, at about four, he went back into his studio until nine at night. He never went out; in fact, he hated social events. Sometimes he dined with friends. He didn't know how to drive and never took pictures, and he never went on vacation. All he did was paint. He was always in a state of great mental tension. At night, before going to bed, he smoked a cigarette and never talked about that day's work. Besides, no one was allowed to go into his studio. When my mother came back from the market, my father would take all the packaging, which he sometimes incorporated into his paintings.

PD: Did your mother talk about painting with him?

DM: No, she didn't enter his world. But outside of his work, my father didn't have a single notion about daily life. He always said, 'Without Pilar, I would be an orphan. She's my guardian angel.'

PD: Is it true that he was very superstitious?

DM: Yes. He was wary of the number thirteen and dates such as Friday the thirteenth. He hated even numbers with such a passion that when illustrating a book he aimed to produce an odd number of prints for its pages. For good luck he always had carob or olive-tree leaves on hand.

PD: How did he spend the last years of his life?

DM: Two years before he died, he had an embolism and went blind. He had a cataract operation and regained his sight, but it was horrible. He died on Christmas Day, 1974, at three o'clock in the afternoon. The end of his life was very sad.

PD: Before he died, he decided to create a foundation in Palma de Mallorca...

DM: He couldn't stand the idea of his paintings ending up in the dining rooms of rich financiers. He often said, 'People don't see paintings, they only see dollars.' That made him angry. He wanted everybody to be able to see his paintings. That was why he decided to open his Palma studios, where he worked from 1956 on, to the public. Today, the studios have become the Pilar and Joan Miró Foundation. Visitors can wander through these rooms and discover his last pieces, as well as the works of young painters. It's not a museum, but a living, thriving place for artistic creation.

Interview by Pépita Dupont

Painting, sculpture, ceramics: Joan Miró's oeuvre spans a vast territory of the arts; too vast to discuss in merely a few words—several books would be needed to take its diversity into account. Painting, sculpture, and ceramics are, like music, autonomous languages sufficient unto themselves. Discussing Miró's abstract images is similar to translating poetry into another language—the flavor of the original is inevitably lost in the conversion from one medium to another. What we can do is to describe these colorful, biomorphic and strange forms that inhabit his paintings in a way that will aid us in understanding the artist's ideas. But again, we have to analyze his technique, which isn't easy either. First, because I'm not an expert on technique, and second because discovering Miró's methods would not reveal his secret. Technique is necessary, but insufficient to explain a body of work. It is after or beyond technique that the personality and soul of a work emerges. Taking an inventory, establishing a catalogue of works, is the most we can accomplish, and becomes our incentive to further explore an oeuvre. In order to convey what we have understood, it is best to make a painting of the painting. Even if the painting of the painting is very clumsy, it has the advantage of being silent and of interpreting what we have understood or have thought to have understood in its silence. The rest is chatter. Consider the silence of a painting. But in this silence, there is a choreographed pantomime, a ballet, voice, and form. In Miró's work, we are witnessing events. Painting that "moves" is rarer than we think, but characteristic of Miró. What he shows us, especially in his sculpture, is the hidden, latent face of things. We think to ourselves as we look at a Miró, "It's true, the world resembles this and I never realized it. What I took for unseemly is natural."

Miró is a sculptor and a painter of the fantastic. The fantastic aspect of reality in the work of other painters, writers, or composers is most often nightmarish. In Miró's paintings, the fantastic is humorous, delightful, and manifested by surprising, amorphous creatures and objects, although not always benign. His compositions are spacious, ethereal, and large; they are portals into the world of God. He makes us believe or understand that creation was, and continues to be, a game for God. Miró plays this game, accepts it, and plays with the objects that are God's toys.

There is no trace of pessimism in Miró's work. Humor and irony abound in these canvases. He heightens the improbability or unreality of objects yet maintains an aspect of the real. Not socialist realism or naturalism, since Realism (reality is not realist) is a school and a convention. Realism is not real. It's what underlies or is behind Realism that is real. Miró caricatured creation and at the same time seemed to attempt an alternate visual reality. It is perhaps possible that Surrealism provoked him to explore and create alternative modes of visual recognition, but he went well beyond Surrealism, which became banal, dramatic, or academic, in the same way as Realism. Surrealism is no longer free, it has its styles and recipes, whereas Miró is freedom itself. Miró excels at the art of playing a metaphysical game. Is an egg on a stool, a fork coming out of a table, a blue mark underlined by a black semi-circle, or something that resembles a faucet—less real than nature, than naturalist nature? Miró uncovers an unlimited realm of possibilities; this is also why he brings us into a world where the relationship between object and form seems as likely or more likely than a naturalism, realism, or symbolism that is densely and logically symbolic. It is Miró's inexplicability that seems to best describe the world, or rather what appears to us to be more correct and normal in the abnormality of the world. Miró makes us understand that the normal is not normal, that the world can be entirely other.

Miró suggests that, yes, other displays of the creative force are possible; their number is unlimited. The painter compels us to imagine others, to prepare ourselves to accept our multi-faceted physical universe. He challenges God in terms of invention, or rather, he invites God to create new forms, new relationships between new things, to use other elements or other mediums for constructing other worlds.

He accomplishes all of this with the greatest freedom. In Miró's work there is a combination of humor, malice, mischief, and grace. In the image of God, Miró creates out of pleasure, for his own and for our sense of curiosity.

—Eugène Ionesco
Académie Française

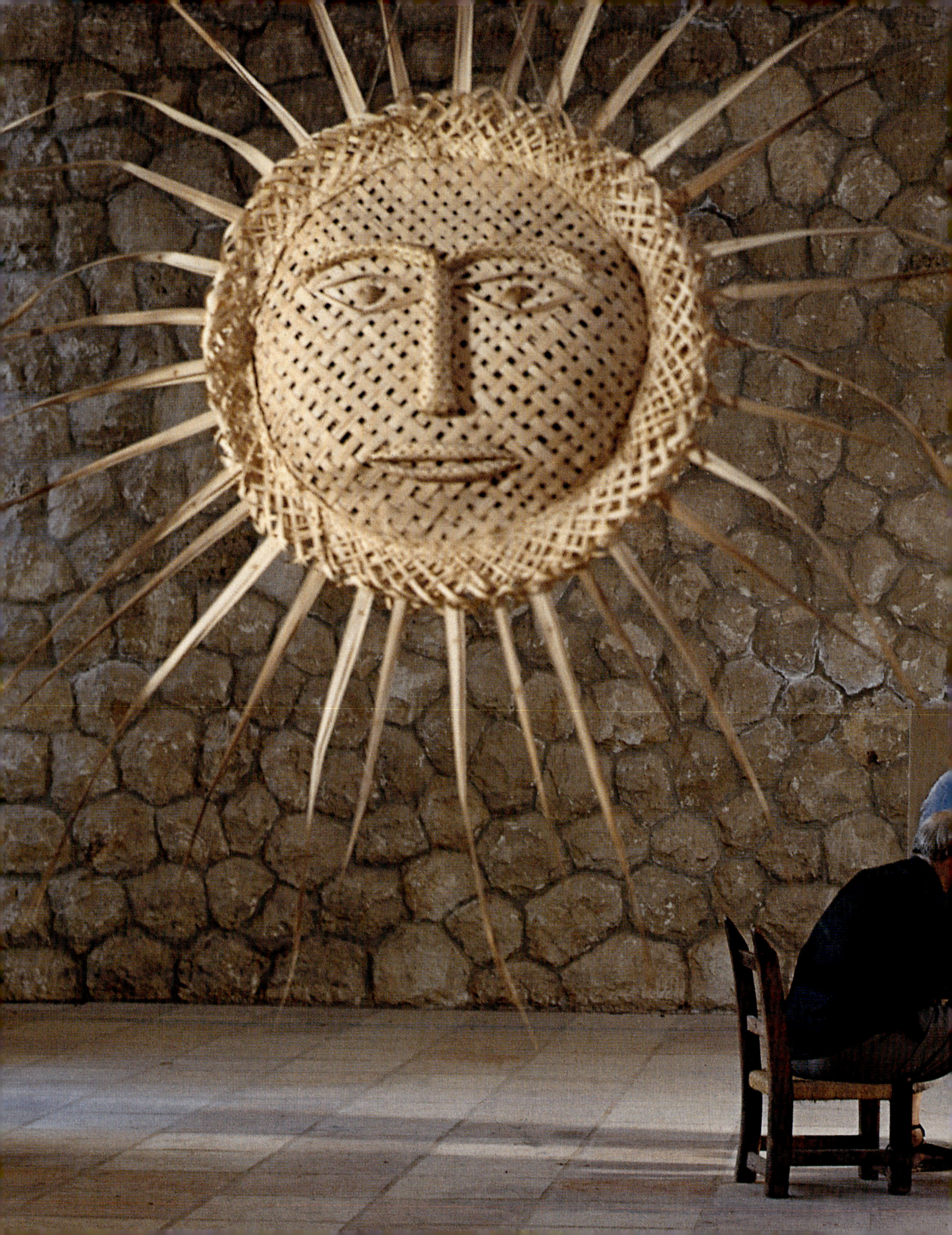

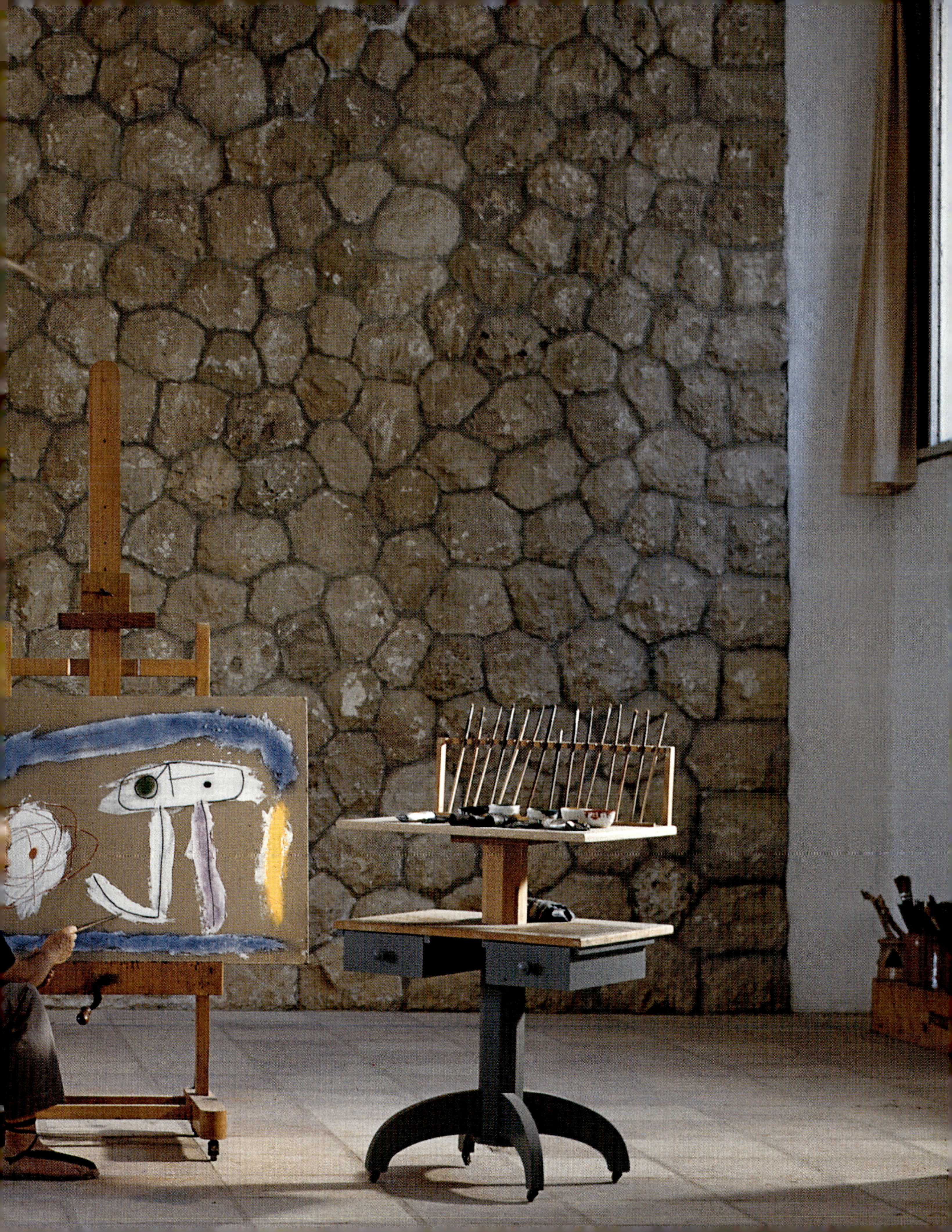

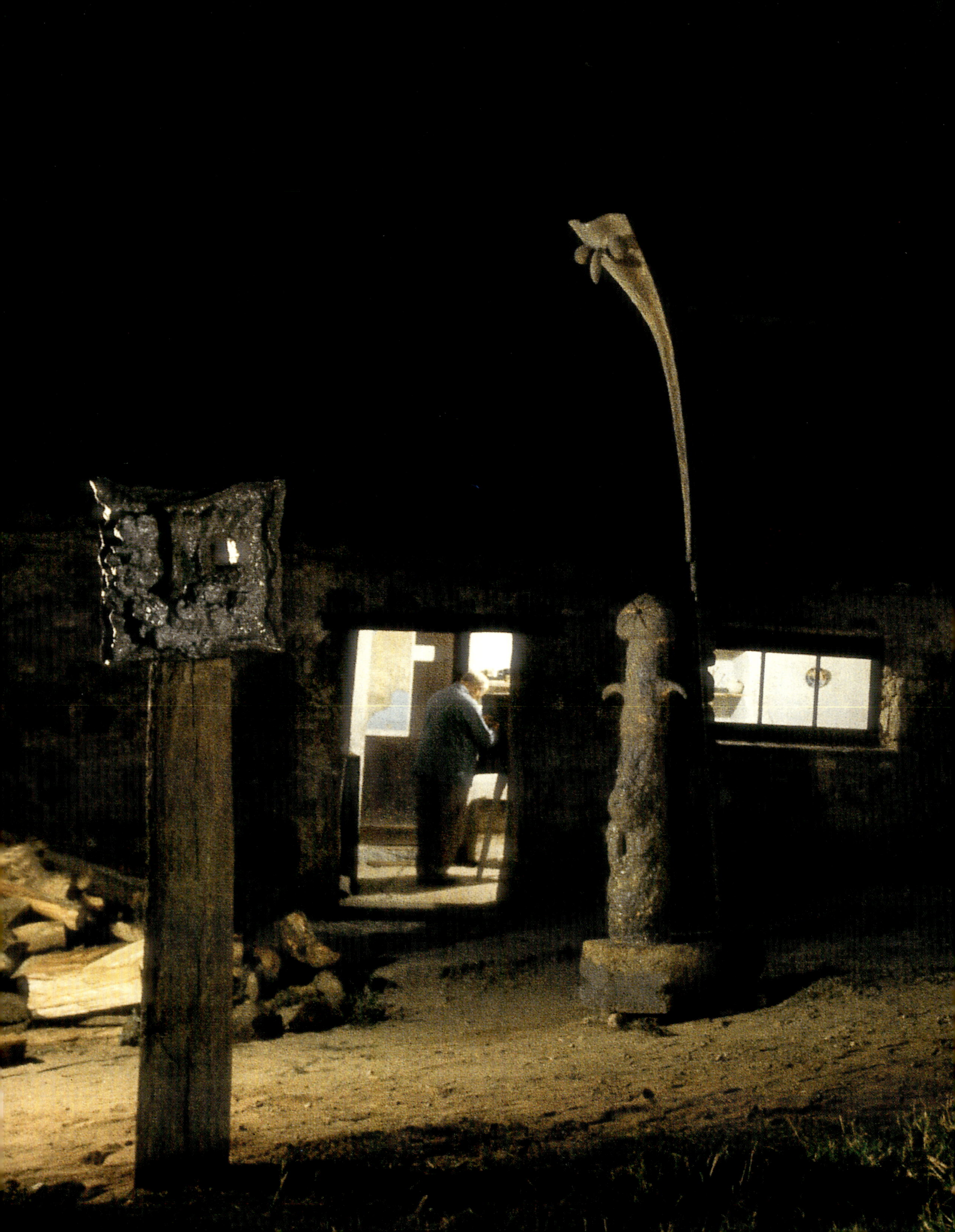

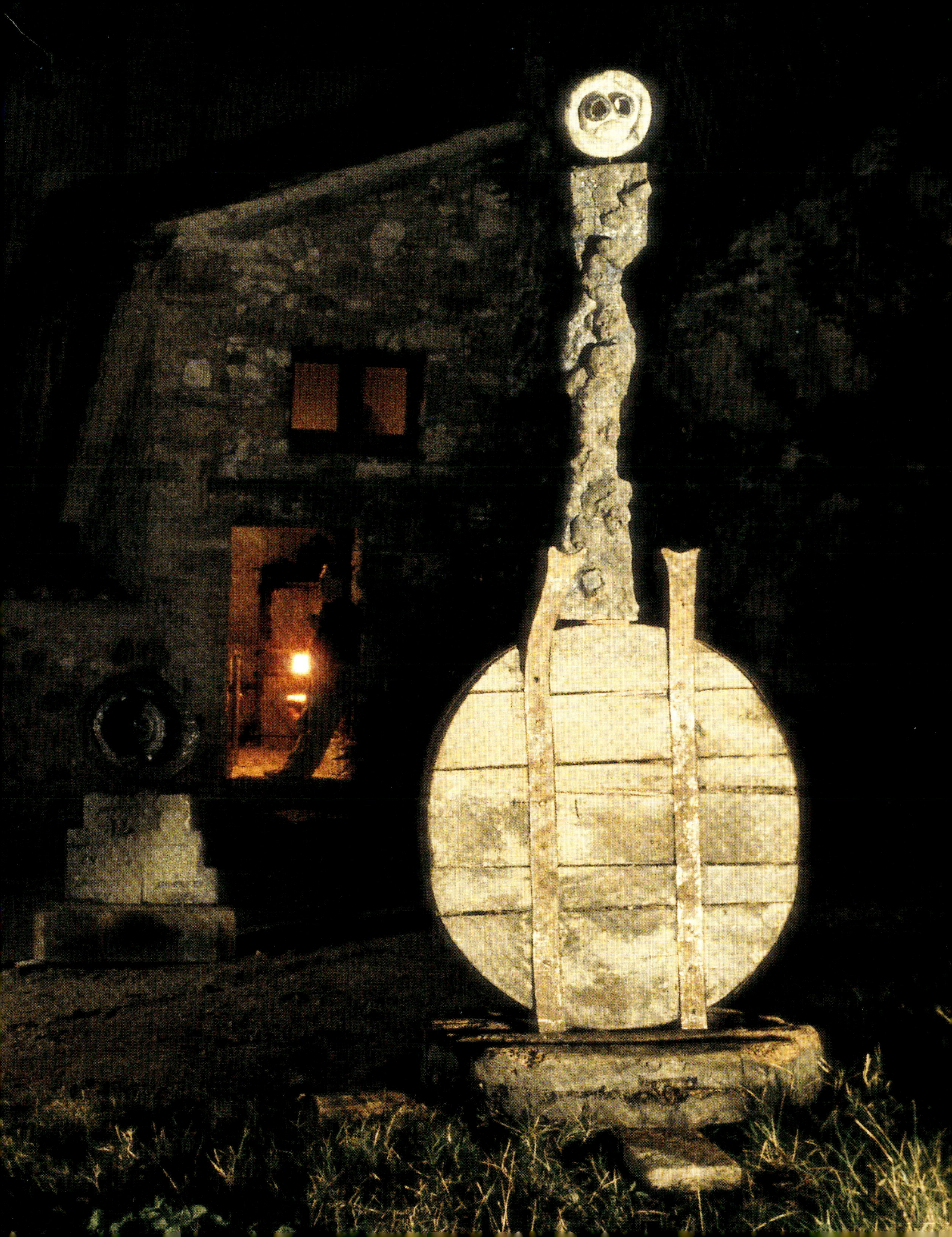

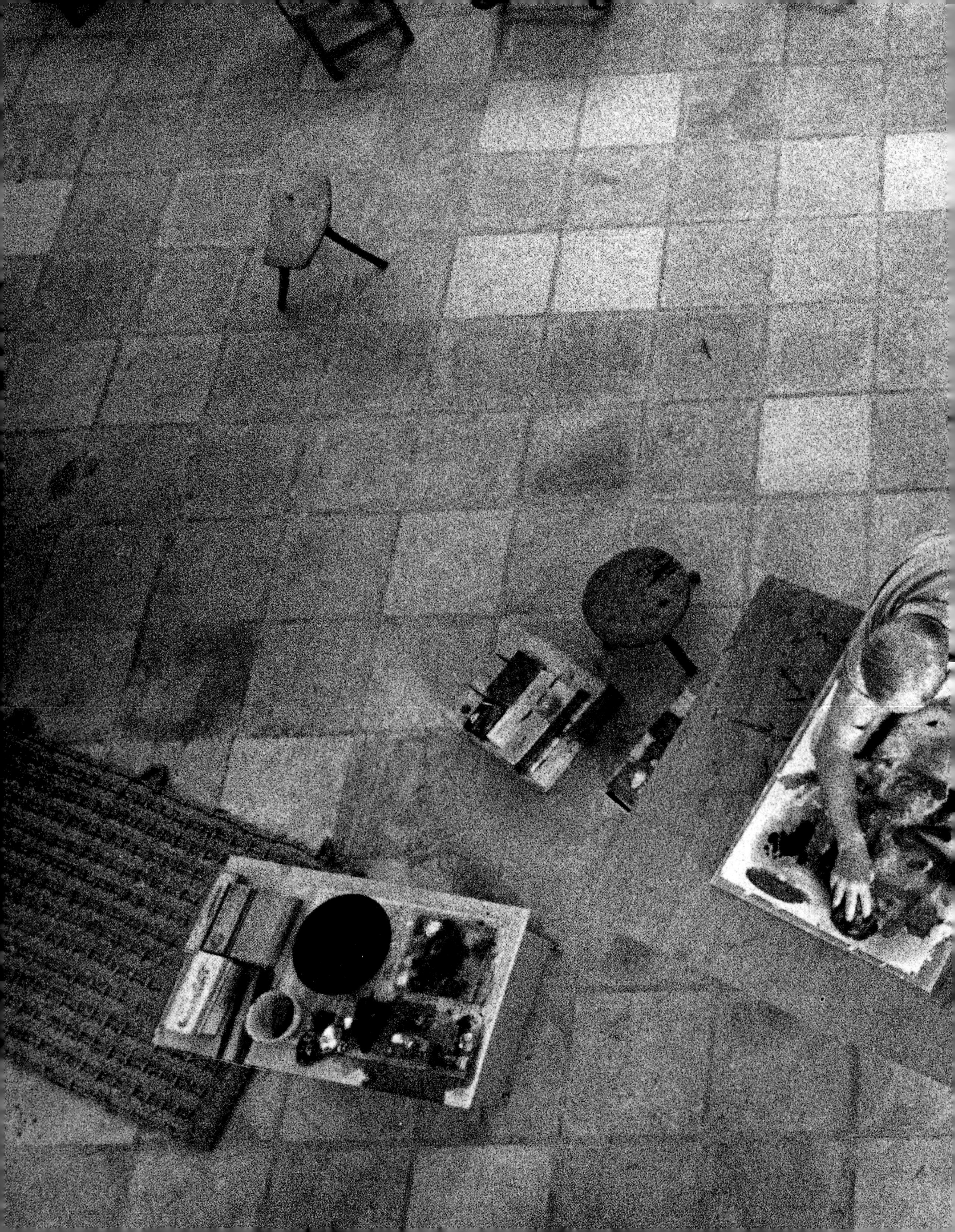

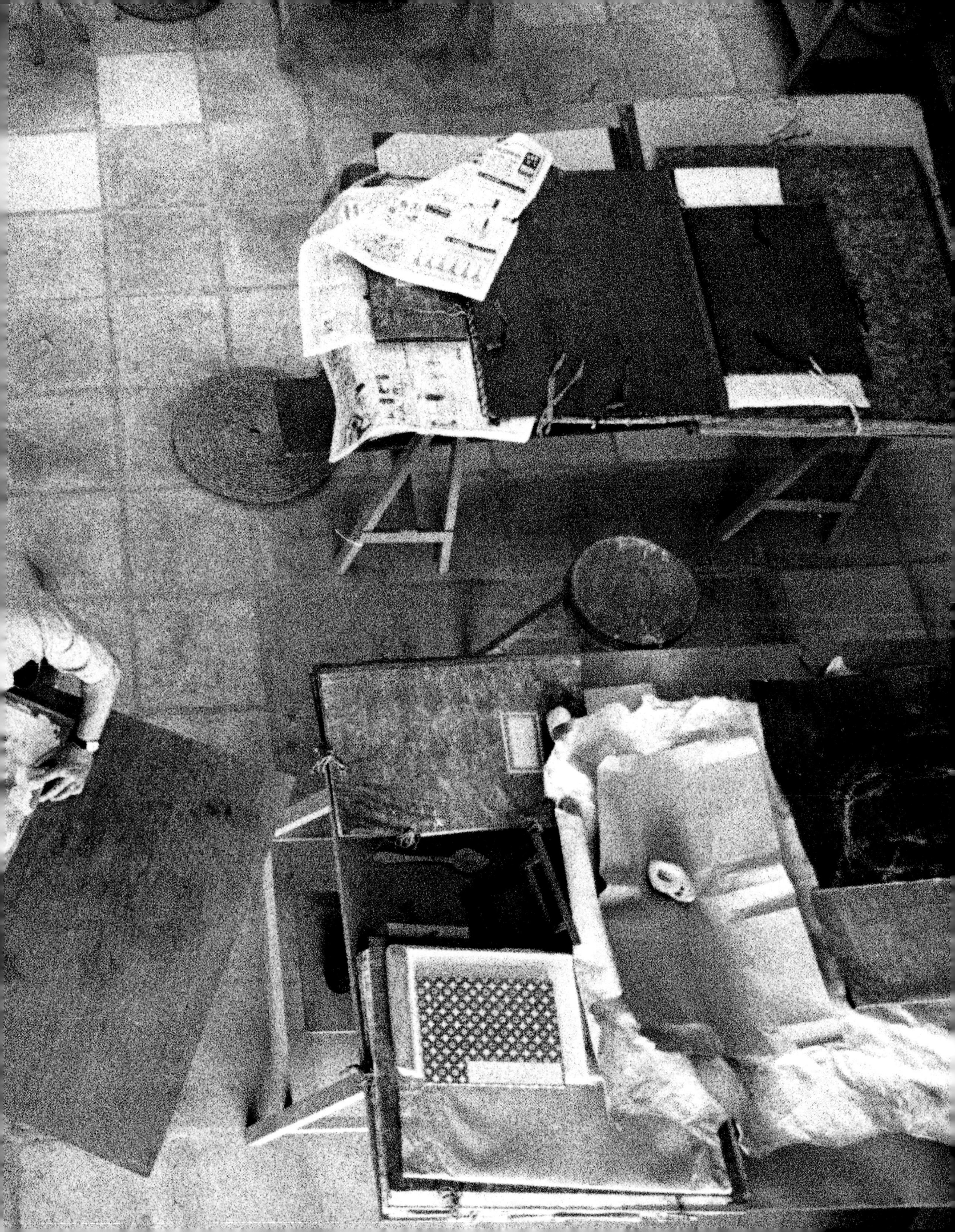

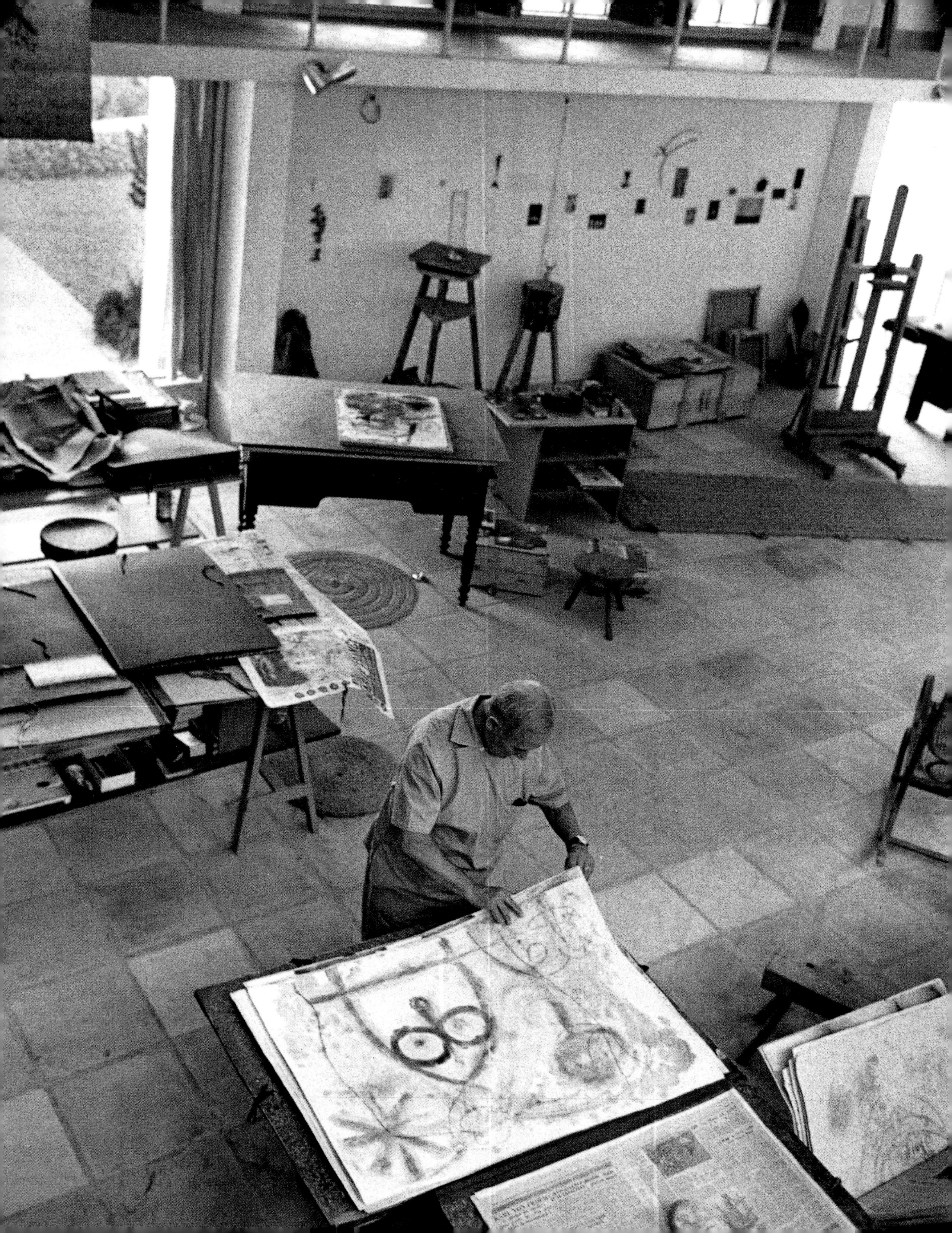

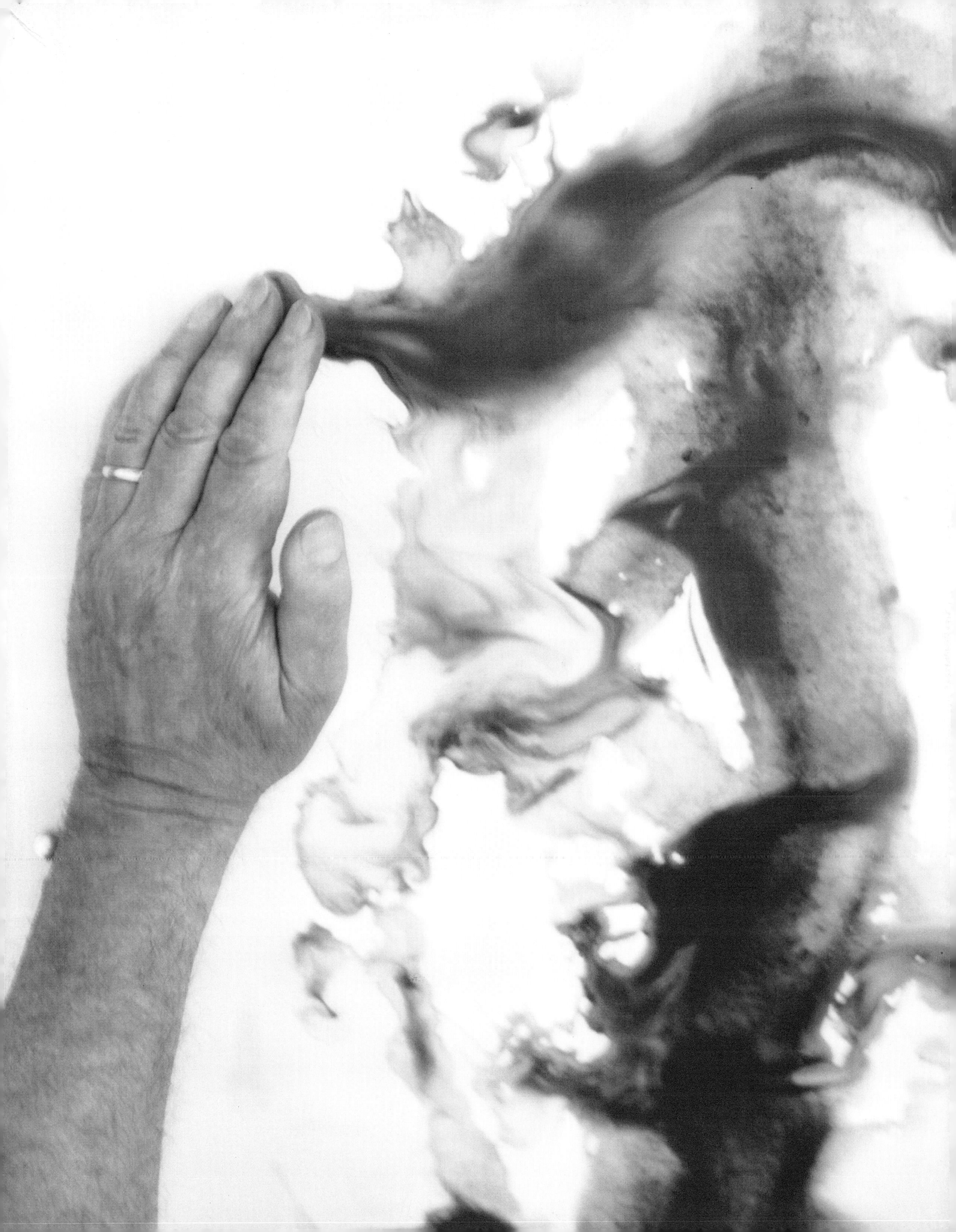

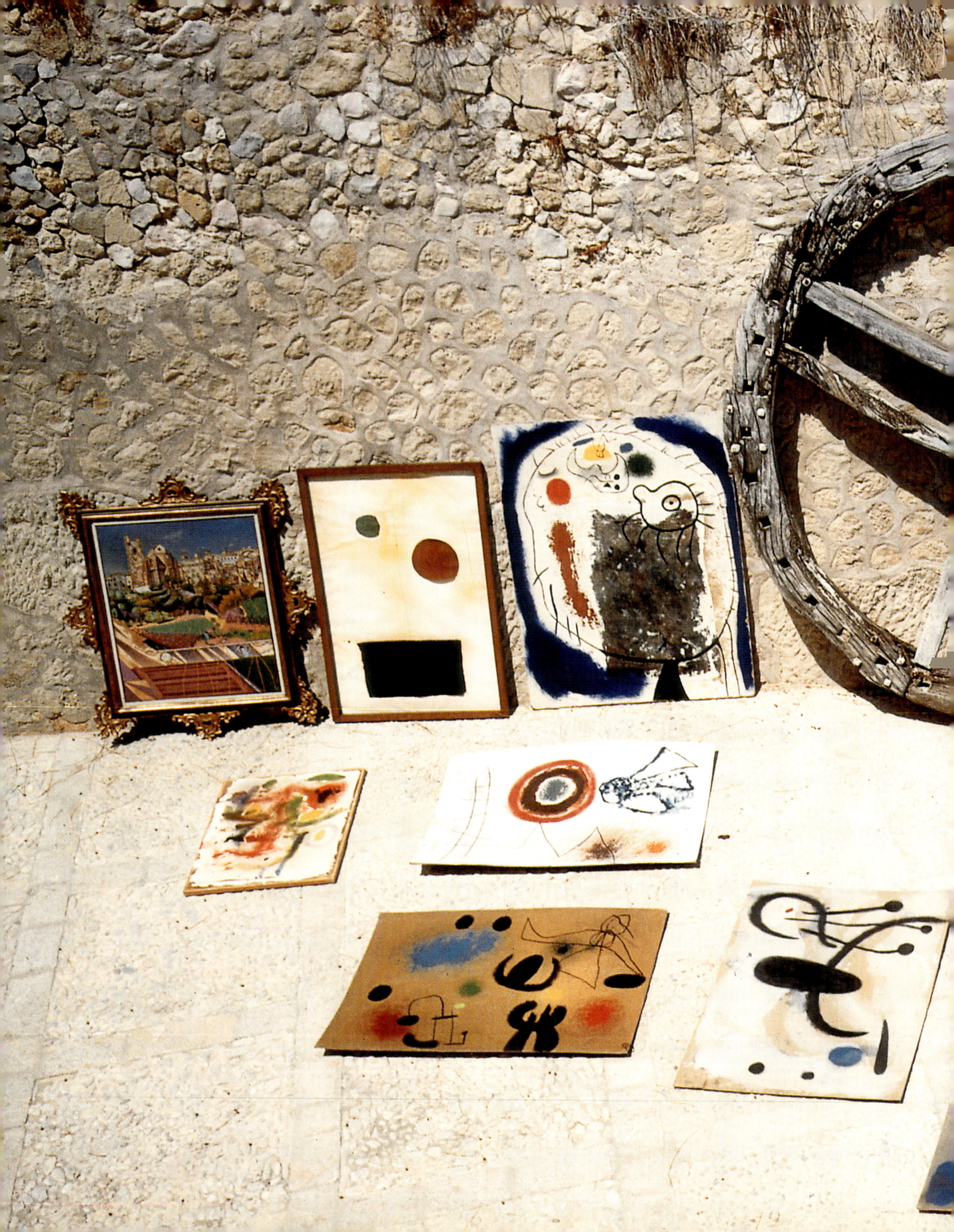

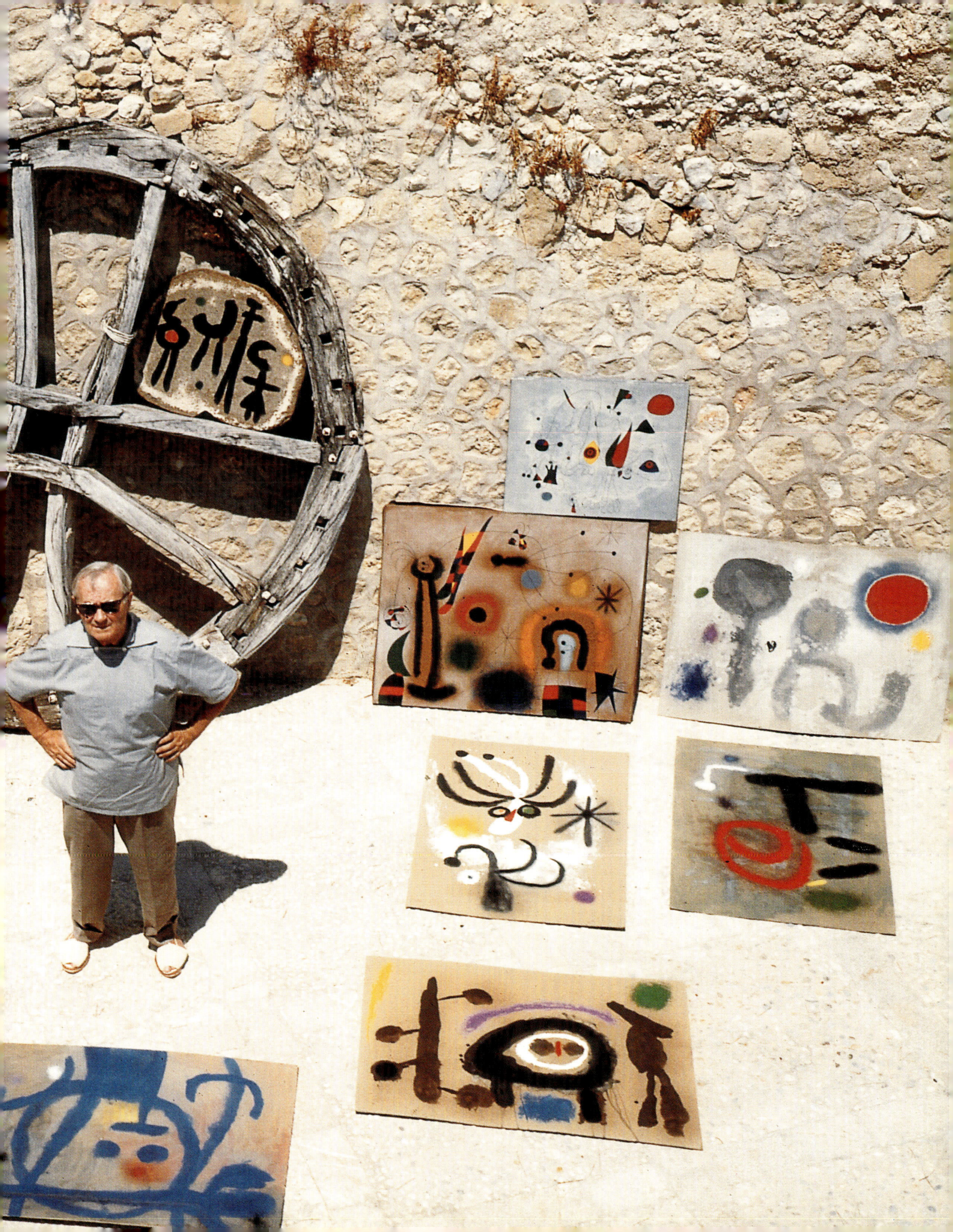

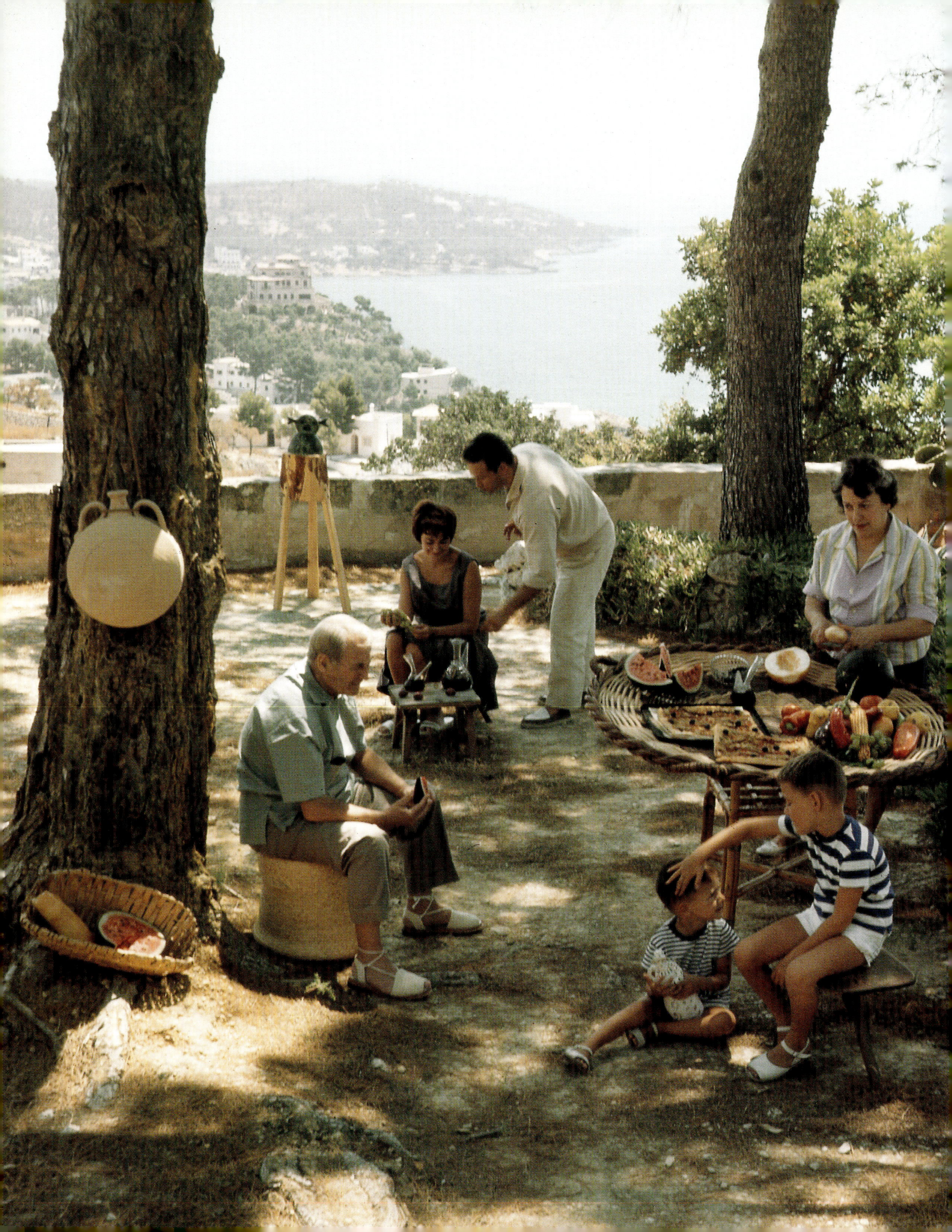

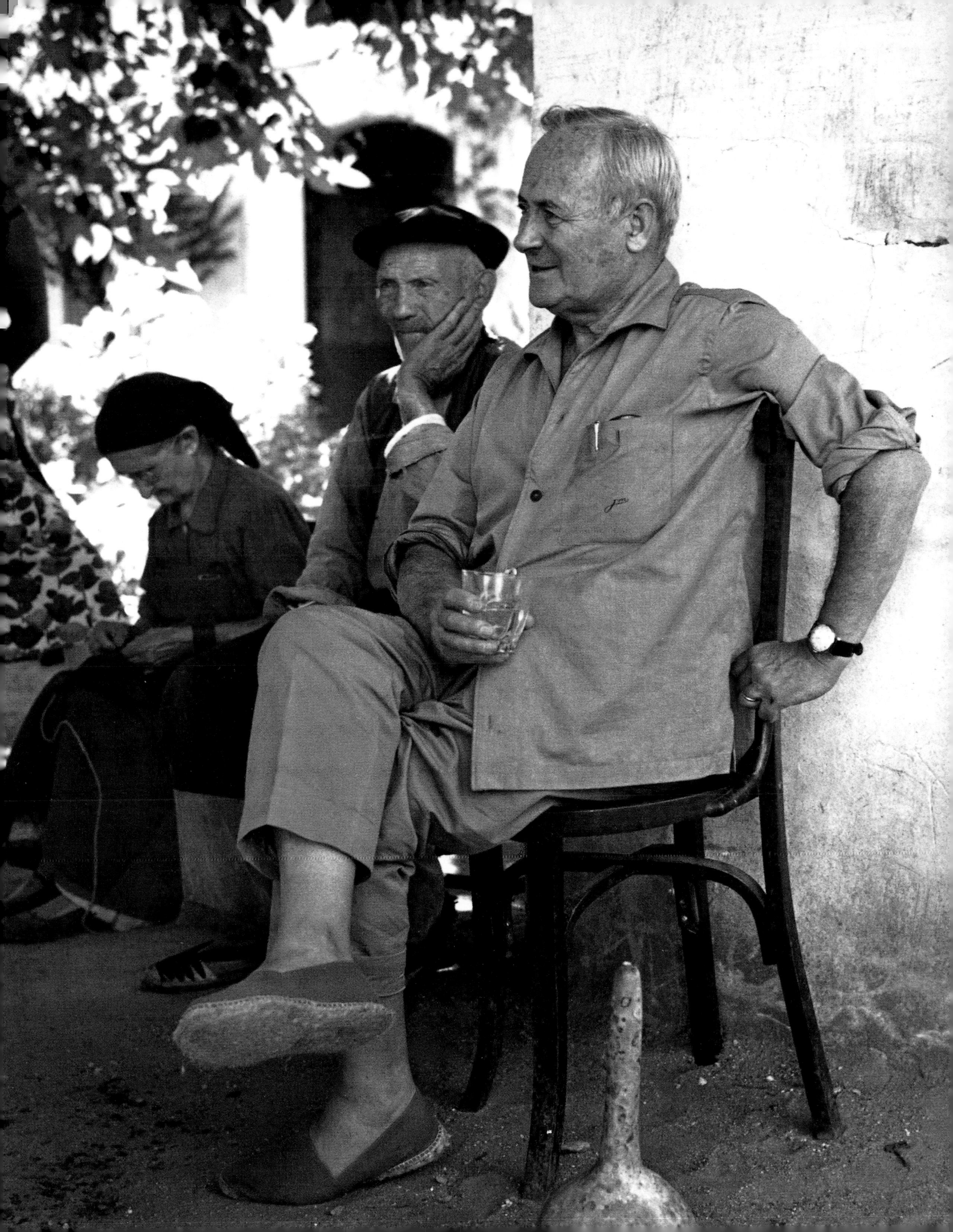

Delvaux

Segonzac/
Gibey 1969

Under Paul Delvaux's broad brow, fantasies lurk, waiting to be transformed into canvases.

Delvaux's studio in Brussels. A mirror to his left reflects his painting from a different angle.

Delvaux's clothes are sleeveless, allowing him freedom of movement to go with his freedom of inspiration as he paints a portrait of his model, Danielle.

Delvaux enters a painting in which soulless girls pose in front of Greek columns.

The apartment is snowed under with paintings, and the kitchen is full of paintbrushes. "My women," he declares, "come from the very roots of art." Delvaux's unearthly sleepwalkers are now a part of art history.

A canvas hung above Delvaux's piano depicts a group of women carrying oil lamps—a vision from the painter's childhood.

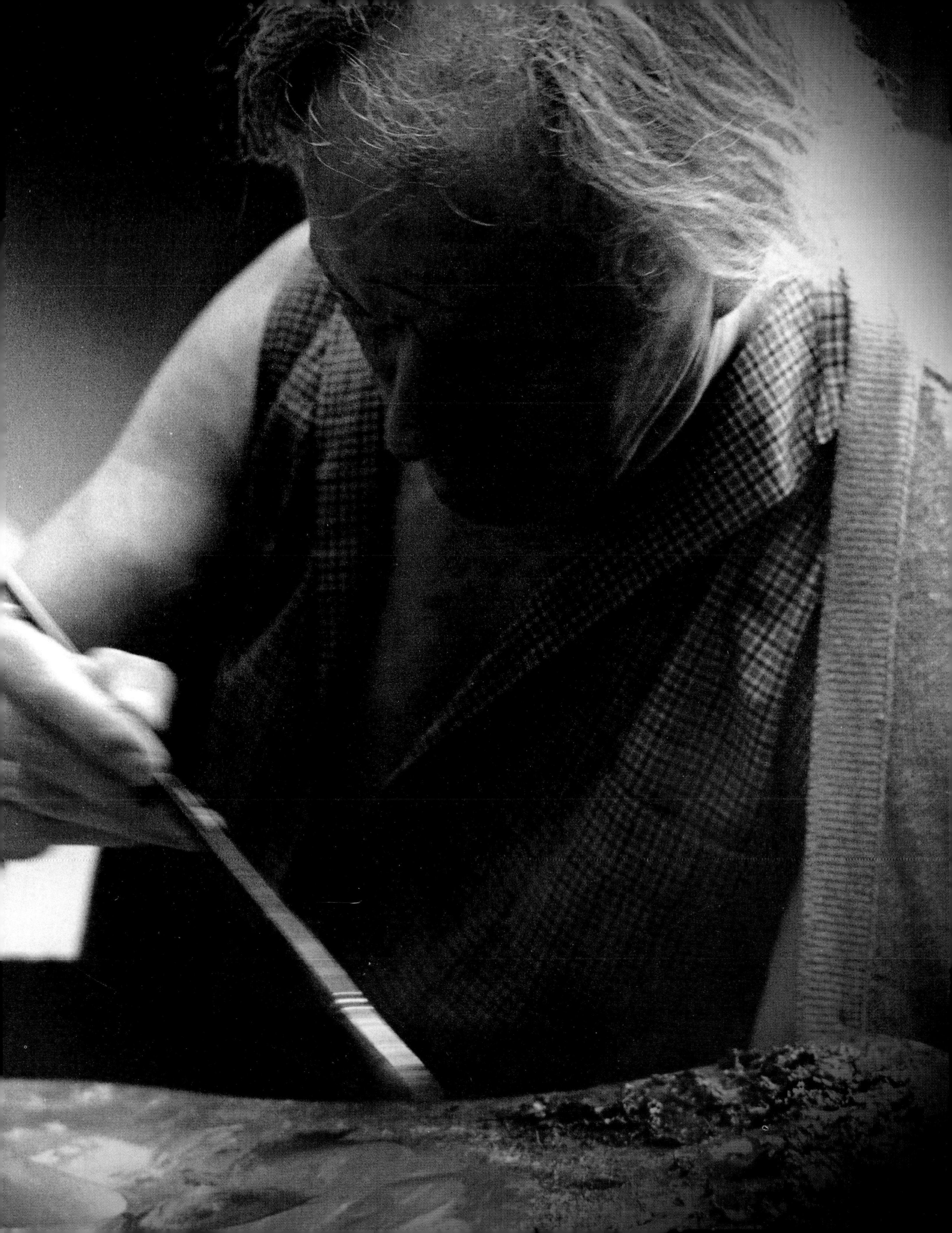

Marie-France Saurat: You first started painting seventy years ago. Looking at your work, what sort of continuity do you see in it?

Paul Delvaux: To begin with, I did impressionist work, paintings of nature, landscapes, and seascapes. Then I tackled figurative art and that altered both the appearance and the psychological content of my pictures. That's when I started doing larger compositions with people in them. I eventually destroyed all my big early paintings, but the ball was already rolling.

M-FS: What made you do something so radical?

PD: I wasn't happy with them. They didn't measure up to what I'd expected. They were bad.

M-FS: Did you tell anyone about these doubts?

PD: I never tried to hide my opinion of myself, which was never high. I've known doubt, the feeling of not being as good as I wanted to be, of not arriving at the truth.

M-FS: So you continued to paint large compositions.

PD: Yes. I perfected them and introduced Surrealism in such a way as to give the subject a special, strange quality, one that was sometimes greater than its real quality: that's what Surrealism felt like to me. After that I wanted to go back to Surrealism, but in a different way, by trying to inject a Surrealist sensation into something natural. That was between 1940 and 1945. I poured my personal feelings of sadness and joy into that mould, notably in pictures like *La Mélancholie, Le train de nuit,* and *Les Grandes sirènes:* they were a part of my surrealist apprenticeship. But I came out with something extra, something that is neither seen nor felt but which is nevertheless in the paintings and gives the figures their quality. I've persisted ever since along similar lines: I didn't want Surrealism to be apparent in my paintings, I wanted it to remain hidden in their general atmosphere.

M-FS: Is that why you've so often refused the label of surrealist?

PD: I concluded that Surrealism was a theory, and the one thing I wanted to stay away from was theory. In the early days I flirted a little with that side of things. I did a picture of a triumphal arch with lamps on it, which was accidentally destroyed in London. That was definitely a surrealist painting. But later I abandoned it. *Le Cortège en dentelles* was no longer surrealist, it was something else, and it was my first worthwhile picture. I never wanted to be part of the group. I preferred to stay independent, taking from Surrealism only what I thought might come in useful. Nude women in avenues carrying lamps was quite a curious concept, rather extraordinary. It's the light that is beautiful...I was accused of meaning to represent a phallus in the lamp, which is nonsense. When I was a child, there was a lighted lamp on the table at home. Ours was a family atmosphere, with a warm, human feeling about it.

M-FS: Your works are bathed in an atmosphere of otherworldliness. How do you lure the spectator into such a world?

PD: It's another consequence of what I just said—the triumphal arch with the lamps, then the women in lace. Little by little I emerged from the well of surrealism to discover my own brand of it.

M-FS: Certain persistent themes reverberate throughout your work. First of all, female figures, sometimes clothed, more often naked. Where do they come from?

PD: (A prolonged peal of laughter.) It's quite straightforward, my dear. As human beings, women are born quite naked. Why should I dress them, which would place them in some kind of contemporary situation? Where do they come from? They come from the very roots of the history of art. They just arrive. Do you see? They're naked because I can't dress them as if they belonged to some particular era of history. They're timeless.

M-FS: And men? You've painted a few men.

PD: The men are either completely dressed, belonging to certain clearly defined elements of our time, or else... in any case, they're very rarely naked.

M-FS: In the *Green Sofa,* the man is naked.

PD: The Green Sofa required a nude male, not a female. What men have I painted with clothes on? Well, I did Lidenbrock, a sage. I came across him in the work of Jules Verne, whom I greatly admire. I used to have an engraving of Lidenbrock in my studio, along with pictures of other wise men and astronomers. But in my opinion men are less amenable to painting than women.

M-FS: The men in your pictures look detached, even anxious.

PD: In *La Ville inquiète,* the main figure in the foreground is a man. It's a self-portrait. I lay down on the ground and copied myself so I wouldn't make a mistake. In that picture my self-portrait represented all the anxiety in the world. It was done during the war.

M-FS: The decor—the porticoes and colonnades—are they there to give a sense of the infinite, the eternal?

PD: Certainly not. I was merely inspired by antiquity. All those Doric and Ionic columns are so beautiful—that was why I painted them. That's all there is to it.

M-FS: And the railway stations remembered from your childhood, with the trains that seem to have no specific destination—what's the significance of the trains?

PD: There is none. They're just trains moving to and fro. It's the way they look that interests me, not where they're going or their symbolic meaning. I couldn't care less about those aspects. I think of the compartment in the carriage, the tiny light playing on the ceiling, the whistle of the locomotive leaving a station. Those are straightforward things, childhood memories that evolved as I grew older.

M-FS: In the early years, were you influenced by other painters?

PD: Lots of painters influenced me. James Ensor in particular, who I think was one of the greatest modern artists. There was Constant Permeke too, and Gustav De Smet, a very modest man. Yet everything he did was beautiful, so beautiful, it smelled of the land...Giorgio de Chirico, also. De Chirico's cityscapes are silent poems.

M-FS: Have you influenced other painters?

PD: I doubt it very much. I don't know. Picasso, now, I can understand why people copied him: he created revolutionary art forms. All I ever did was follow the forms of nature.

M-FS: For many years your only female model was Danielle Canneel.

PD: Yes, for twenty years. She was an intelligent, cultivated, and sensitive person. There are some models who are quite the opposite, you know. I stayed with her until just before I arrived here at Veurne in 1984.

M-FS: Your wife, Tam, who was such a strong presence in your life, is curiously absent from your work.

PD: It's true, I never did a painting of her, only drawings. I should have painted her portrait. Often in life the most obvious things simply don't occur to you. I never did commissioned portraits, either. I'm not a portraitist.

M-FS: The exhibition at the Grand Palais organized by Solange de Turenne and Charles van Deun, with a hundred and twelve pictures, is the biggest retrospective of your work ever assembled.

PD: Yes, and my first show was at the Palais des Beaux-Arts in Brussels, in 1936.

M-FS: Are you happy with the Paris exhibition? What are your feelings about it?

PD: Ca va, ma chère, ça va.

M-FS: Do you still have ideas for paintings?

PD: I still dream of painting. I did drawings for years, while I still had the faculty to do so. These days I try not to imagine too much; it would be awful if I did. In any event, just being alive is a way of dreaming.

Interview by
Marie-France Saurat

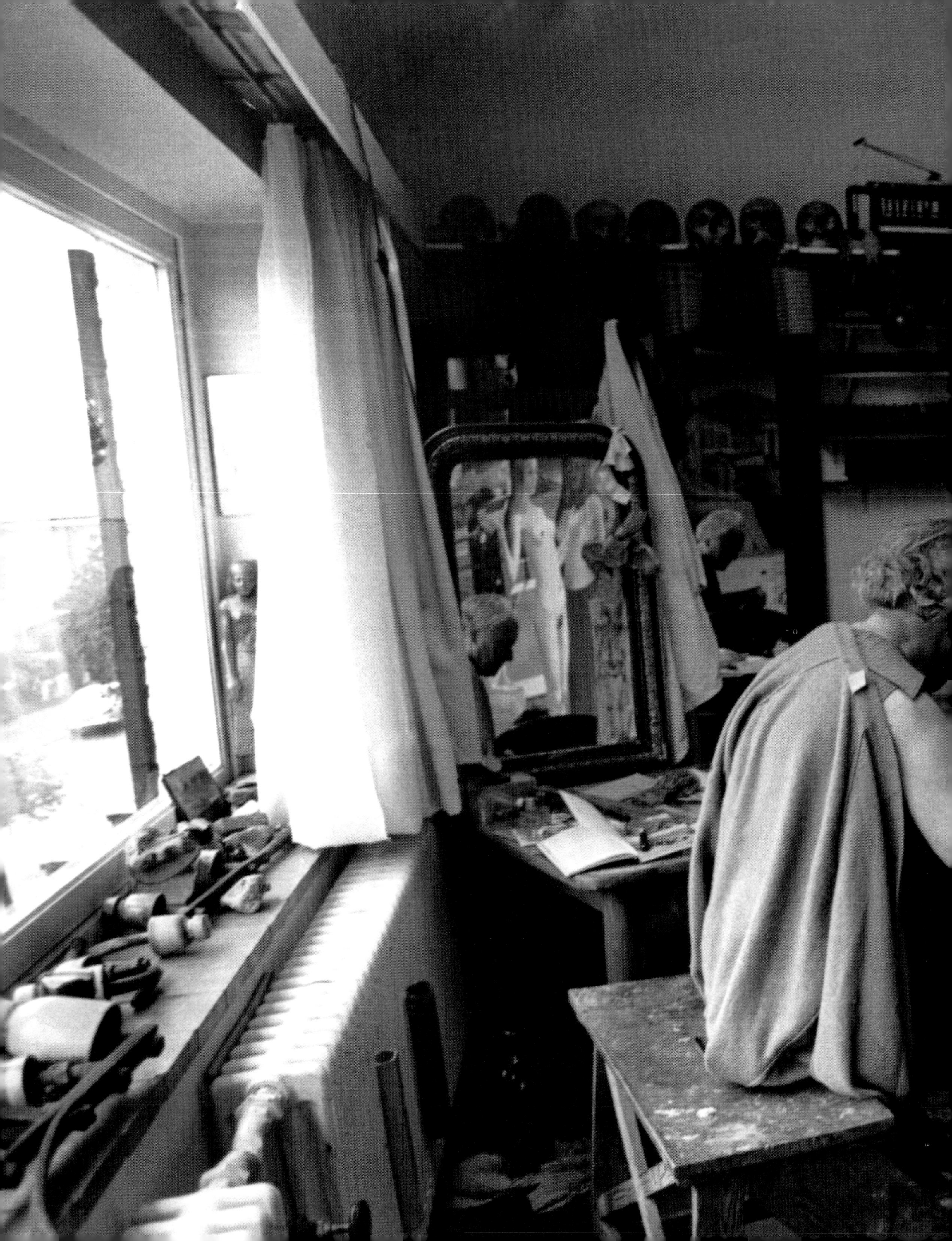

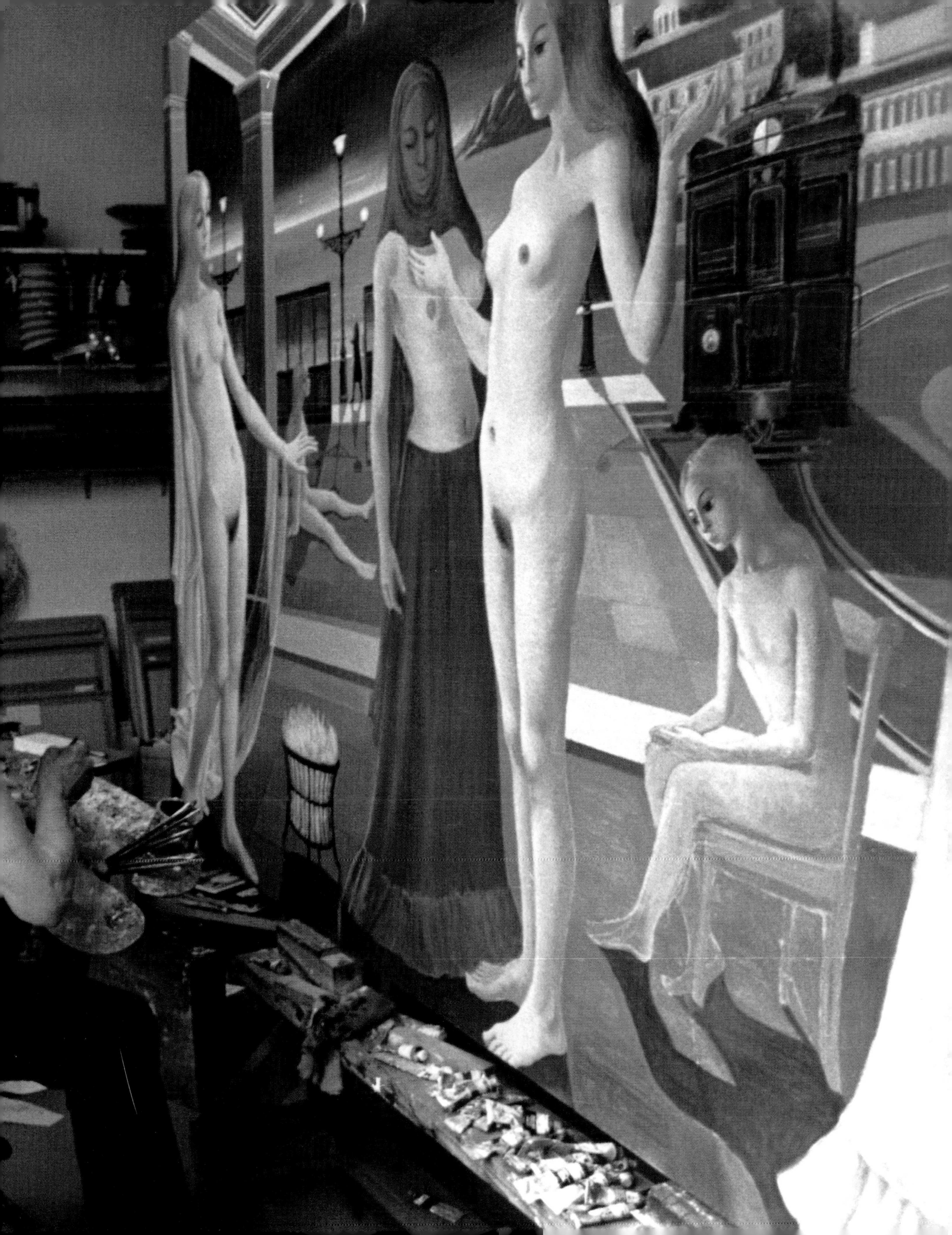

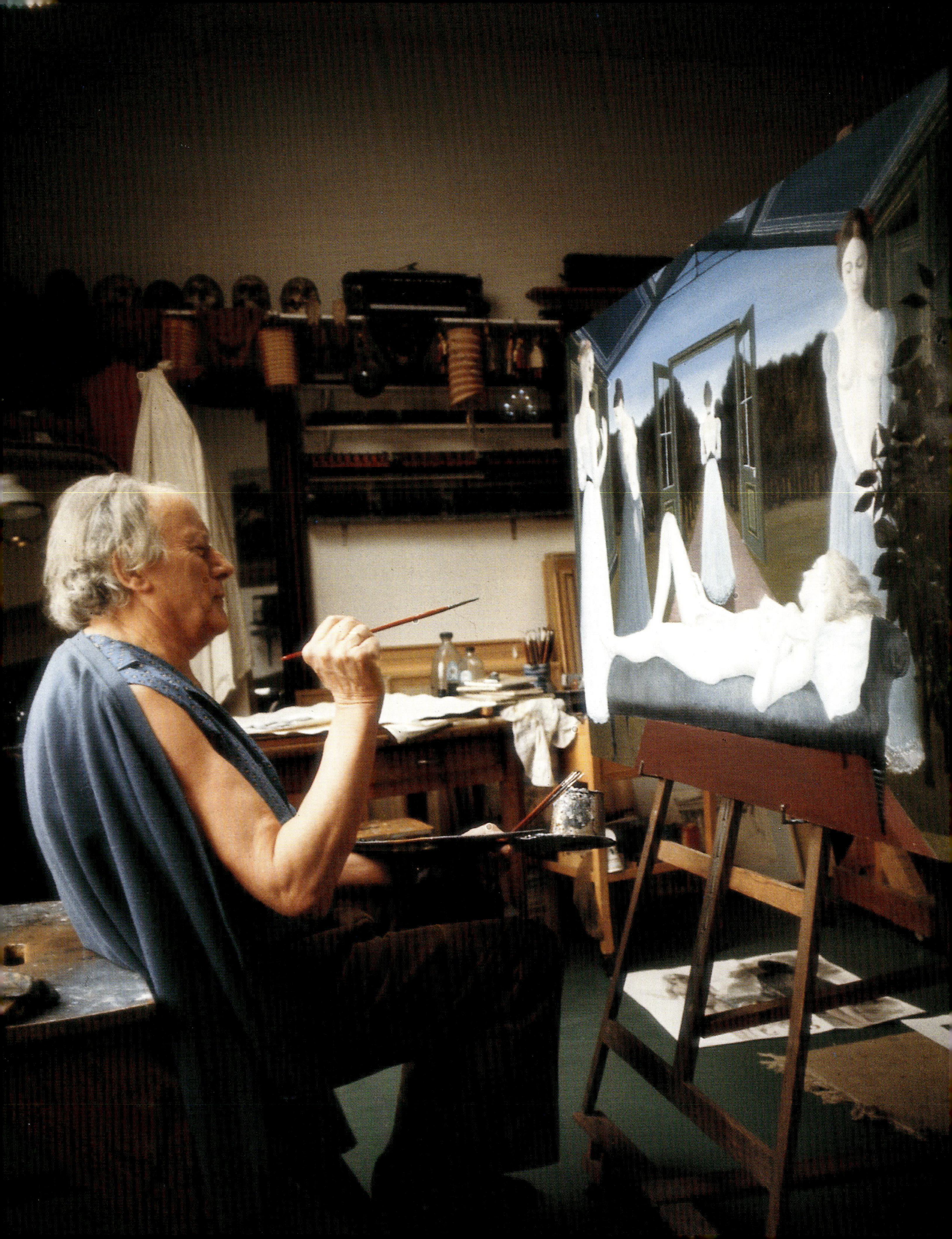

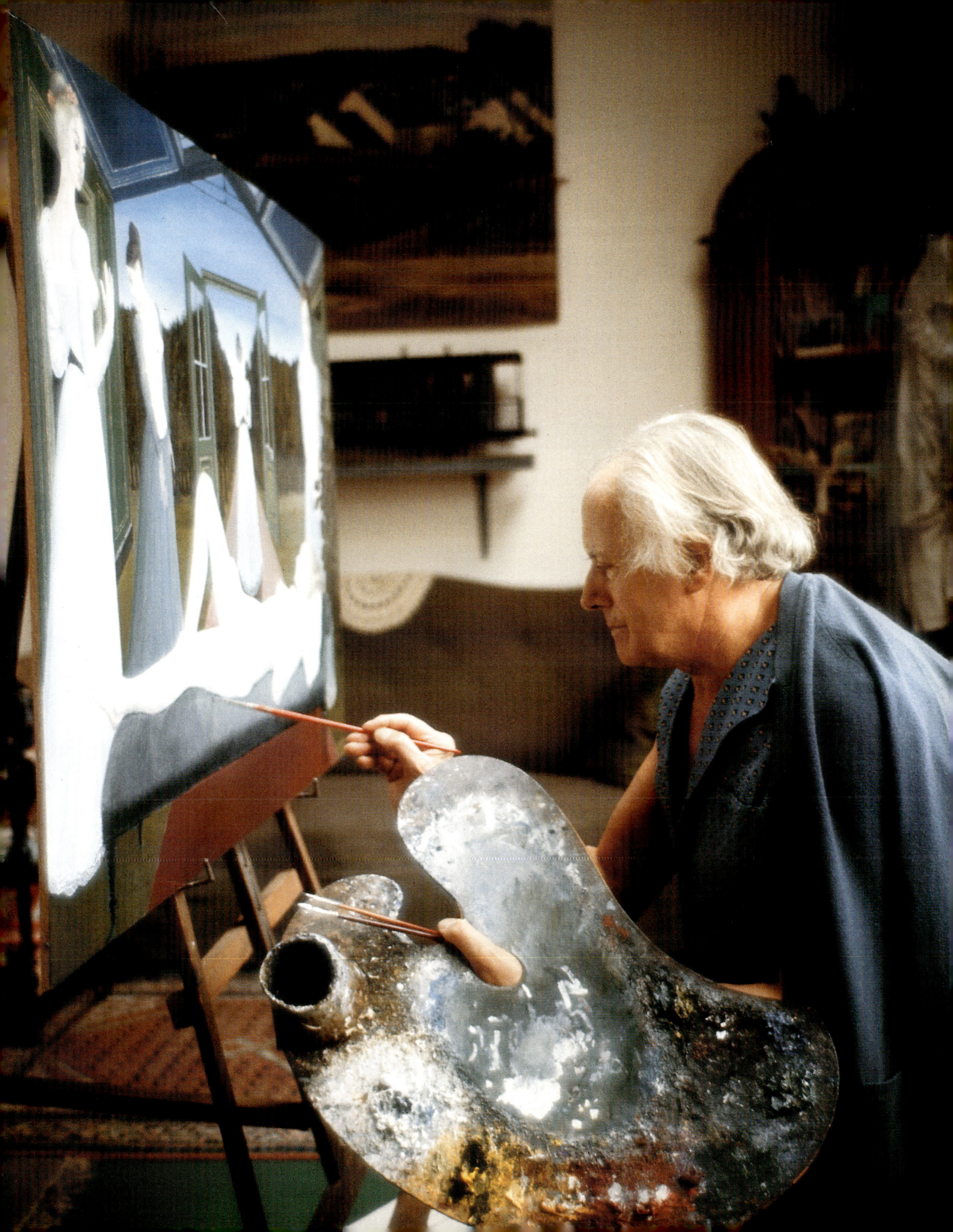

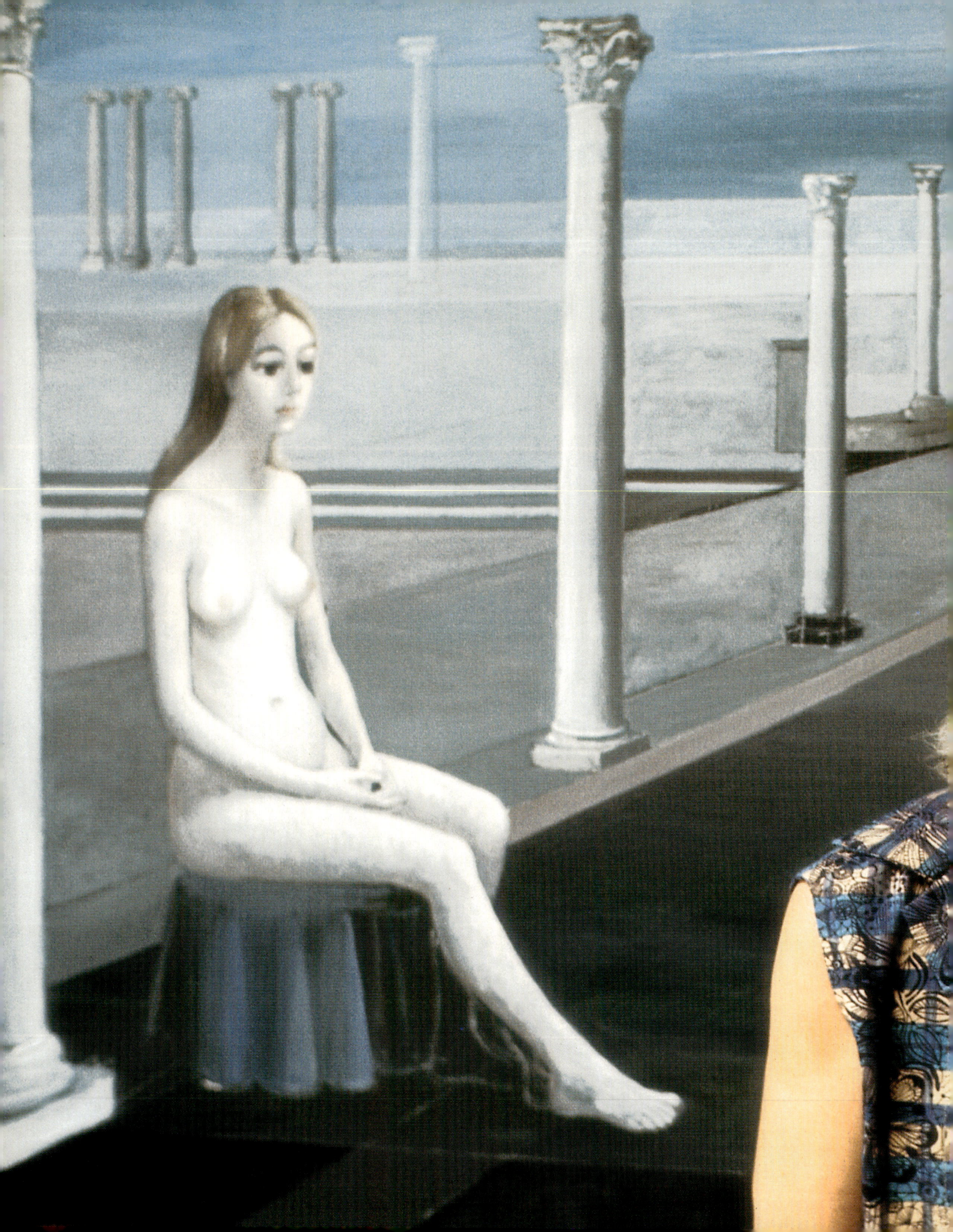

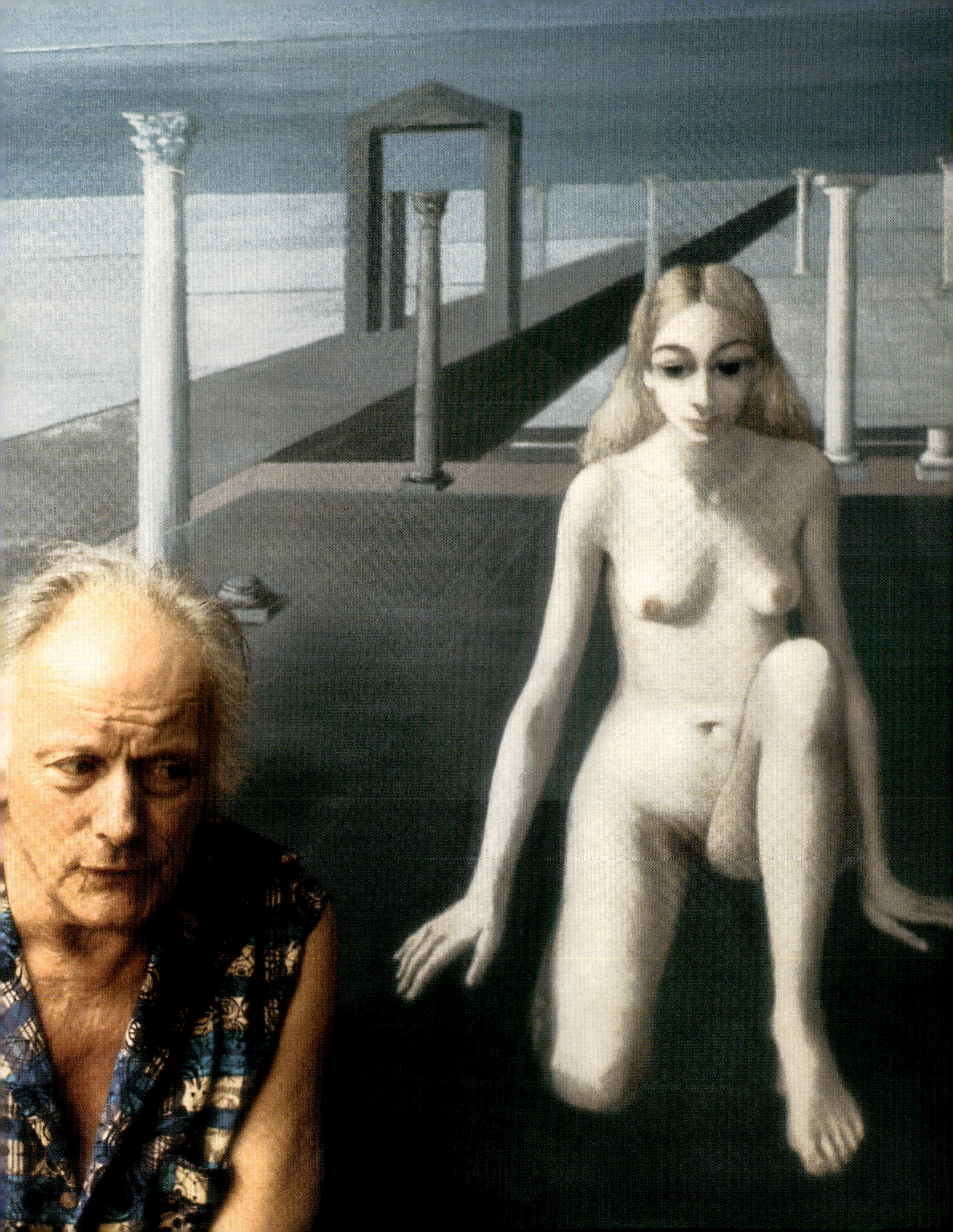

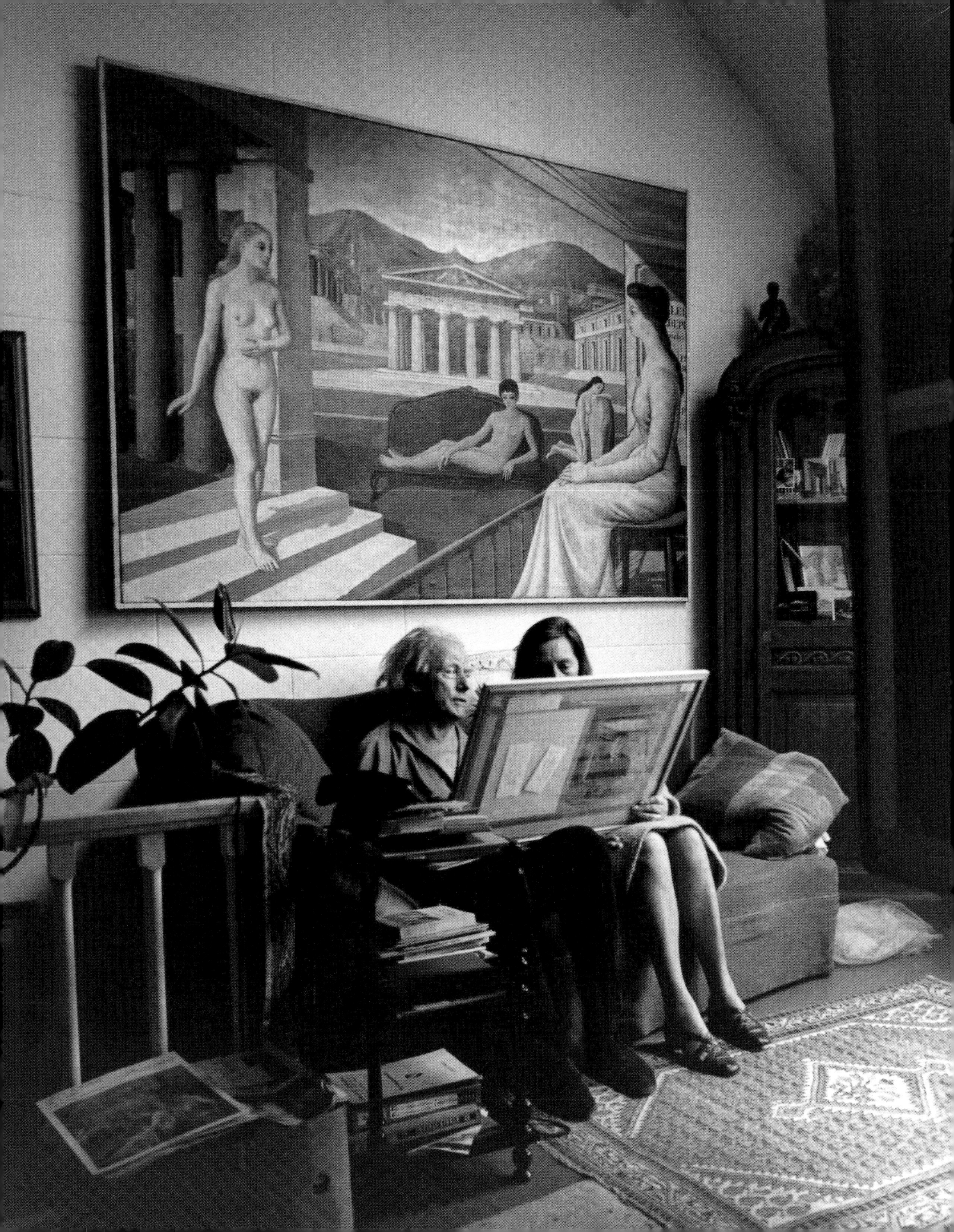

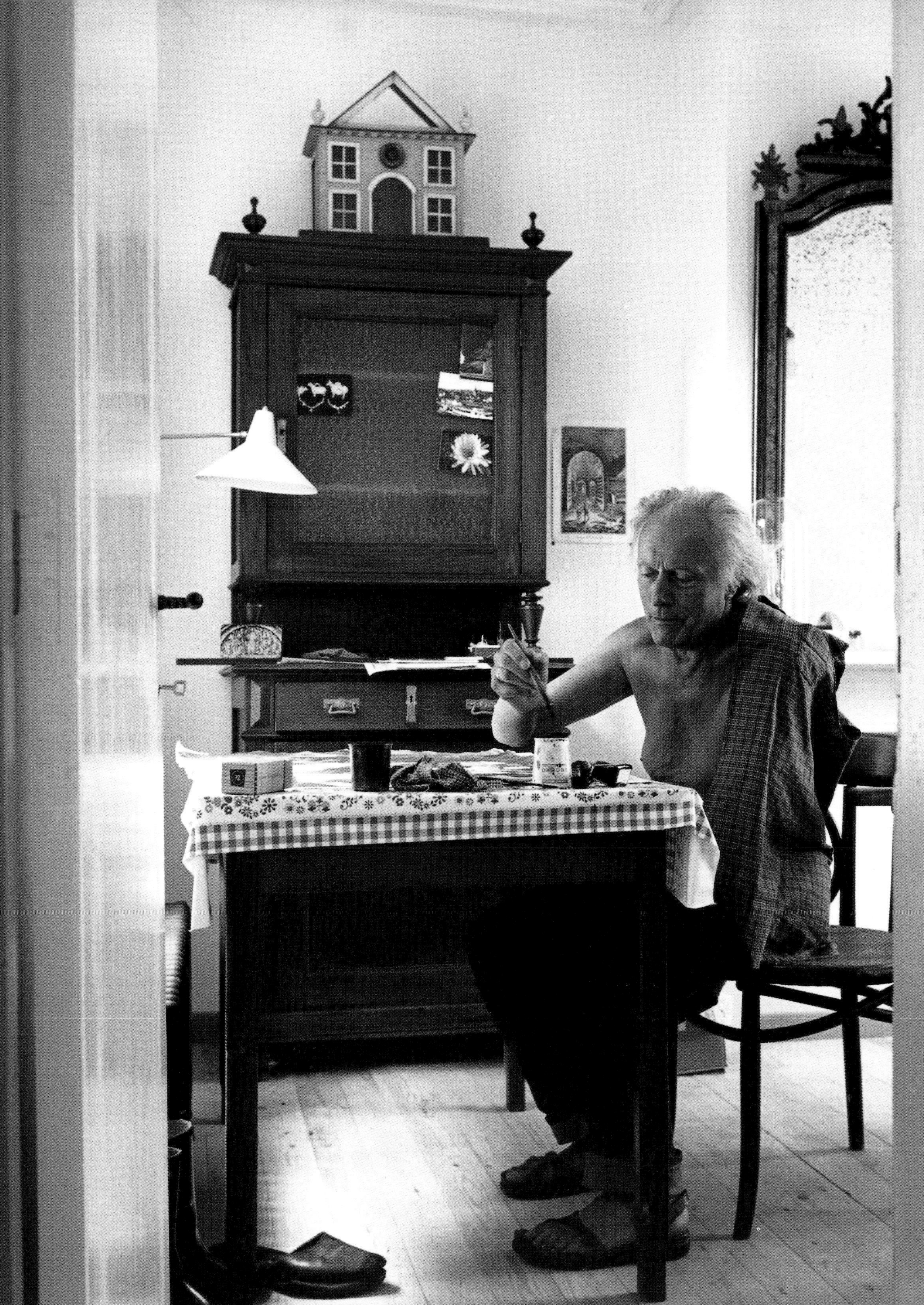

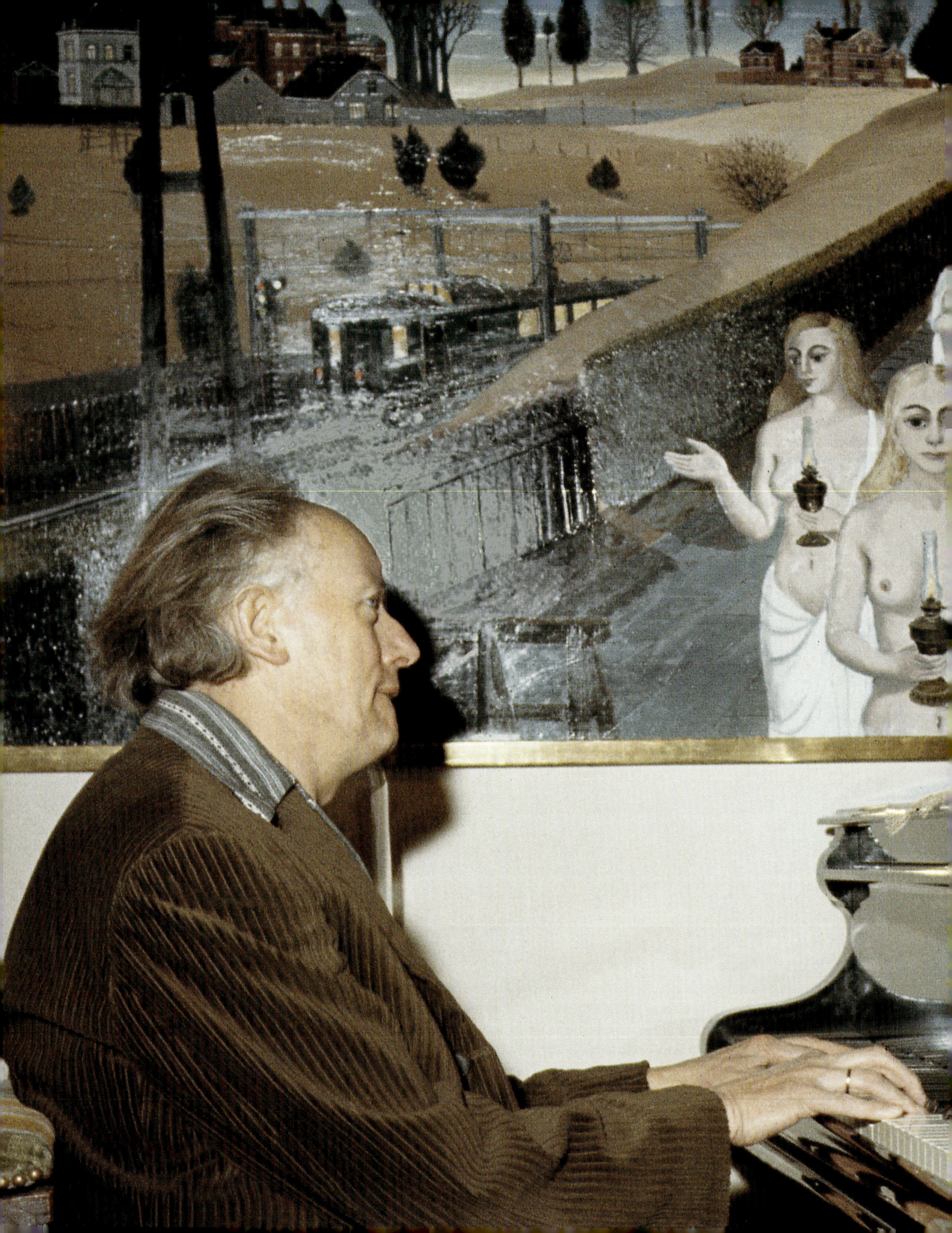

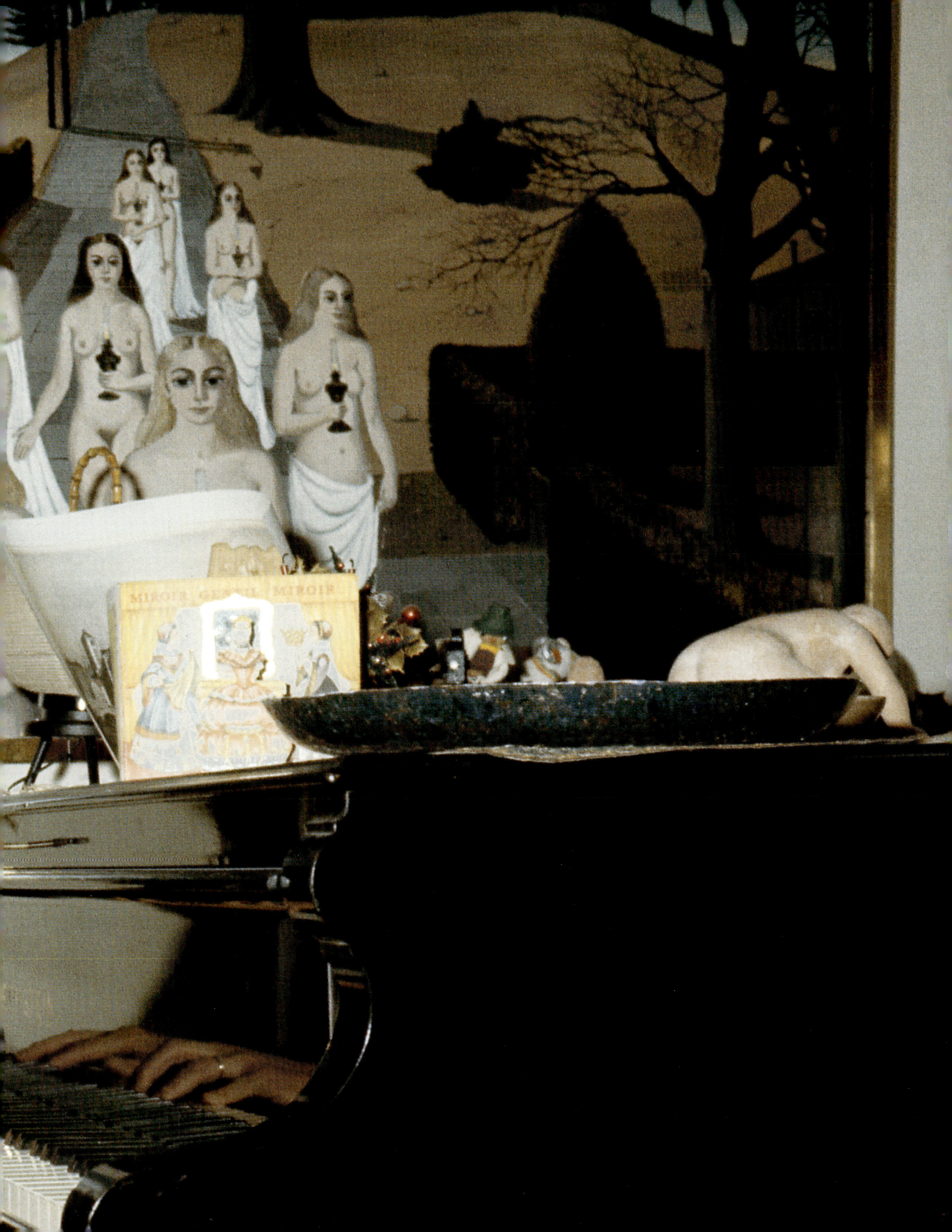

Léger

Robert Doisneau 1937/47/54

Fernand Léger was the "primitive of modern times." Here, he sits under the Gif-sur-Yvette sun.

Léger at the French café Dôme in 1937. He is the Sunday morning painter, the painter of May Day and Bastille Day, as the poet Jacques Prévert said. Léger founded an academy where he worked together with his students. Americans came to film him there—did they know he was a member of the Communist party?

At 86 rue Notre-Dame-des-Champs, his postwar studio in 1947. "It's when I'm doing nothing that I work the most," he says.

The artist in his studio at Gif-sur-Yvette, 1954. "Art must not participate in the battle, it must rather be a respite from daily struggle."

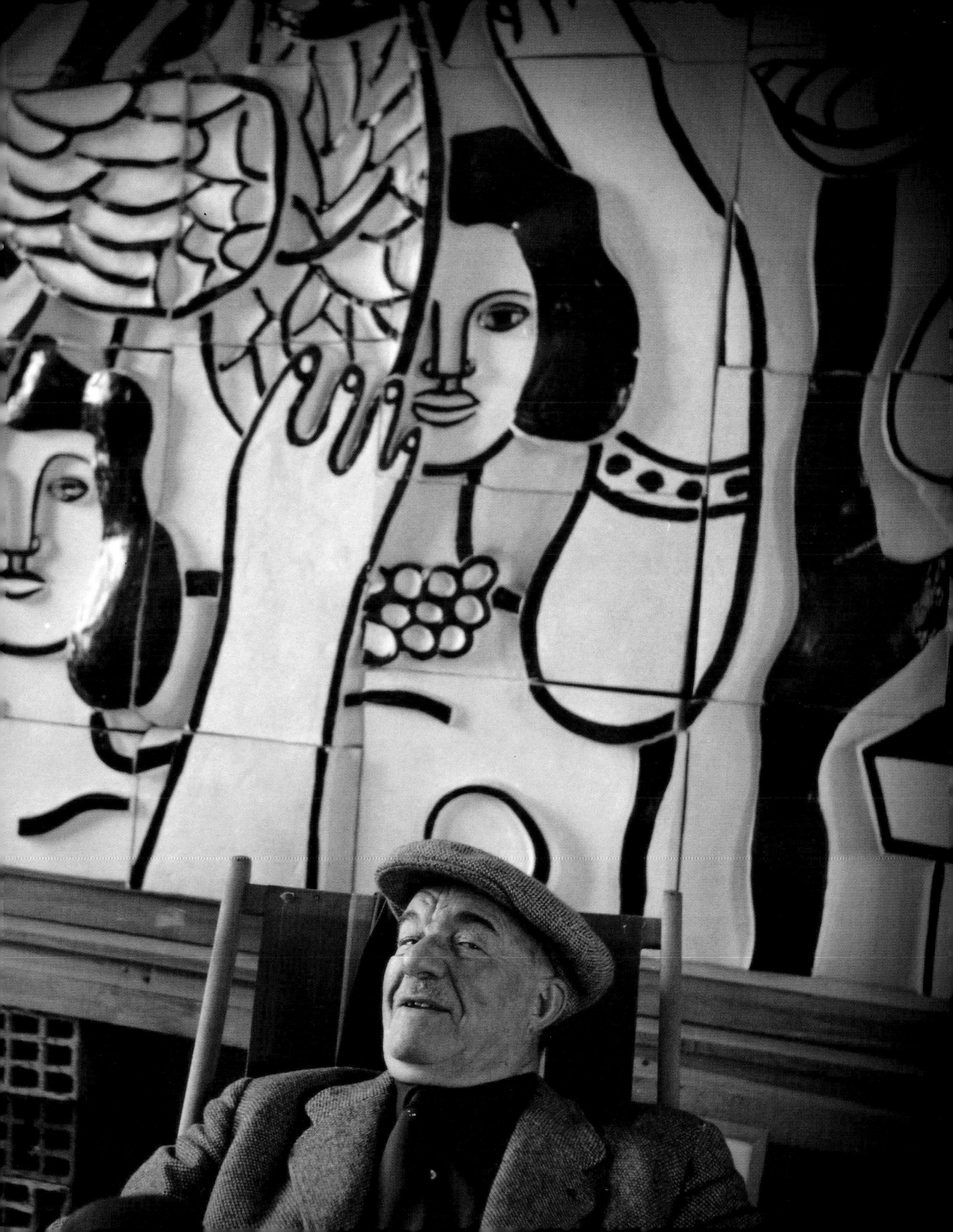

"In this man, whose tall stature suggested power, there was without question a guarded tenderness that pierces through many of his works, discretely distributed through different periods, a tenderness that is evidence of a long and sensitive vision that, as he went, he was able to cast over the world."

—Pierre Reverdy, 1955

The son of a cattle breeder from Normandy, Fernand Léger began his career as an apprentice at architectural firms in Caen and Paris, and throughout the course of his life came to know the extremes of both poverty and wealth. Léger's early paintings contributed to the spread of classic Cubism, but he is most recognized for employing his own visual language of industrial forms to render the new modern world. The city of Paris paid him homage by exhibiting his work at the Grand Palais.

Léger met his wife, Jeanne Lohy, in 1919 while she cycled along the boulevard Montparnasse in her wedding gown. She was a whirlwind of pink and white, an image from a surrealist painting. The pedaling creature was a woman from Normandy, married that very morning to the son of a lawyer. Among her wedding gifts was a bicycle. She wanted to try it. She sat on the seat and took off unaware that she would never return to her groom of that morning. Her legs and lungs were so strong that she reached Paris before she knew it. Seated at the Closerie des Lilas with her friends, a man took note of her, his mouth opened in awe. He had broad shoulders, large arms, and, under a wool cap, a ruddy peasant's face with a strong nose. The cyclist stopped before him. He eventually married her. This is how Léger met Jeanne Lohy and how, together, they went toward a future that pulsated with sun, color, and form. As for the bicycle, painted in white and cadmium red, it reappeared in several paintings—a symbol of work and leisure, an image revealing the "mechanical" soul of Fernand Léger.

Léger's career focused on depicting the urban environment as a world in which humankind fit in among a scenic landscape of levers, gears, ironworks, and the smooth surfaces of sheet metal. His divine industrial reality captured the simple geometries of new modern objects and inventions. "It was while driving on the road every night to Chevreuse that I was struck by the idea of painting the *Constructors*. A factory was being built in the fields there. I saw man as small as a flea, still seemingly lost in inventions, with the sky above him. I wanted to render the contrast between the worker and all that metal architecture, that permanence, that ironwork, those bolts and rivets. I consciously positioned the clouds to contrast with the beams and girders. I brought the *Constructors* to the Renault factories where it was installed in the building's canteen. At noon the men arrived to eat their lunch. While they ate, they looked at the figures in the painting. Some sniggered: 'Look at them! They'll never be able to work with hands like that!' Put simply, they were judging by comparison. My paintings seemed funny to them. They didn't understand anything. I listened to their criticisms and sadly sipped my soup. A week later, I went back to the lunchroom. The atmosphere had changed. The men weren't laughing anymore. They weren't paying attention to the painting. However, several of them lifted their eyes while eating, looked at my painting for a moment, and then lowered their eyes again to their plate. Who knows? Perhaps they were intrigued by what they saw. On my way out, one man said to me, 'You're the artist, aren't you? My friends will realize, once they take down your painting and the walls are bare again, they'll realize what's in your colors.' This made me happy."

Journalist: "Would you have liked to have been something other than a painter, Monsieur Léger?"

Léger: "A cattle breeder like my father, but I don't regret painting."

Journalist: "Do you have a favorite artist?"

Léger: "Myself."

Here is Léger growing like the sun
during Tertiary times
And he hardens
And he sets
The still life
The crust of the earth
The liquid
The foggy
All that tarnishes
The cloudy geometry...
And here
The painter becomes an enormous thing
That moves
Wheel
Life
Machine
Human soul
A 75 breech
My portrait.

—Blaise Cendrars

In 1919 Fernand Léger was known across the globe. All of life's banality was behind him for once. Poor since his fathers death, his life had been difficult. The son of a Norman peasant, half breeder, half horse dealer, and half bull himself (that's three halves you say, but the Léger family always had broader shoulders than everyone), Léger began his career as an architectural draftsman and photograph restorer, but it was painting that interested him. In 1903, after failing to gain admission into the celebrated Ecole des Beaux-Arts in Paris, he attended the Ecole des Arts Décoratifs and then entered the Académie Julian. It's uncertain whether he earned enough money to be able to eat before 1914. There was one thing, however, that stopped him from complaining: the example of his forefathers. "When I think of those years, I realize that the Impressionists waged an amazing revolution. Their revolution was much greater than ours. Those five or six brave artists who were starving to death made it through circumstances that were much more bleak than the ones we experienced."

"Five or six brave artists," an accurate expression that compares to the one he used to describe his war companions from the Argonne and Verdun forests: "Ah! Those big guys! I was big too, and I wasn't scared. They became my comrades. Even when they asked me to go deep into the front in camouflage, I didn't want to leave them. 'I'm staying,' I said."

Whether with painters or soldiers, this was Léger. What he brought to painting is perhaps this: the vivid feeling of fraternity behind form. Once, before 1914, Léger went to the Salon de l'Aviation accompanied by Marcel Duchamp and Constantin Brancusi. The three men wandered through the propellers and motors. All of a sudden, Duchamp cried out to Brancusi: "Painting is finished! Who will do better than this propeller? Tell me, can you do this?" Although Brancusi continued to create sculpture, Duchamp devoted himself to mechanics, optics, and chess much more than to painting. As for Léger, he thought long and hard and gradually came up with the only valid answer to Duchamp's propeller: "My times surround me with perfectly made objects. What's important is not to copy it all, but to do as well...A painter should not seek to reproduce something beautiful, but to make sure that his painting is something beautiful."

When war broke out, Léger left for America and, upon his return he was more famous than before. In 1945 he was most certainly one of the five or six painters who mattered. But victory gave the other artists an air of glory. It neither gave nor took anything away from Léger. He lived his painter's life without budging an inch. In shirt sleeves, munching on bits of smoked ham, he painted throughout the day, unconcerned about gossip and rumors. Having never built anything for money, having never driven a car, and probably having never put a good nail into a wall (this is his little man-machine paradox), he worked peacefully by gas light.

In 1950, after the death of his wife, Jeanne, he married Nadine Khodossevitch, one of his first admirers. In Smolensk in 1921, Nadine saw reproductions of Léger's paintings and decided to take the train to Paris to be taught by this "truly extraordinary" artist.

Léger faced mortality with the strong soul and resignation of a countryman. "We won't see each other again," he said to Blaise Cendrars three days before his death. Yet for fifty years, he had welcomed all of his friends, all of his students, with the same two words: "How's life?" He knew that it would be difficult to leave.

Journalist: "Do you have a favorite color?"

Léger: "Yes, yellow. During one of my exhibitions in 1926, I was frightened when I saw yellow in all of my paintings."

One beautiful summer day in 1955, two black horses brought him to his resting place; his favorite color—everywhere in the fields—was there to watch him pass. "Come on! Come on! A color doesn't see," the wise Léger would have surely objected.

True indeed, we could have answered, but what can you do, comrade Léger, if those who loved you wanted to mourn you on that day.

—Pierre Joffroy

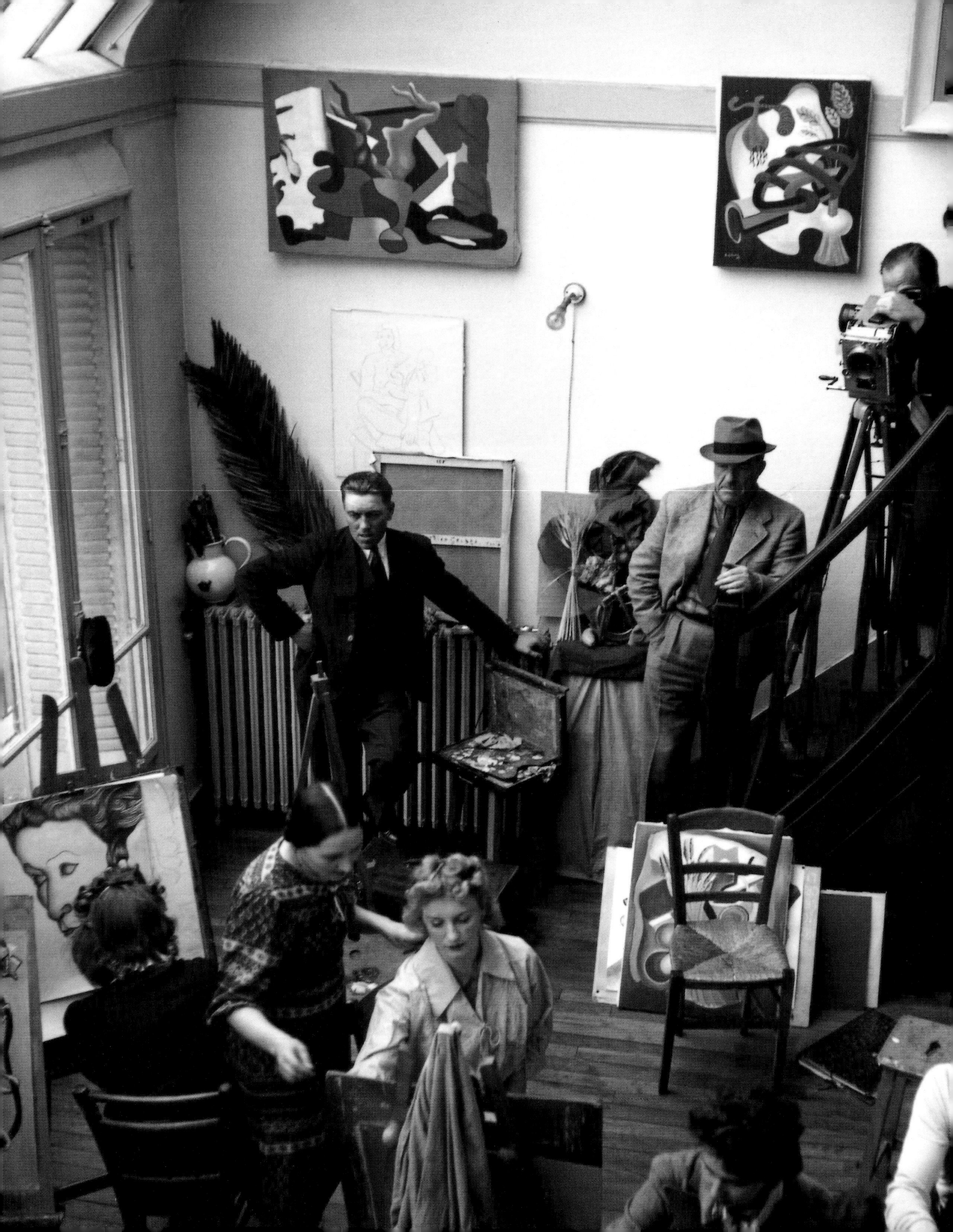

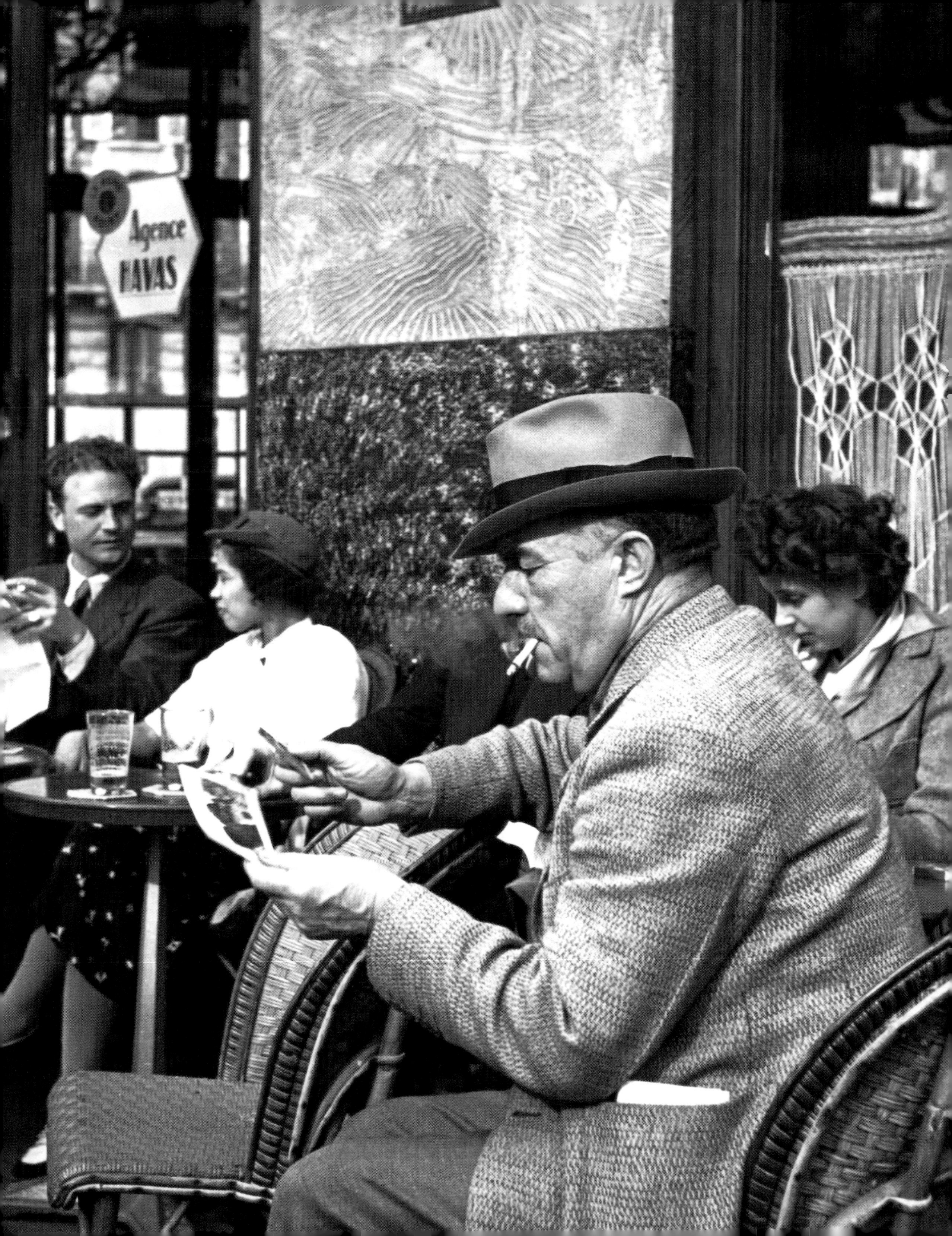
Agence
HAVAS

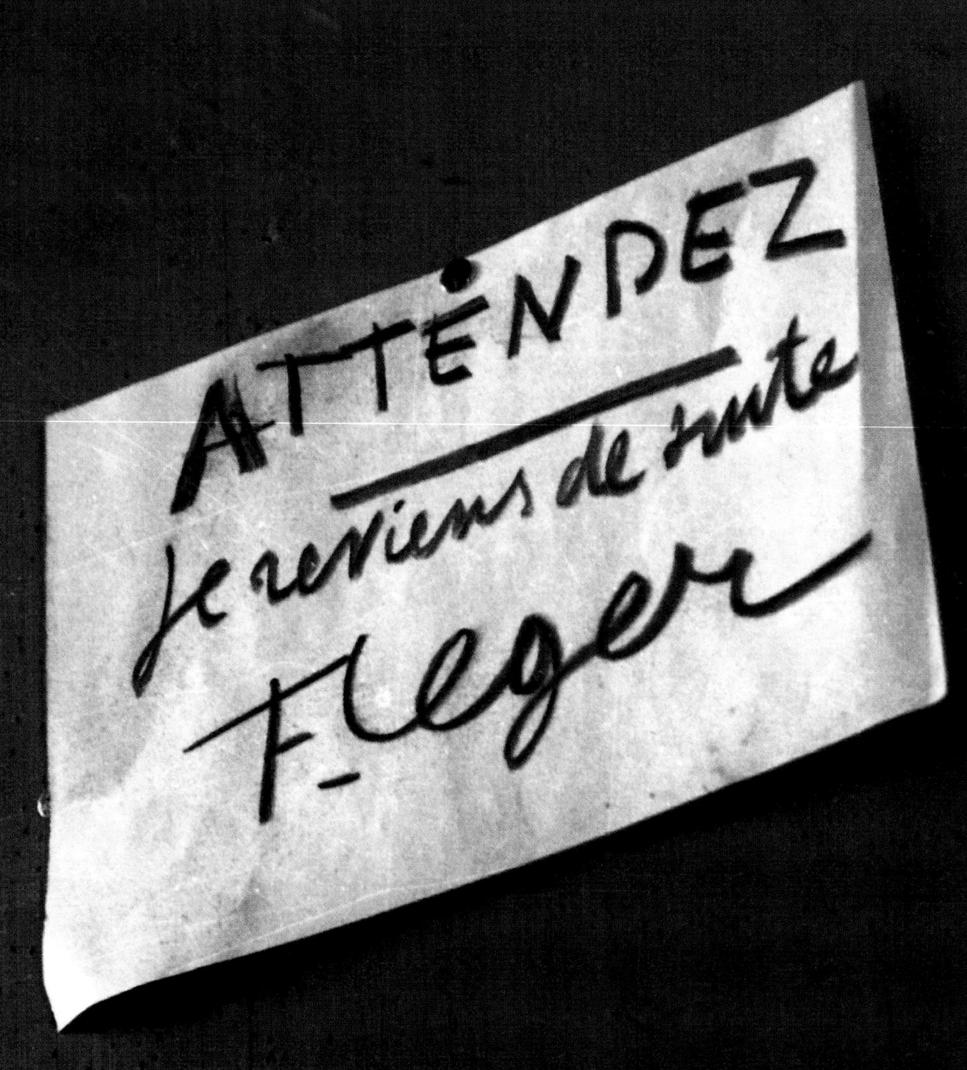
ATTENDEZ
Je reviens de suite
F. Leger

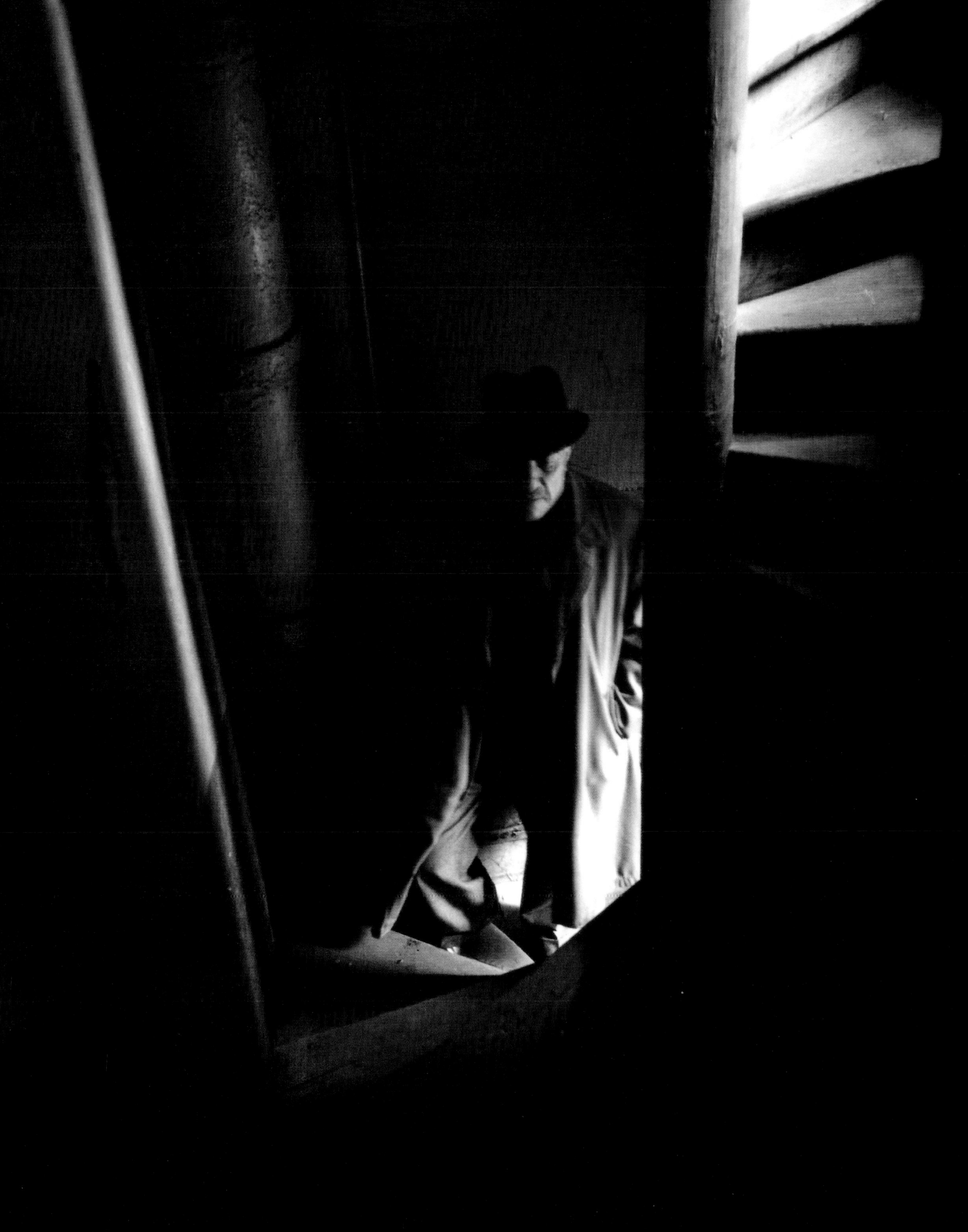

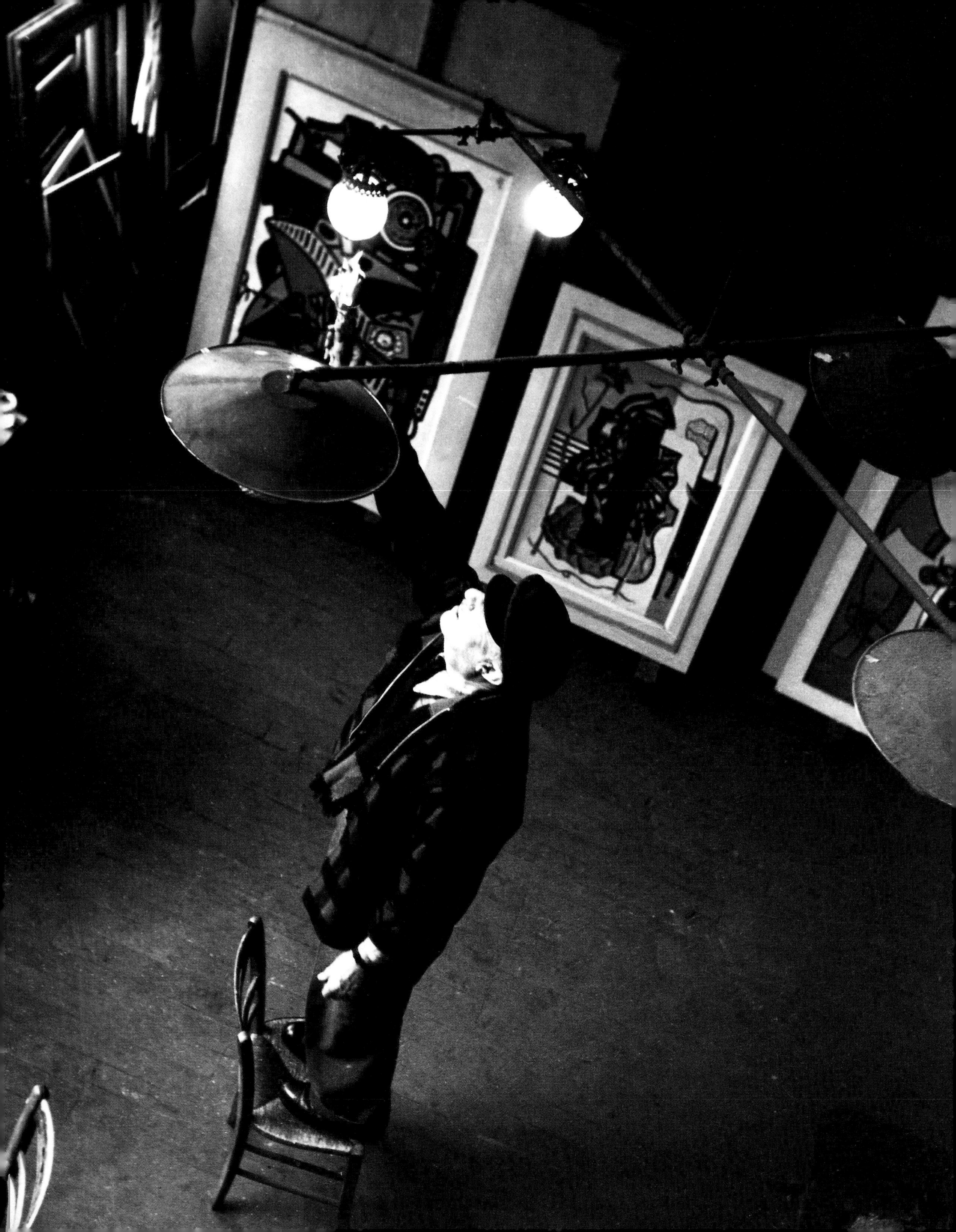

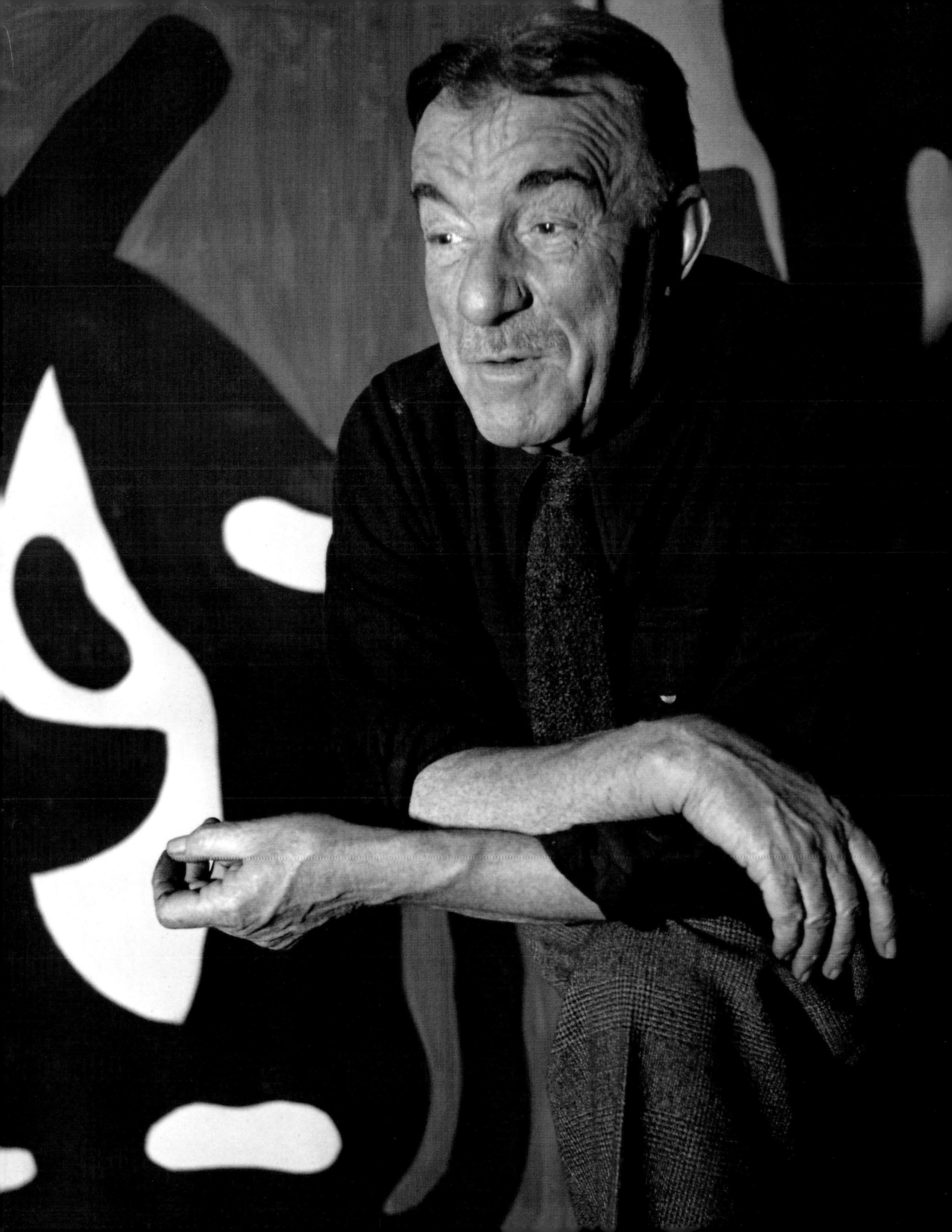

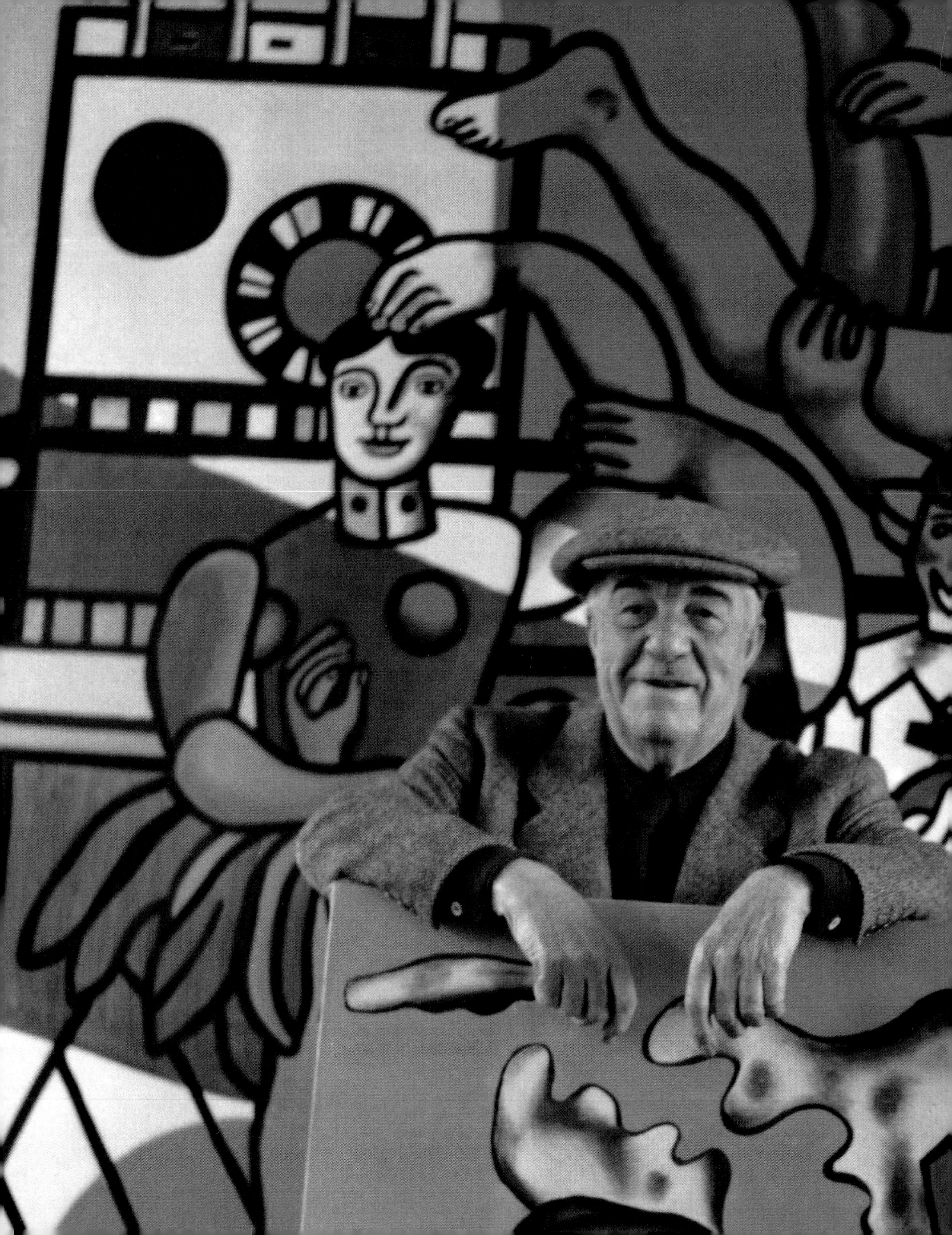

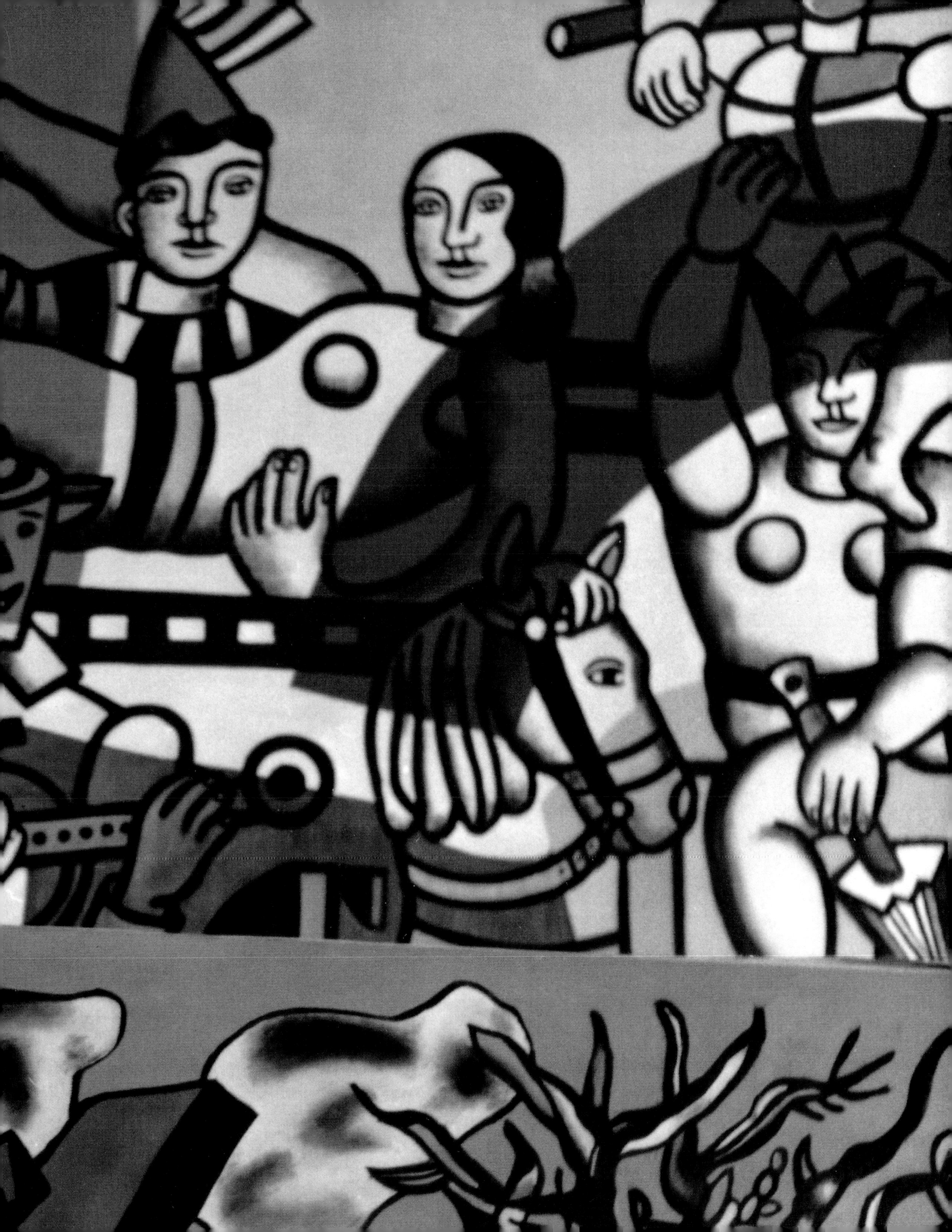

Balthus

Alvaro
Canovas
1998

Count Balthazar Klossowski de Rola enjoys looking at this first image of himself. The greatest living artist begins his day in the pale blue of dawn, with a cigarette.

As the sun rises, his happiness is complete. His wife, Setsuko, and their daughter, Harumi, have prepared an exquisite breakfast.

At the Grand Chalet, the studio awaits the master painter. Setsuko prepares his palette and watches silently as he sets to work at his easel.

Mice love tubes of paint, particularly the red and black ones. "Just like Stendhal," says Balthus.

At ninety years of age, Balthus needs no spectacles to begin the day's work on *Landscape at Monte Calvello.* His hand unfailingly knows what to do.

At the end of the day, he thanks his young model, Anna, captured on canvas for eternity.

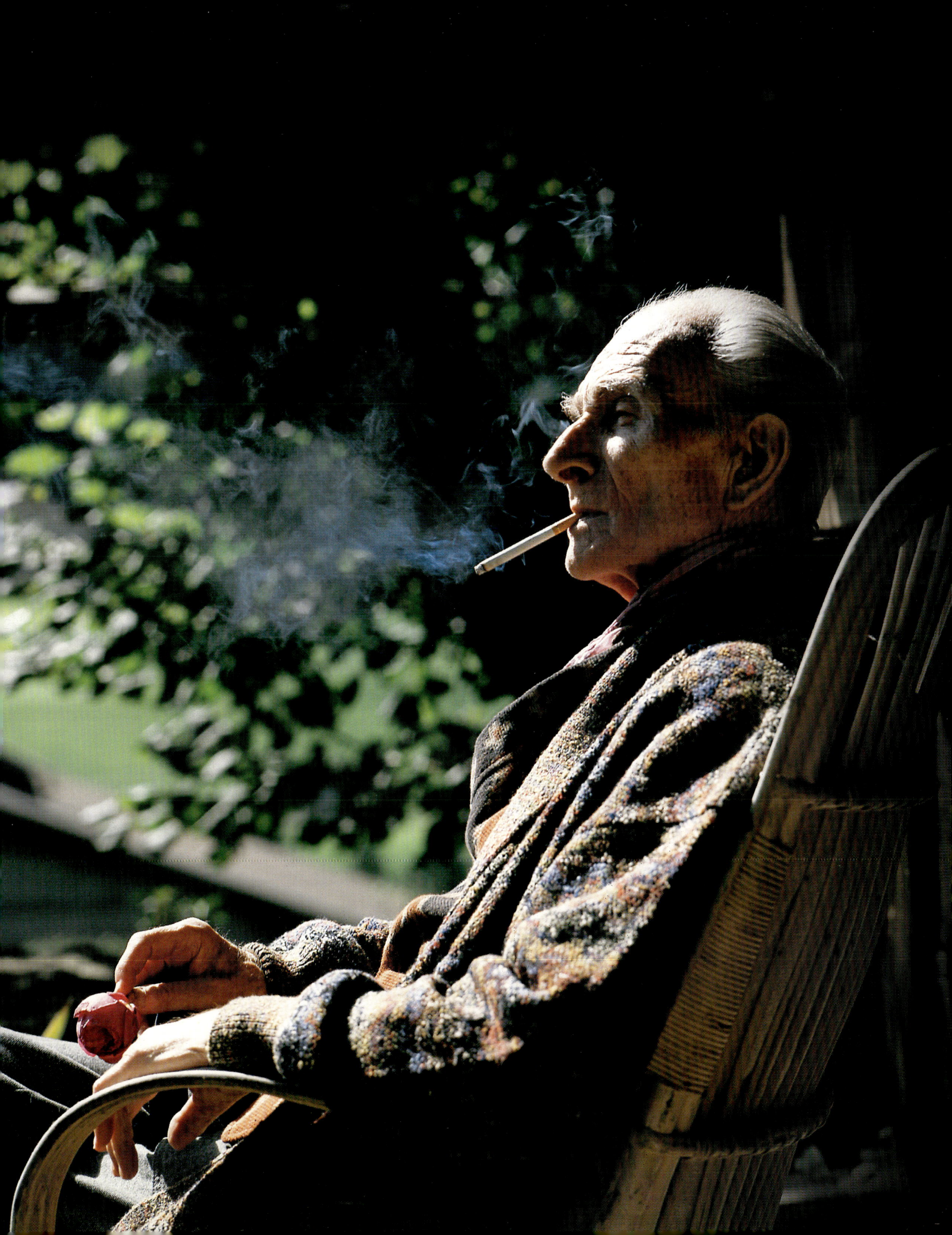

Balthus celebrated his ninetieth year at the snow-covered Grand Chalet, his eighteenth-century home in Switzerland. This is the house where the last surviving giant of twentieth-century art continues to work in seclusion, protected and cared for by his family. Balthus's wife, Setsuko, describes to Alvaro Canovas how moved she is to learn new things every day from a man who has never grown old.

Alvaro Canovas: Where does Balthus find his energy?

Setsuko Klossowski de Rola: As soon as he feels like painting, Balthus seems drawn magnetically toward his canvas. The force appears to come from without rather than within. His need to paint is like a perpetual and ever-growing fire. It is particularly strong in his latest painting. His motivation also seems to come from a profound need to improve on the previous day's work.

AC: Can you describe a typical day for Balthus?

SKR: He works best in the morning. If the light is good he starts painting straight after we have breakfast, and we often gather again for lunch in the studio. He carries on until five o'clock. At this time of year the snow lends a wonderful pearlescent quality to the light. He doesn't talk at all while he's working; he's in a world of his own and has no grasp of what's going on around him. He remains silent even when he's finished for the day and comes to have tea. In a sense, he never stops working, and looks at everything in terms of his work: light, color, and contrast. It affects his whole way of looking at the world.

AC: What is a day like when you are together in the studio?

SKR: First he looks at what he did the day before. He will take a mirror and study the painting through its reflection to see if anything needs changing. It's a way of looking at a picture with new eyes. The artist becomes so involved in what he's doing that his thoughts can become too concentrated, and the mirror offers a fresh critical view of the work in progress. While he's doing that I often wash his brushes for him, which can take a long time. It's essential to Balthus to start with clean brushes.

AC: But don't you clean them the day before?

SKR: Yes, they are soaked overnight in turpentine, and in the morning I wash them out in hot water.

AC: Do you prepare his colors too?

SKR: He'll begin by approaching the canvas and saying, "It needs some Egyptian violet there, and some burnt sienna over here." Some pigments come in powder form, and he will ask me to prepare them for him, always very carefully. He looks first at the canvas, and then considers the colors he will need to get his palette ready...it's amazing to watch. As soon as I have mixed the colors, he starts to see nuances of tone and will ask me to add this or that pigment. It's a very delicate operation.

He always prepares his palette himself. For example, if he's painting a landscape with poplar trees, he prepares a shade of Prussian blue mixed with a warm grey. His instructions are always very precise; he tries it on the canvas, and, if it's not right, the mixture has to be changed immediately. I'm always struck by the fact that in everyday life his eyesight is not very good, but as soon as he's working—it must come from experience—he is aware of the slightest change in tone, the tiniest error: "There it will have to be longer, lower down, further to the left or to the right," he occasionally comments. "I am always astonished by the sharpness of his vision. Sometimes he'll come into my studio and ask me why I've used such and such a mixture of colors, and will often offer his suggestions on different color combinations. He shows me things that no one else would notice. The same goes for composition too: "There's that line on the left; it's a pity it's broken in the center," he might say. He notices every change I make and talks to me about it.

AC: Does he remember everything he sees?

SKR: Everything. A while ago, I was working on a portrait of Emmanuel de Savoie, and I told Balthus that I was frustrated by its progress. He came into my studio and said, "Put a small highlight on the tip of his nose." It was the simplest touch on a tiny portrait, but it transformed the image into the face of Emmanuel.

AC: So that little touch brought the portrait to life...

SKR: Yes, it was exactly what it needed. After about fifty attempts I felt I was so nearly there, but not quite. I couldn't see it, I didn't understand what was wrong. It just didn't look quite like him.

AC: You said you still have thousands of things to learn from Balthus...

SKR: Yes, I learn something new every day. It's so moving just to see the touch of his paintbrush on the canvas. He often says that he identifies completely with his subject. When he paints a mountain, he becomes a mountain. When he paints a girl, it's as if he is physically that girl. It's very moving. Now that he's old, handling the paintbrush causes some difficulties, but his inner force is so strong that it shines out of his paintings. You can feel a burning intensity just by watching him paint.

AC: When his palette is ready and he starts to paint, do you work at his side?

SKR: That depends. Sometimes I watch him at work,

just to absorb some of that extraordinary skill of line that has taken his hand a lifetime's worth of experience to acquire. It's like the way a musician remembers sounds, and for me, watching him paint is like listening to music. He has a rhythm, and it makes me realize just how far I am from possessing that power and how much I still have to learn. So I watch him while he paints, particularly the way he handles his brush, trying to look in on his private world.

AC: Is he no longer aware of you then?

SKR: No, he only sees what he's doing, that's his world.

AC: So nothing will bring him back from his world except the fading light in the studio as evening approaches…

SKR: Sometimes, if he needs to change his palette, for example, to change his brushes, or work out what colors he's going to need later on.

AC: At the moment he's adding the finishing touches to *Landscape at Monte Calvello,* which I thought he had finished some weeks ago. Does he always take so long to complete a painting?

SKR: It can go on for years. Each painting has a long history. There are battles, victories, and defeats going on all the time. Figures, animals, and many other elements can appear in his pictures only to disappear later. For example, in *The Card-players,* there were originally two figures. Another one was added in the middle, which Balthus later turned into a chair! Only the main subject stays the same.

AC: Each painting seems to have gone through several lives before completion. If the layers of paint were removed one by one, they would tell a long story.

SKR: Yes, just one small part of the great story of the life of Balthus. Each painting is like an entire book, the fruit of long experience and a constant search after truth.

AC: Tell me about the Balthus Klossowski de Rola Foundation that you're planning to establish with help from the local authorities.

SKR: I want to get to work on the construction of the building, which will be not too far from the chalet, in harmony with its natural surroundings and the village itself. We have already found three old barns that are going to be demolished. We plan to take them down and put them up again here, near the Grand Chalet. Father Schweizer and Pierre Danger, who both know a lot about traditional timber construction, are going to oversee the work and the organization of the project.

AC: How will the different aspects of the foundation's work be divided among the three spaces?

SKR: One of the barns will be devoted to a permanent collection of Balthus's work. He's going to design the layout and the lighting himself. The remaining space will be for communal activities, music, and theater performances.

AC: Today is March 1, 1998, the anniversary of Balthus's non-birthday. Is he planning to celebrate?

SKR: Balthus was born on February 29, 1908, and only celebrates his birthday during leap years. That's why he says everything seems so long to him—one year for most people is four years for Balthus. We won't be celebrating his non-birthday, but I really want us to celebrate his next real birthday together in the year 2000.

—Alvaro Canovas

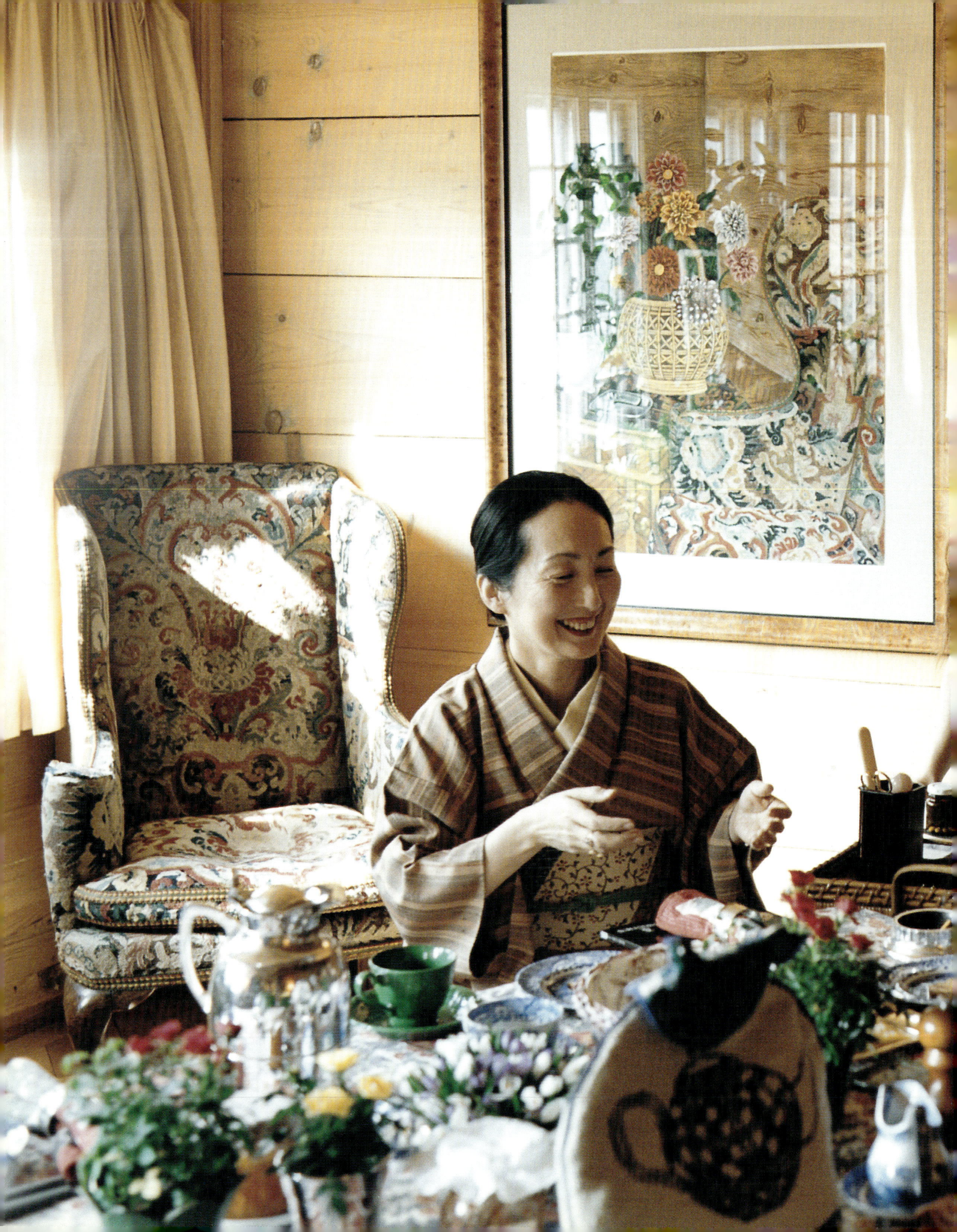

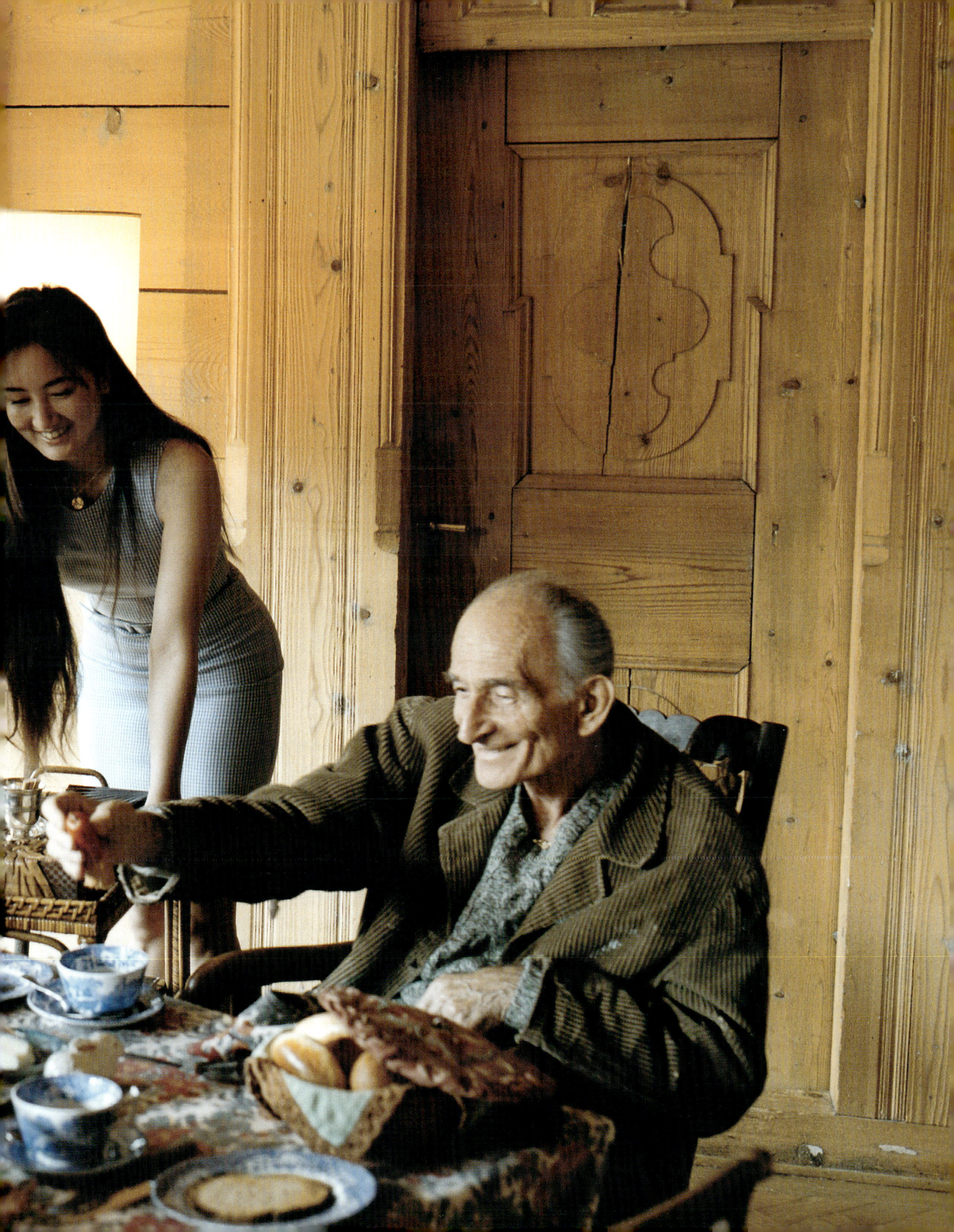

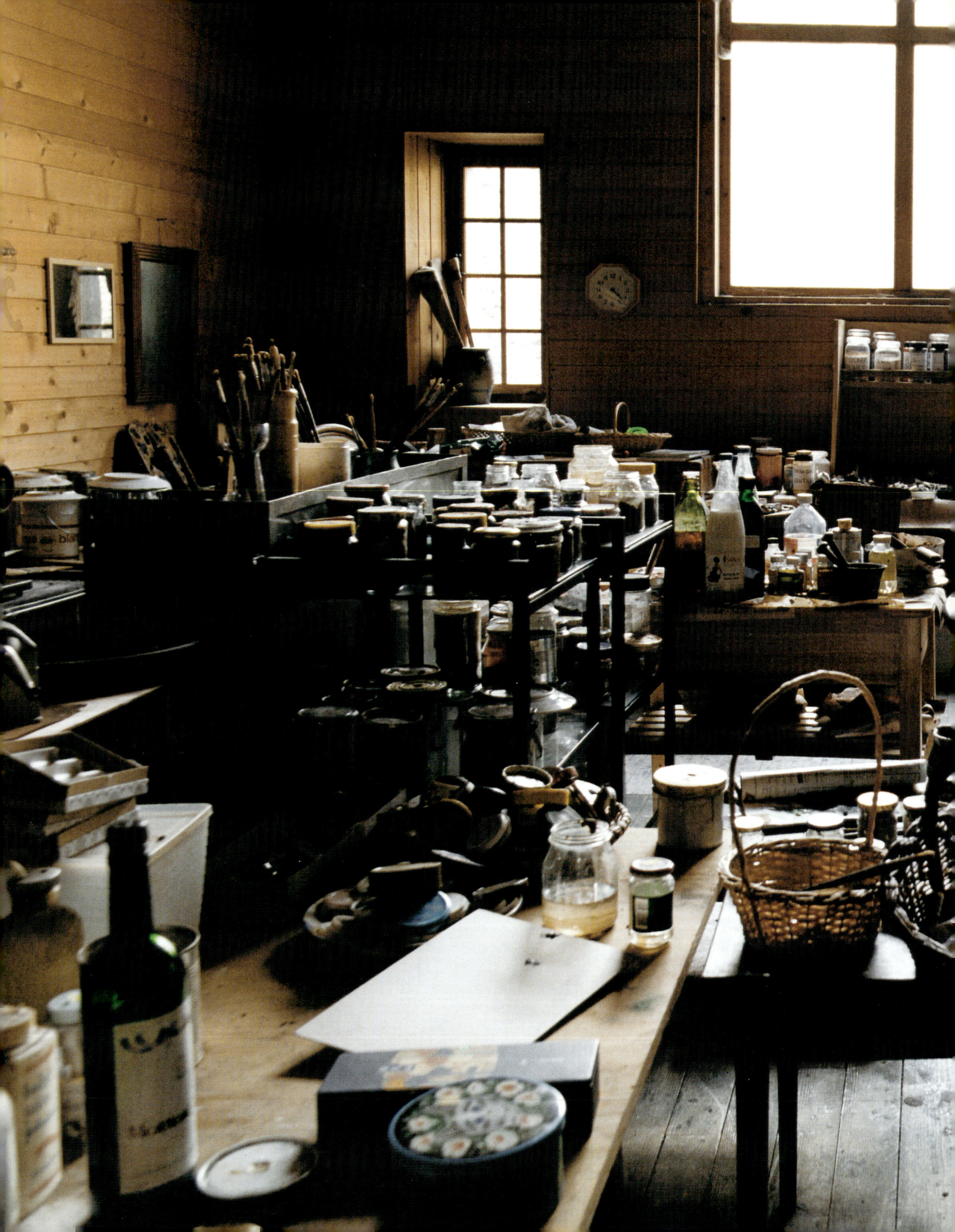

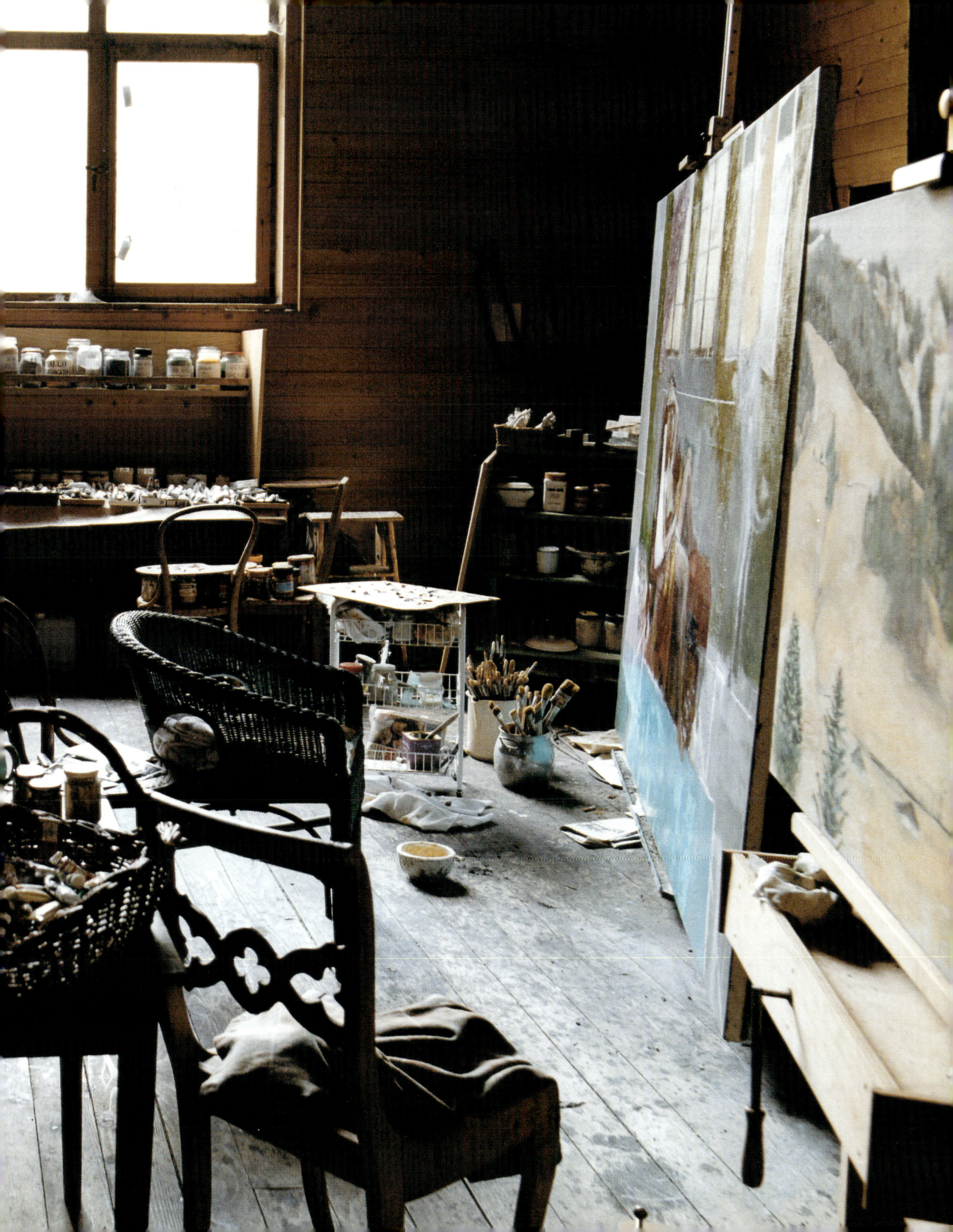

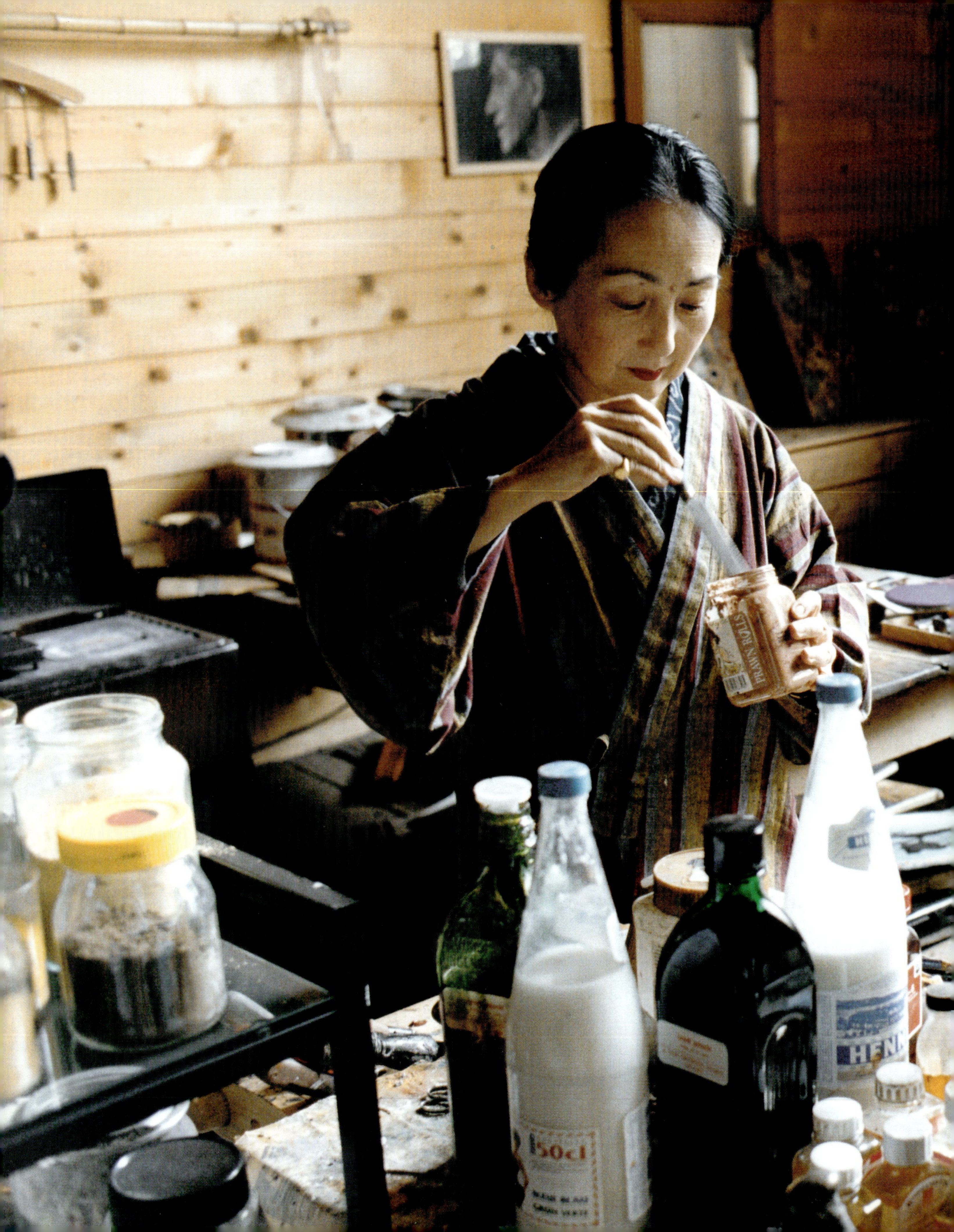
PRAWN ROLLS
50cl

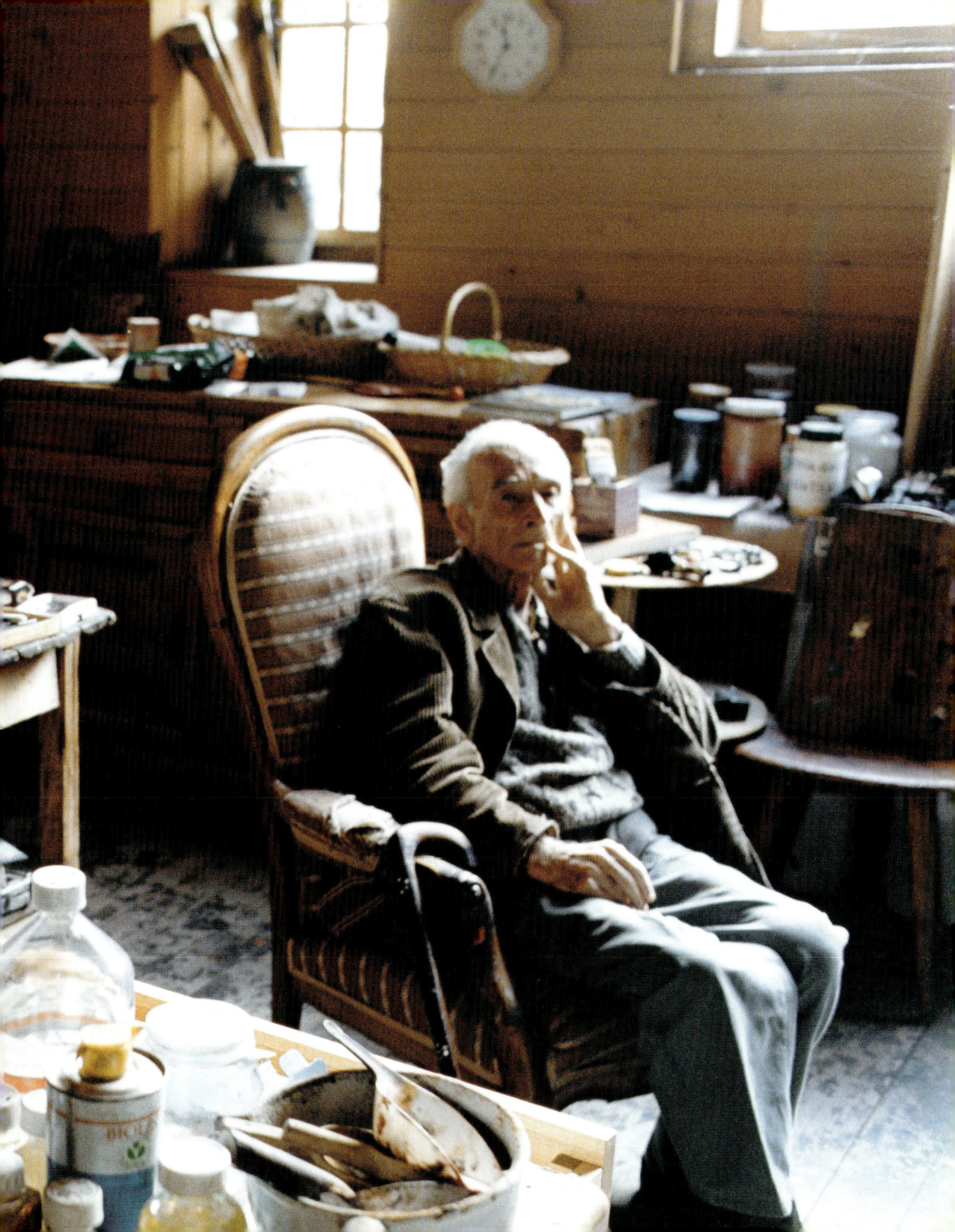

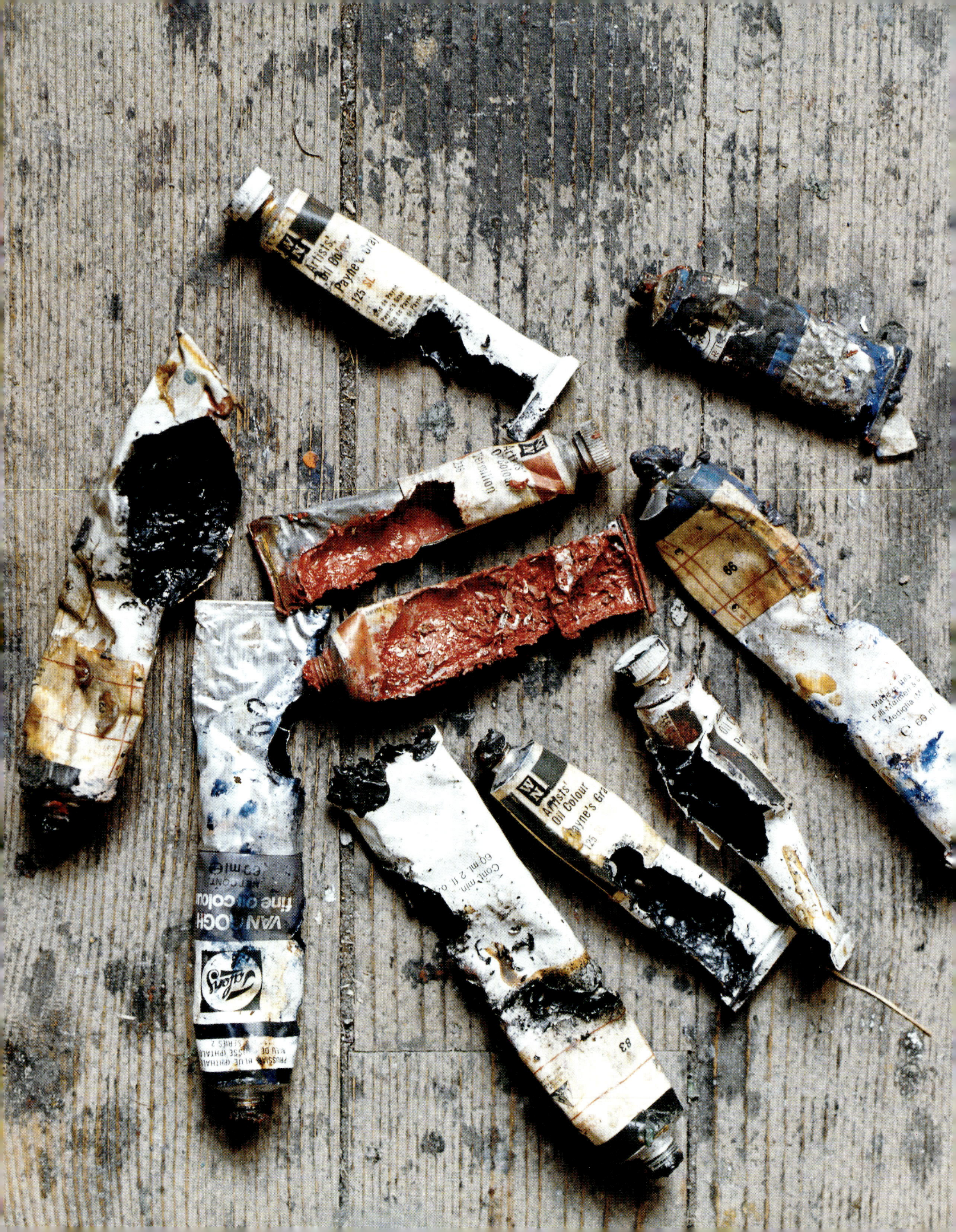
Artists'
Oil Colour
Payne's Gray
VAN GOGH
fine oil colour

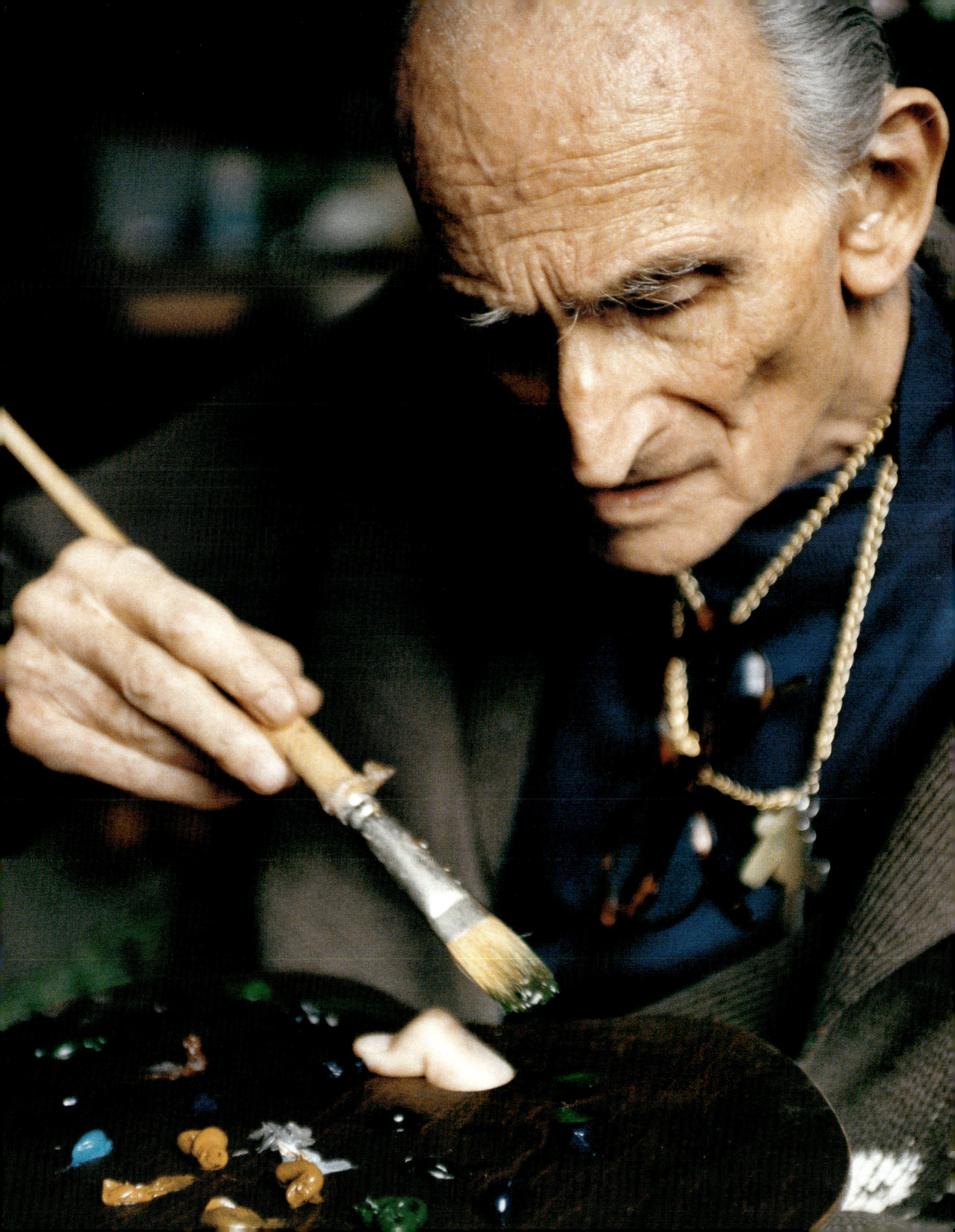

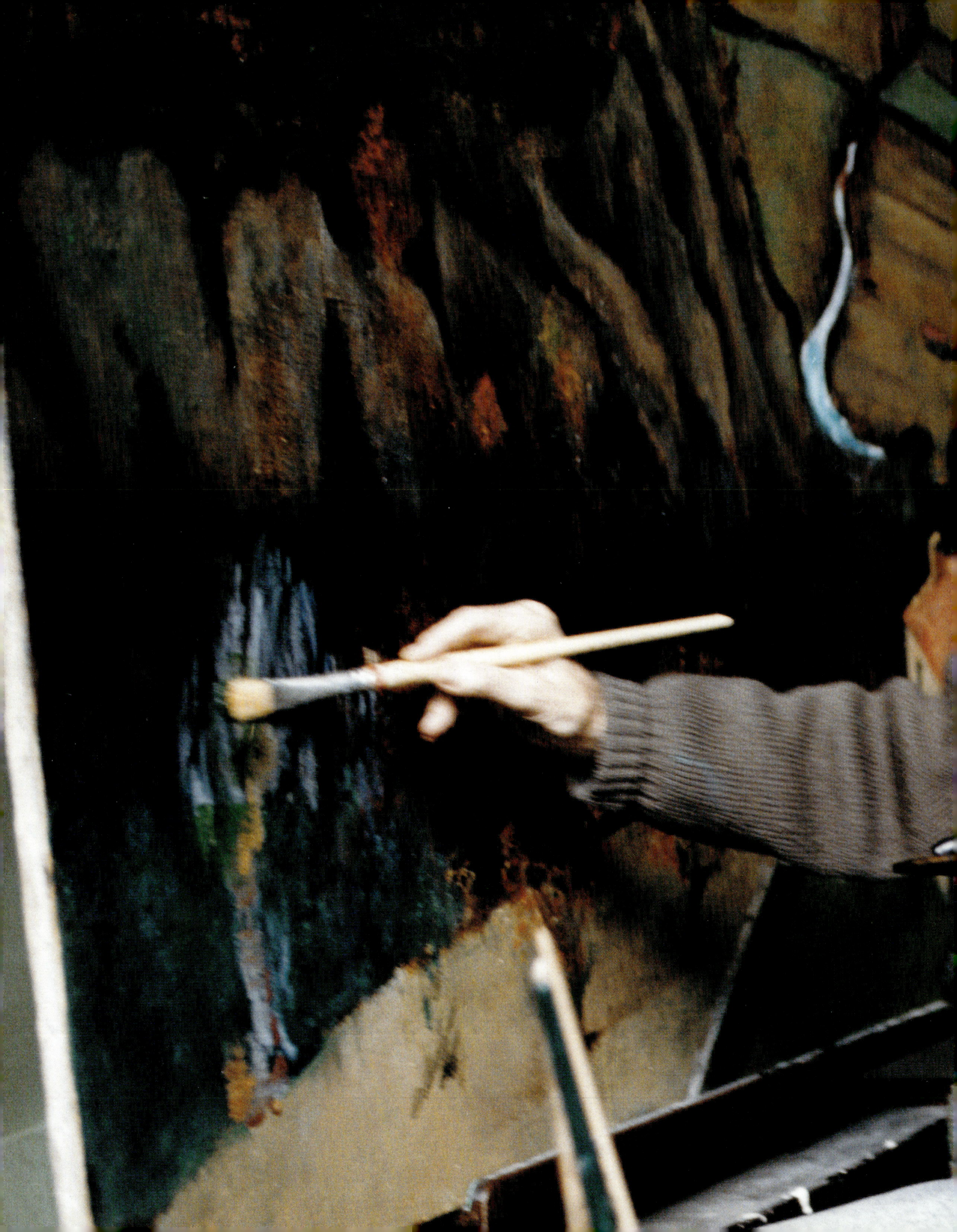

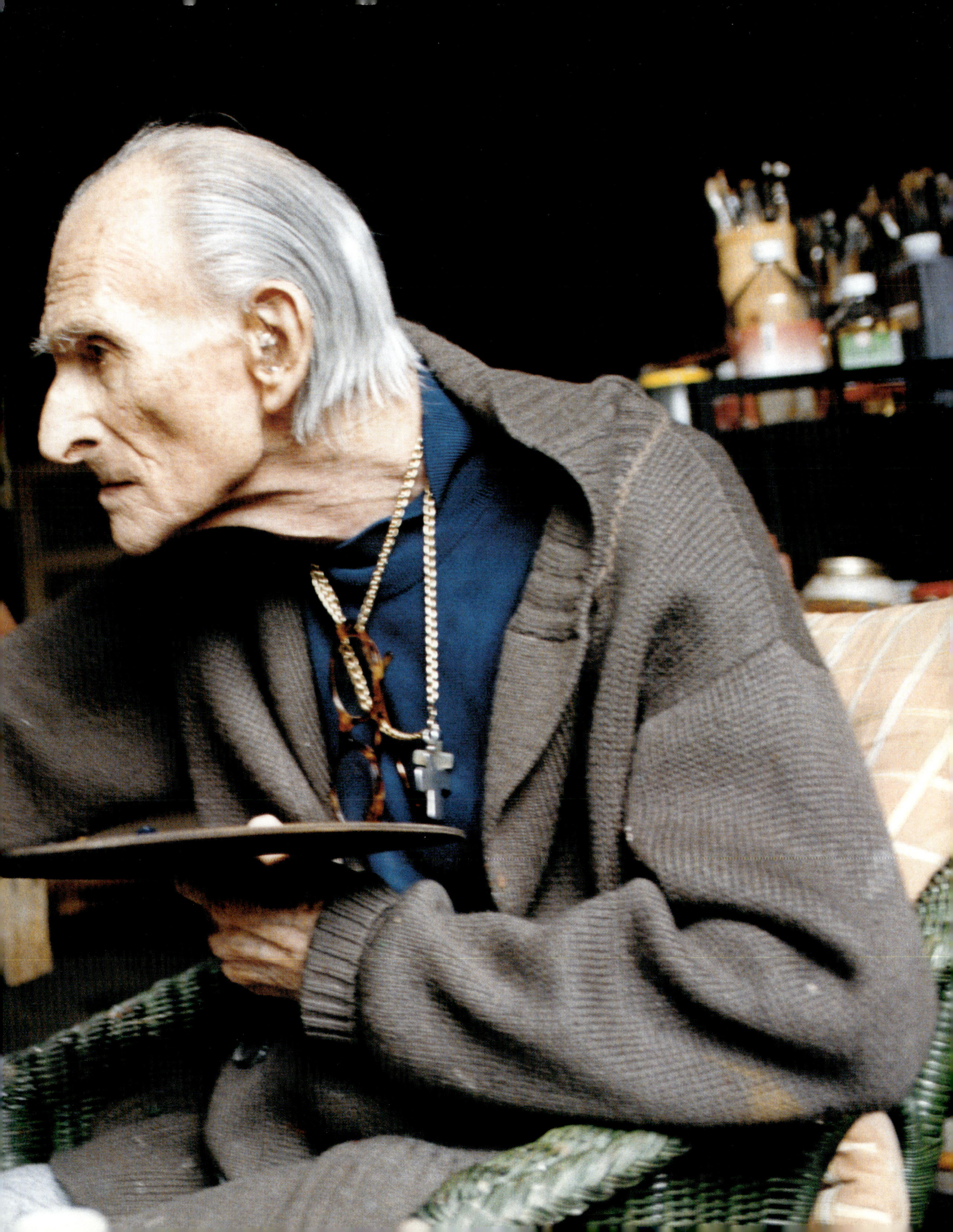

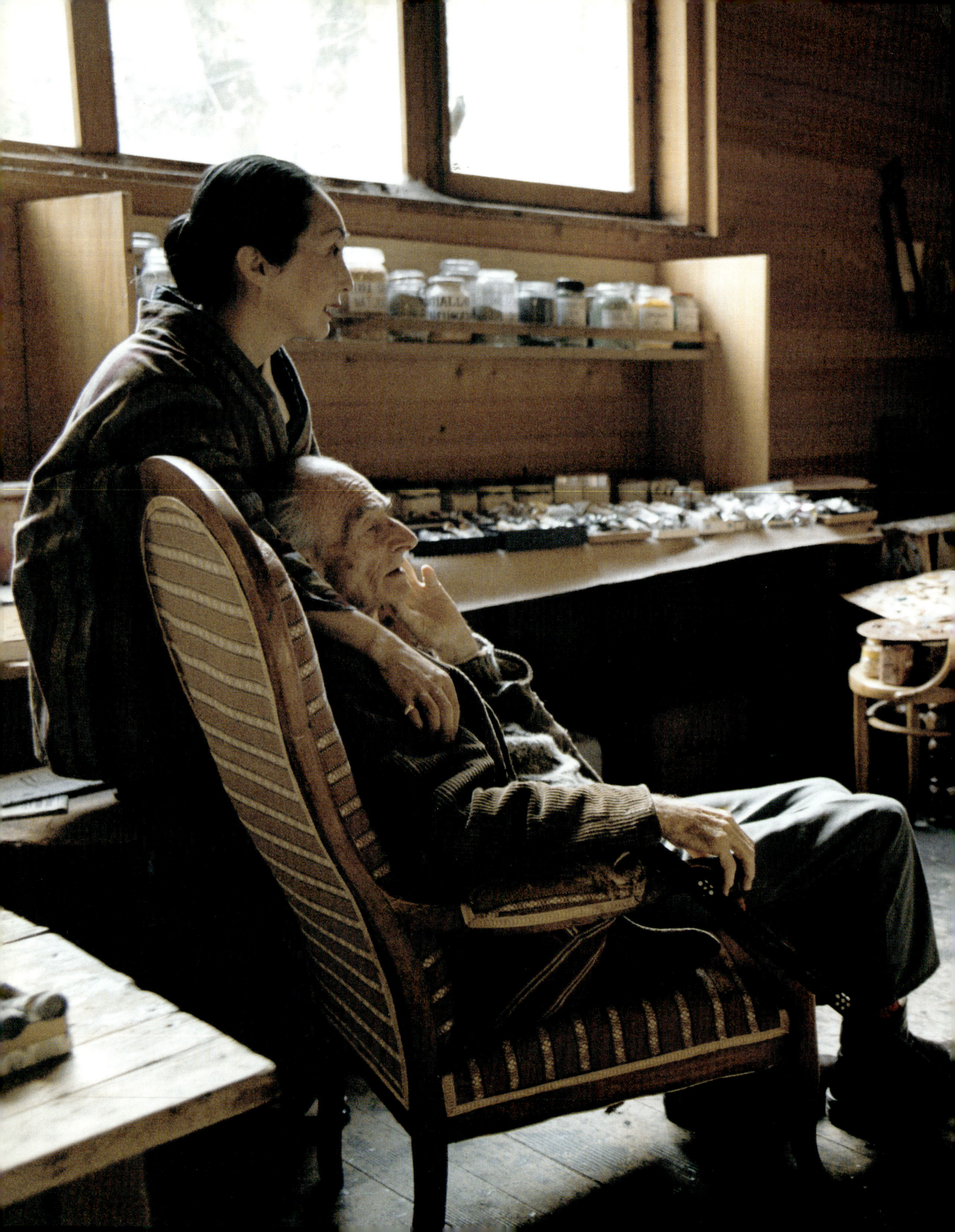

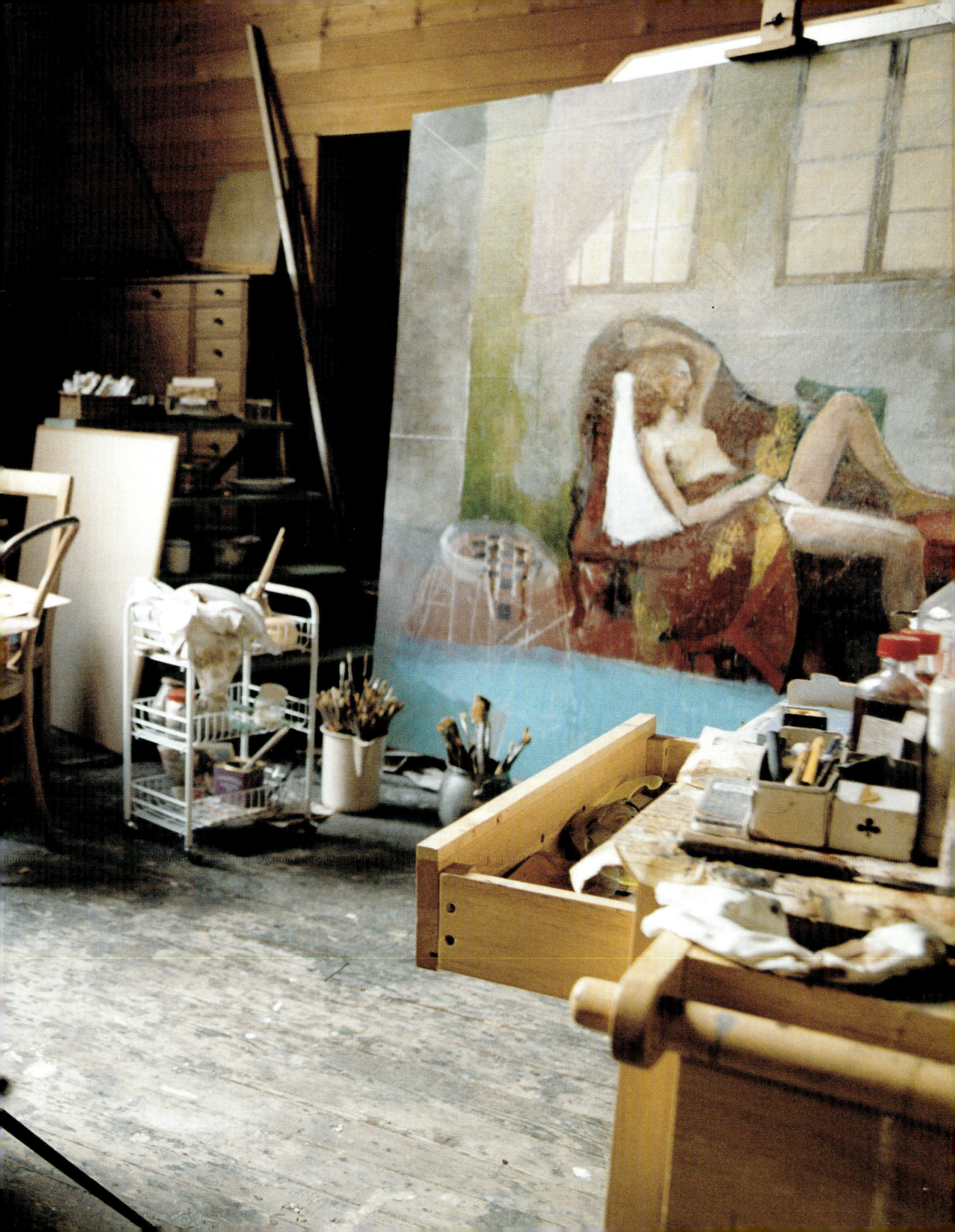

Balthus never lost touch with childhood, a time of natural grace and unadulterated inhibitions. His own remark that he never abandoned his ability to look at the world through childlike eyes is both revealing and enlightening. Circumstance and unerring intuition have always led him toward people and places that allowed him to blossom. He was born in Paris in 1908 and remembers the Old World charm of the city—at that time still peopled by craftsmen and artisans. His parents were amateur painters and literati and counted among their friends the writer André Gide, and the Nabi painter Pierre Bonnard. The vicissitudes of war took Balthus to Switzerland where, amid astounding natural beauty, he remained in Geneva for the most part, but also traveled to Zürich and to Bern. He spent his holidays at Beatenberg, a magnificent Alpine resort overlooking Lake Thun. It was here, among the peasants and shepherds of the mountains, that he came to love the country life and culture that was to inspire his great painting of 1937, *The Mountain,* now the precious possession of the Metropolitan Museum of Art in New York.

For twelve years Balthus was closely associated with the German poet Rainer Maria Rilke, who wrote the introduction to his first collection of drawings entitled *Mitsou.* Rilke's preface expressed admiration for the artist's talent and his exceptional knowledge of Far Eastern culture. Early on in life Balthus traveled to Great Britain and Ireland, and admired the values and the literature he found there. He also traveled extensively in Tuscany and Umbria before being sent to Morocco to serve in the military. His two studios in Paris, the first on the rue de Furstenberg, was visited by the French poet and director Antonin Artaud, and the writers Pierre-Jean Jouve, and Julien Green, and the second in the Cour de Rohan, where the painters André Derain and Joan Miró posed, were both havens of calm within historic quarters of the city. After returning from war on the Alsatian front, he took up residence at Champrovent in 1940 in a *ferme-manoir,* a large and handsome farmhouse typical of the Bugey region of France. In 1943 he moved to a townhouse in Fribourg and next, in 1945, he moved on to the Villa Diodati, an Italianate residence in Geneva, where Byron had once stayed. Once back in Paris, he returned to an earlier passion: designing sets and costumes for the theater, ballet, and opera. For him, the music of Mozart was the perfect example of the kind of flexible modulation that should govern painting.

From 1953 to 1960 Balthus withdrew to the Château de Chassy, a well-appointed gentleman's residence dating back to feudal times and set in the fine landscape of the Morvan Mountains. Every window offered a splendid view, and at each of them he sat and painted, bringing to the canvas his own echoes of China and of the classically ideal renderings of Nicolas Poussin. In 1961 Balthus was summoned by André Malraux, then French Minister of Culture, to follow in the steps of Ingres and head the Académie de France in Rome, where he remained until 1977. He was an inspired director who also undertook, with perfect taste, the renovation of the Academy's prestigious home, the Villa Medici, set on the Pincio Hill amid gardens Velázquez once painted.

In 1962 Balthus was entrusted with an official mission, the first of six incredible journeys to Japan—voyages of exploration to discover the country's treasures. There he met Setsuko. His marriage to this young woman who combined perfect Japanese refinement with the discipline of a Chinese education, allowed him at last to gain true contact with aspects of an ideal civilization that had fascinated him from childhood: its art, its exoticism, and its truly universal vision. His last visit to Japan was in 1991, when he received the imperial prize for painting. He will be making his seventh visit in November when an exhibition of his work opens in Tokyo. For the occasion he is making final changes to the third version of *Cat with Mirror.* This 1989–94 panel is the largest, quite certainly the best, and the most daring of the three in terms of color. In it the model Anna, in a sort of radiant stupor, holds up a mirror to her feline companion.

Since the fall of 1977 Balthus has been living in Rossinière, a picturesque village well off the tourist routes in the Vaudois, or *pays d'en haut.* His house is called the Grand Chalet, a name fully justified by its sheer size, but which is one of the most beautiful in Switzerland, exquisitely proportioned and in a breathtaking mountain setting. Inside, everything blends together in perfect harmony: decor, furniture, and fabrics, and with arrangements of flowers everywhere that are changed each day. Setsuko has incorporated an awareness of her own roots into the house, keeping the traditional clothing and customs of her native Japan. Balthus falls in with this willingly, his aristocratic profile taking on the look of an Oriental sage which, beneath its intrinsic humor, reveals the depth of the artist's mind.

Setsuko has become an accomplished painter in her own right, intimate and poetic. Already she has had successful exhibitions in Rome, Lausanne, New York, London, and Tokyo. At the moment she is illustrating a Japanese novel for an American edition, and, in 1991, she followed in the famous tradition of many great artists when she designed the French vintner Mouton-Rothschild's label for that year's vintage. Her illustration work began with pictures to accompany stories for her daughter, Harumi. In the chalet where cats, Balthus's symbolic beasts, used to reign supreme, Harumi has introduced Fandor, a friendly and exuberant dalmation.

—Jean Leymarie

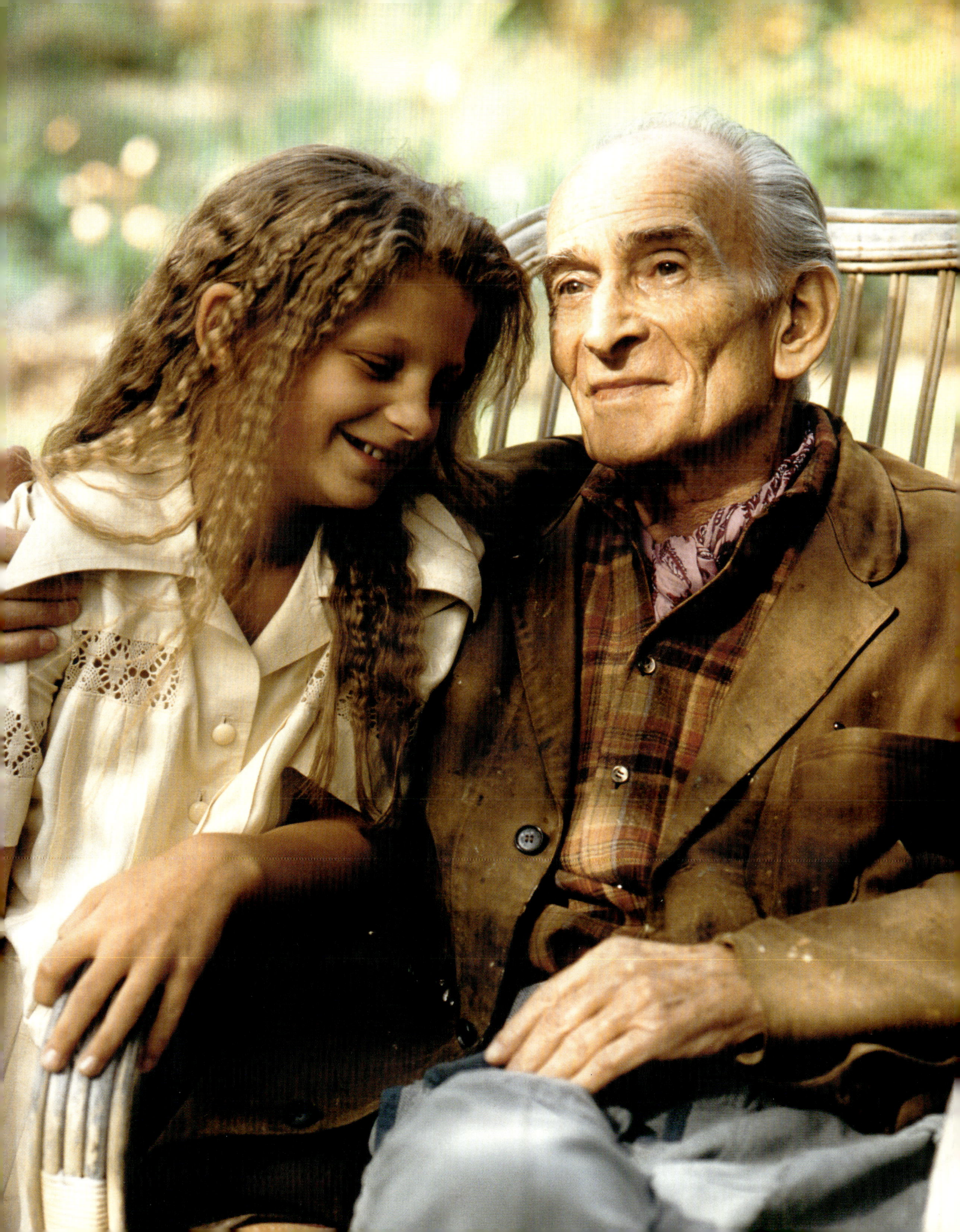

This collection of treasures from the archives of *Paris Match* are an homage to the photographers of the great *Paris Match* team from the 1950s, '60s, and '70s, and the new initiates of the 1980s, '90s, and the year 2000. Many of the featured photographers live on through the publication of this book. Not forgetting our friends outside of *Match,* whose images enrich our archives, one must remember the photographers' partners, the journalists of *Paris Match,* who often opened the doors to celebrities and captured in words what these photographs illustrate. The campaigns and victories of this impressive group of contributors will forever live on in the chambers of our archives.

Acknowledgments

The publishers would like to thank Florence Rossier, director of the Photothèque, and Fernande Ricordeau, head of the Research Department at *Paris Match* for their gracious help. Sincere thanks to Didier Rapeau and Pierre Vergnol at the *Paris Match* photography department, and to the staff at the archives of *Paris Match*—Claude Barthe, Pascal Beno, Yvo Chorne, Geneviève Musitelli, Dominique d'Orglandes, and Gérard Ratineaud.

Following is a list of dates for which the articles gathered here first appeared in *Paris Match.*

Matisse Sacrifices 800 Million..., May 6, 1950,
By Edmonde Charles-Roux, October 21, 1999.

Dalí
By Julien Green, September 2, 1989.

Bacon
By Barry Joule, June 27, 1996.
By Peter Beard, December 1988.

Picasso
By Hélène Parmelin, extract from *Picasso Says,* December 3, 1966.

Chagall
By Jean Diwo, July 5, 1958.
By Maurice Rheims, December 4, 1985.

Braque
By Henriette Chandet, June 5, 1954.

Van Dongen
By Jean-François Chabrun, October 10, 1959.

Miró
By Eugène Ionesco, November 10, 1978.
Dolorès Miró interviewed by Pépita Dupont, June 3, 1993.

Legér
By Pierre Joffroy, November 23, 1971.

Delvaux
Paul Delvaux interviewed by Marie-France Saurat, November 14, 1991.

Balthus
By Jean Leymarie, June 27, 1993.
Setsuko Klossowski de Rola interviewed by Alvaro Canovas, March 19, 1998.

Photograph Credits

Jacket front: © 2000 ADAGP, Paris; jacket back: © 2000 ADAGP, Paris; pages 9–23: © 2000 H. Matisse estate; 25–33: © 2000 Gala & Salvador Dalí Foundation/ ADAGP, Paris; 35–43, 46, 47: © 2000 ADAGP, Paris; 49–59: © Am Rhyn-Haus Picasso Museum; Rosengart Donation-Lucerne.© 2000 Estate of Pablo Picasso; 61–79: © 2000 ADAGP, Paris; 95, 98, 99, 100, 101, 102, 103, 104, 105: © 2000 ADAGP, Paris; 107–121: © 2000 ADAGP, Paris; 123, 126, 127, 129, 130, 131, 132, 133, 134, 135: © 2000 Paul Delvaux Foundation/ ADAGP, Paris; 137–147: Agence Rapho © 2000 ADAGP, Paris; 149–165: © 2000 ADAGP, Paris.